LEARNING IN THE FAST LANE

Fast Lane

The Past, Present, and Future of Advanced Placement

Chester E. Finn, Jr., and
Andrew E. Scanlan

PRINCETON UNIVERSITY PRESS
PRINCETON AND OXFORD

Requests for permission to reproduce material from this work
should be sent to permissions@press.princeton.edu

Published by Princeton University Press
41 William Street, Princeton, New Jersey 08540
6 Oxford Street, Woodstock, Oxfordshire OX20 1TR

press.princeton.edu

ISBN 978-0-691-17872-1
Library of Congress Control Number: 2019942780

British Library Cataloging-in-Publication Data is available

Editorial: Peter Dougherty and Alena Chekanov
Production Editorial: Karen Carter
Jacket/Cover Design: Layla Mc Rory
Production: Erin Suydam
Publicity: Tayler Lord and Kate Farquhar-Thomson

This book has been composed in Adobe Text and Gotham

Printed on acid-free paper. ∞

Printed in the United States of America

10 9 8 7 6 5 4 3 2 1

*With gratitude and love for the families that nudged us into faster lanes,
and have done their best to keep us there.*

CONTENTS

ACKNOWLEDGMENTS

We knew from the outset that this study could not proceed very far without the cooperation of the College Board and its bottomless trove of data, research, and historical lore, and Trevor Packer and his colleagues didn't disappoint. Even more generously, they helped without trying to recast or "spin" our findings and conclusions. Veteran AP majordomo Packer was himself invaluable. Also aiding us were more individuals than we can name, but let us at least recognize the contributions of Lawrence Charap, David Coleman, Crystal Morales Coto, Maureen Ewing, Jessica Howell, Sherby Jean-Leger, Liam Julian, Daryl Morris, Jeff Olson, Stefanie Sanford (also a Fordham Institute trustee), Ellen Sawtell, former College Board scholar-in-residence Ben Wildavsky, and John Williamson.

As we embarked on fieldwork around the United States, we leaned hard on—and took inexcusable advantage of—many, many people. Our deepest thanks to them all, including (but not limited to):

In Fort Worth: Stacy Burrell, Michael Calder, Kristin Compton, Walter Dansby, Carrie Grant, John Hamilton, Colin Jenney, Patricia Linares, Sharon Meng, Theresa Mossige, Barbara Ozuna, Omar Ramos, Gregg Ruthart, Kent Paredes Scribner, Michael Sorum, Sarah Weeks, and a high school parent who prefers to remain anonymous.

At the University of Texas: Rebecca Karoff, Harrison Keller, Rachel Martin, Elizabeth Mayer, Wanda Mercer, and Julie Schell.

At Educate Texas: Luzelma Canales, the inimitable and irrepressible John Fitzpatrick, Kelty Garbee, Shelly Haines, Kristin Kuhne, and George Tang.

Elsewhere in Texas: Christine Bailie, Shasta Buchanan, Paul Cruz, Carolyn Bacon Dickson, Pascal Forgione, Jacob Fraire, David Gardner, Eric Harslem, Tom Luce, Mitch Morken, Raymund Paredes, Penny Schwinn, Craig Shapiro, and Joanna Slaton.

In New York City: Suzette Dyer, Kristin Ferrales, Kristin Kearns Jordan, David Krulwich, Ashley LaCavalla, Diana Moldovan, Mort Orlov and John Smolenski (both then with the National Math and Science Initiative), Flavio

Puello Perdomo, Joshua Smith, and Merilee Valentino, as well as a high school principal who prefers to remain anonymous.

In Dublin, Ohio: Craig Heath, Todd Hoadley, Jessica Kroetz, Lori Marple, Dusty Miller, Jill Reinhart, Bob Scott, and Mike Ulring.

In Montgomery County, Maryland: Kecia Addison, Henry Johnson, Erick Lang, Libby Rogovoy, Brian Scriven, super-superintendent Jack Smith, Darryl Williams, and Janet Wilson.

In the charter-school sector: Peter Bezanson, Yasmin Bhatia, Jack Chorowsky, Jesse Corburn, Daniel Fishman, Mike Franco, Richard Harrison, Megan Heron, Ana Martinez, Charlie Ticer, and Tom Torkelson.

At the National Math and Science Initiative: Ken Cohen, Gregg Fleisher, and Leighton Watts.

At Equal Opportunity Schools: Alison Gazarek, visionary founding CEO Reid Saaris, and Leslie St. Pierre.

In a dozen other places: Mark Cavone, Dylan Conger, Elizabeth Dolan, John Fink, Peter Gow, Susanna Jones, Tim Lacy, Karen Lassey, Mark Long, David Steiner, Tristan Stobie, Jennifer Zinth, and a veteran university admissions officer who prefers to go unnamed.

Special thanks to John Schneider of MassInsight for hosting us at an AP summer institute for teachers; Nat Malkus of the American Enterprise Institute for reviewing part of our draft as well as his own fine AP research; and the *Washington Post*'s Jay Mathews for beaucoup encouragement, insight, and leads into the Advanced Placement program that he has followed so closely for many years as well as the inspiring Escalante story.

At our home base, the Thomas B. Fordham Institute, this protracted project was enhanced and supported in a hundred ways by Mike Petrilli, Gary LaBelle, Brandon Wright, Nicholas Munyan-Penney, former Fordham staffers Alyssa Schwenk and Caryn Morgan, and many others, including the greatest interns ever.

We couldn't have done it without the financial assistance of the Sid Richardson Foundation (special thanks to Pete Geren and Bill Koehler, himself a world authority on education in Fort Worth); the Jack Kent Cooke Foundation (especially Jennifer Glynn, Ricshawn Adkins Roane, and the late, great, Harold Levy); the ExxonMobil Foundation (Kerri Briggs!); and another funder who prefers to remain anonymous.

We're grateful to two nameless reviewers of our final manuscript, both of whom provided expert analysis and valuable suggestions.

We owe deep appreciation on so many fronts to ace editor (and old friend) Peter Dougherty at Princeton University Press, who saw the potential in this venture, improved it along the way, and meticulously ushered it into production with the help of a crackerjack team that included Bob Bettendorf, Karen L. Carter, Alena Chekanov, and Dawn Hall.

Finally, words cannot encompass our debt and affection for Renu Virmani and Lara Bryfonski, loving spouses, helpmates, victims of late nights and working weekends, and patient (or not) frequent utterers of "So how is that book coming along?"

Indebted as we are to so many others, we alone are responsible for all that follows.

LEARNING IN THE FAST LANE

Introduction

Amid the enduring mediocrity of American secondary schooling and the nonstop caravan of reforms, experiments, and pilot programs intended to fix it, there lurks a sixty-year-old success that has not drawn the attention or plaudits that it deserves. Now engaging nearly three million high school students who sit for some five million exams every year, the Advanced Placement program has quietly worked its way into the offerings of most public and private schools, the policies of many states and districts, the admissions and placement decisions of hundreds of universities, the educational aspirations of countless families, and the academic programs of innumerable college students. Along the way, it has emerged as a nearly unique standard of rigor and quality for the K–12 system, a source of professional gratification for myriad teachers, and—remarkable in these fractured and politicized times—a de facto national high school curriculum joined to a battery of exacting tests that are widely deemed "worth teaching to."

Unlike charter schools, "dropout recovery" schools, and virtual schools, Advanced Placement is not a newfangled institutional form. Unlike—though intersecting with—today's enthusiasms for personalized learning and online instruction, AP is not a pedagogical or technological novelty. Unlike "No Child Left Behind" and "Race to the Top," AP is not a federal program or mandate. Unlike the "Common Core," it is not something that states impose on reluctant school systems and teachers. Rather, it's a privately operated, mostly privately financed, and almost entirely voluntary curricular option for high schools and their teachers and students, one that's been competently

1

managed and adroitly led by the nonprofit, nonpartisan College Board. As such, AP enjoys an excellent reputation and is broadly popular among both parents and educators, including many who bridle at other items on today's reform agendas. It has mostly avoided the politics and fads that roil contemporary American public education, even as it has gradually evolved into a significant player in the longest-running and most compelling reform impulse of all: to widen educational opportunity and foster upward mobility for disadvantaged youngsters.

For several decades after its founding in the mid-twentieth century, AP was a modest venture, scarcely visible on the K–12 scene, that conferred extra advantages on a relative handful of already-fortunate kids attending a short list of exclusive private and posh suburban public high schools. Within those well-heeled surrounds, AP offered college-level courses to able, motivated pupils in a limited array of subjects, followed by exams that gauged their mastery of that material, potentially leading to degree credit on matriculation. (Author Finn used it in 1962 to skip his freshman year of college.)

Today, however, Advanced Placement's profile is far higher and markedly different: A host of policies, auxiliary programs, and booster organizations have widened access to it. Not only is its scale vastly greater, its cadres are also much more diverse, both demographically and geographically, and it's being deployed strategically in many places to strengthen the secondary schooling and postsecondary prospects of poor and minority youngsters who long lacked access to high-level coursework.

For them, as for its original population of course- and exam-takers, participation in Advanced Placement can bring multiple benefits: One's scores may yield stronger odds of gaining admission to the university of one's choice, the chance to skip entry-level classes after matriculating, and actual credit toward one's degree. Along the way, AP supplies intellectual challenges to able students, affords them additional academic choices, and enables them to go further and deeper in subjects that interest them than is possible in standard curricula. It creates opportunities for motivated teachers to stretch themselves while gaining valuable professional development and colleagueship. Carefully deployed, it can tone up and revitalize entire high schools and, sometimes, the middle schools that feed them. For College Board leaders, as *New York Times* columnist Thomas Friedman recently noted, it's even a means for ensuring that more young people enter adulthood having already accessed the "two codes" they view as central to successful lives and good citizenship in today's America: computer science and the US Constitution.[1]

As it shoulders these multiple missions, however, and pursues goals that go far beyond its initial raison d'être, the AP program confronts sizable challenges. It must navigate the ideological and curricular rapids that flow from academe into the K–12 system, and it must seek viable truces in the culture wars that rock a number of disciplines so that its courses can continue both to satisfy the demands of universal public education at the secondary level and to qualify for course credits and placements at the college level.

Delivering on AP's promise also grows palpably harder as the program expands and diversifies: finding—and preparing—a sufficiency of qualified and willing teachers across the almost forty subjects in the current catalog; ensuring that school principals and district leaders are fully bought into the multiple challenges both of implementing AP in the high schools and satisfactorily preparing more youngsters before they even get there; fending off critics who would rather devote all available resources to low achievers and struggling learners; retaining the loyalty of upscale parents who fear that their kids' AP experience (and advantage) may be dimmed by the inclusion of "those other" students; dealing with the blowback from AP's democratization as some exclusive private schools and colleges begin to shun it; and contending with a surge of rival offerings (notably "dual enrollment" programs) that seem to promise easier access to surer college credit.

How is the College Board handling such dilemmas? Can one program juggle so many balls? As AP enlarges its footprint and extends its mission, how well is it preserving the features that made it worth expanding in the first place, particularly its unapologetic rigor, its commitment to liberal education, and its stealthy furnishing of quality education choices? How acute is the tension between accelerating proven high achievers and assisting a diverse population of kids to get a leg up on college? How effective is AP, actually, in those roles today, as it evolves from a low-profile elite option to a big-time reform strategy for policy and philanthropy?

Can AP sustain its acclaimed high standard at a time when most state academic standards are rising even as there's intensifying pressure to ease passing scores, inflate grades, "recover credit," and push everyone through to graduation, matriculation, and college degrees? Can it retain its coast-to-coast acceptance as authority over standards, assessment, and accountability shift from Washington back to the states—and as anything resembling a national curriculum seems politically taboo? Can it sustain its integrity—and expanded market—as competitors get more traction? Can it preserve the respect in which it has been widely held as its very scale and giant revenue stream lead more critics to hurl stones at it?

Closer to the ground, how are actual schools and school systems—both longtime users and those new to the enterprise—dealing with today's Advanced Placement program? How are they accommodating—or initiating—moves to bring it within range of more kids and to advance equity as well as achievement? Why are some private schools turning their backs on it even as some charter-school networks build it into every student's program?

From its modest beginnings, AP has grown enormously in response to popularity among teachers and parents, ambition (and competition) among students, and pressure from many directions to expand access to its courses and add more subjects to its catalog. Today, the College Board estimates, about one-fifth of recent US graduates have scored a "qualifying score" (3 or better on a scale of 1 to 5) on at least one AP test during their high school years.

Many of these young people do in fact obtain some credit and can thereby expedite or deepen their undergraduate education and possibly cut its cost. Yet some colleges—looking to their own revenues, enrollments, and faculty preferences—have lately made this harder to get. Meanwhile, the competition to gain admission to those very institutions has intensified so that even students who don't "qualify" on AP exams are keen to display its courses on their high school transcripts as evidence of their commitment to embracing challenge and grappling with rigor. Still, with large fractions of AP's new participants, particularly black and Latino youngsters, faring poorly on those exams, it's important to ask how much satisfaction to take from wider access when that's accompanied by lower rates of success. This dilemma resurfaces several times in the pages that follow, until we settle our own view of it in the final chapter.

An easy remedy would be to make AP exams easier to pass, but the program's five-point scale may be the closest thing American education has to a "platinum yardstick," an unbending standard of intellectual attainment in high school at a time when state standards, assessments, passing scores, grading practices, and graduation requirements are all in flux. Its association with resolute quality is a major source of AP's popularity with so many families, guidance counselors, policy makers, and philanthropists.

Because Advanced Placement is uniform, externally validated, and respected for its rigor, helping more students participate and succeed in it is the goal of numerous ventures. For many education reformers, opening its gates wider has become a means to equalize opportunity, expand college participation and completion, strengthen America's human capital, and foster upward mobility. Some also prize its ability to assist gifted students who crave more than the standard curriculum and bored kids who otherwise spin their intellectual wheels during the last year or two of high school. Others see AP expansion as a "rising tide" that can lift entire schools. More and more districts and several states cover the costs not only of the AP courses and those who teach them but also of the fees for students taking AP exams.

Although dustups occur now and then over individual subjects, AP's catalog of courses and exams has generally avoided the controversies that typically confound anything that smacks of national curriculum or testing in the United States, although such systems have long existed with minimal ruckus in other high-performing countries. Advanced Placement threads this needle because it's voluntary, not something imposed by government; because its creators and operators serve a private outfit with no political coloration; and because it's not a total curriculum. Rather, it's an array of courses that no school teaches in its entirety and that no student comes close to taking all of. Within each course, a fair amount of discretion is left to classroom teachers, which also causes most educators to value and take pride in teaching it, rather than resenting and opposing it.

Advanced Placement has also functioned as a welcome source of choice within American secondary education—not choice among schools as much as options among courses, teachers, and levels of intellectual challenge. Because it doesn't "threaten the system" like charter schools or vouchers, it hasn't faced the acrimony that we associate with other forms of choice. As it expands, however, and moves more prominently into other reform crusades, draws on more funding, and encounters more competition, it garners greater attention and controversy.

The flood of college-credit options during the high school years also alarms some professors, bursars, and registrars, even as more of their own postsecondary institutions seek to supply (and profit from) such options. At the same time, the still-uneven distribution of these options (and access to them) across the K–12 landscape worries advocates and policy makers who focus on educational equity.

The Advanced Placement program, in short, besides having become a very big deal, has turned into something of an education Rorschach test, playing multiple roles, aspiring to diverse goals, and surfacing a number of fault lines as well as opportunities. One can see in it at least a partial solution to many different problems and can glimpse progress on many fronts. One can also detect signs of reluctance and resistance on a number of those fronts.

Now well into its sixties, AP today warrants a biography—the clear-eyed but friendly kind—and that's what we've undertaken. In the pages that follow, we review its history, examine its workings on the ground, discuss alternatives (and rivals) to it, delve into the major issues that it faces today, and consider the sizable contributions it can—and cannot—make to the future of American education.

Notes

1. Thomas L. Friedman, "The Two Codes Your Kids Need to Know," *New York Times*, February 12, 2019. https://www.nytimes.com/2019/02/12/opinion/college-board-sat-ap.html?action =click&module=Opinion&pgtype=Homepage.

PART I

Brief History

1

Early Days

Accelerated learning opportunities for able, motivated young people have existed on American shores for centuries. Veteran Scarsdale teacher and amateur AP historian Eric Rothschild notes, for example, that "even before 1776, a young immigrant to New York, Alexander Hamilton, walked into King's College and demanded that he be allowed to complete his undergraduate studies in one year."[1] During the nineteenth century, it was normal for students to move through schools and colleges at their own pace, some faster than others, and faster in some subjects than in others.

As high school attendance slowly universalized and democratized, however, it also became more standardized, with prescribed courses attached to specific years in school and grade levels broadly linked to one's age. States passed "compulsory attendance laws" mandating that children attend primary-secondary schools between specified ages (today usually five or six to seventeen or eighteen). Colleges responded by beginning to standardize their admissions procedures, seeking students of roughly the same age who had taken roughly the same courses over roughly the same years of K–12 schooling, although tensions remained strong between those who favored evidence of applicants' "aptitude for learning"—early versions of the SAT exams date to 1926—and those who sought more concrete signs of actual accomplishment in high school and beyond.

What to do with exceptionally strong and ambitious students remained a quandary that elicited no broad consensus. As noted by historian Tim Lacy, throughout the nineteenth century and the first half of the twentieth, educators in both K–12 and higher education worked at such varied strategies as curricular enrichment, acceleration, ability grouping, tracking, and school selectivity, often ending up by either separating advanced students from their pokier peers and instructing them in their own classes or schools or allowing them to skip ahead to more challenging courses, even jump entire school grades or levels of education. Related efforts sought to lubricate the transition of such young people from high school into college with minimal repetition and duplication, even as parallel efforts—including the new SAT—strove to enlarge the pool of prospective college students and draw youngsters from more backgrounds and regions into higher education.[2]

The aftermath of World War II brought further broadening of access, as states made high school mandatory for all and the GI Bill made college affordable for hundreds of thousands of returning servicemen and women, even as the Cold War and, in time, Sputnik (1957) and the National Defense Education Act (1958) focused greater attention on the need for more robust education in general and the development of more scientists and engineers in particular. As Rothschild writes, many people became convinced

> that the upgrading of American education was a matter of survival in a death struggle with communism. We needed engineers and scientists and people of talent in all areas if America was to see another century. Top professionals increasingly needed graduate work and graduate schools needed strong college graduates. If our high schools weren't producing students of talent, America might rot at the core. And if our best high schools and colleges were teaching overlapping material that would be better taught quickly, then somehow we had to speed up the process.[3]

But what should well-educated people study? Should some get a better— or speedier—education than others? Should exceptionally able and hard-charging students get more or move faster than their classmates?

Here we explore the earliest days of AP and the growing pains of its first two decades. In chapter 2, we bring that saga up to the mid-1990s. We dive into more recent developments and the present state of Advanced Placement in chapter 3 and review the program's actual mechanics in chapter 9.

Early Experiments

Through a spin-off called the Fund for the Advancement of Education, the Ford Foundation supported five separate projects during the 1950s—experiments, committee reports, and more—charged with finding better ways of meeting the educational needs of able students via smoother transitions between high school and college. All were meant to push back against "the greatest risk of all—the risk of adhering stubbornly to a clearly imperfect set of practices which are frustrating the development of young talent at a time in history when this nation urgently needs to develop its human resources to the full."[4]

One pilot effort, involving eleven colleges and ultimately some 1,350 students, launched in 1951. It sought to boost high achievers into college two years earlier than the norm, most of them without a high school diploma. After five years, much data, and an elaborate evaluation, it was judged an academic success but it also surfaced some "social adjustment problems," particularly for young males—problems that seem to have consisted mainly of difficulty getting dates with older female students! Although a number of colleges adopted variants of early admission to accelerate a few carefully screened candidates, there was no great enthusiasm for systematically sending large numbers of school-age youngsters onto campus as full-time students.[5]

Two other Ford-supported projects encountered fewer problems and yielded broader consensus among secondary and postsecondary educators— and both loom large in standard accounts of Advanced Placement's genesis. Both were committee-style studies, examining ways to minimize repetition of coursework as students move from high school into college and also to grant strong pupils earlier access to more challenging academics and swifter pathways through their formal education. Instead of sending them to college early, college-level courses would be introduced into their high schools, along with the possibility of finessing those same courses upon matriculation, meaning that one might shorten one's time to a college degree and/or study more advanced material from professors even in one's first year on campus.

One such project gave rise to *General Education in School and College: A Committee Report by Members of the Faculties of Andover, Exeter, Lawrenceville, Harvard, Princeton, and Yale*, published in 1952.[6] Rothschild terms it "a key document for understanding the birth of advanced placement," adding that the document was "unashamedly elitist throughout."[7] Its authors (including the late McGeorge Bundy, soon to be named dean of the Harvard faculty) acknowledged that they were chiefly concerned with "superior students" and "that standards can be pulled up from the top more easily than they can be pushed up from the bottom."[8] In the end, they recommended that schools encourage more independent study for their brightest seniors and that there be launched "a set of achievement examinations . . . which would enable the colleges supporting these examinations to give an entering student advanced placement in a subject like, let us say, chemistry; or credit for the prerequisite to majoring in history."[9]

The other project yielded a more concrete plan—dubbed the "Kenyon Plan" because its leader, Gordon Chalmers, was president of that small private college in central Ohio—for developing college-level courses and standards that high schools could undertake, and recruited academic talent from several disciplines to create "descriptions of college freshman-level courses that college faculty would accept even if taught in high schools."[10] In 1951, leaders of eleven colleges met in Washington to discuss what that plan might look like in practice (including representatives from Bowdoin, Brown, Carleton, Haverford, Kenyon, MIT, Middlebury, Swarthmore, Wabash, Wesleyan, and Williams). Oberlin joined the following year.

"Pioneer Schools"

These discussions yielded a pilot program that commenced in 1952, beginning with seven public and private high schools, expanding to twenty-seven by 1954.[11] These "pioneer schools" introduced advanced courses across ten disciplines (biology, chemistry, English composition, French, German, Latin, literature, mathematics, and Spanish). In May 1954, the first common exams were administered to 532 students in these schools, and identical exams were taken by freshmen in the participating colleges. Both were evaluated by the Educational Testing Service (ETS). It turned out, in Rothschild's words, that "the high school students had acquitted themselves very well."[12]

A brief tussle arose over how this endeavor would be sustained and managed in the future, with Chalmers wanting to keep it based at Kenyon while others urged the College Board to take it on—not least because of the continuing need for test development, administration, and scoring by ETS, which was practically a subsidiary of the College Board.

The Board's then president, Frank Bowles, resisted for a time, partly due to the infant program's high unit cost and partly because doing AP right meant resuming a mode of assessment that the SAT had discarded in favor of objective multiple-choice testing, namely (in Bowles's words), reinstating "the definition of requirements, the syllabi, the written examinations made up in advance by committees of examiners and read by committees of readers."[13] But he soon changed his mind and persuaded his colleagues at the College Board to take on the project. In a 1965 memoir, Bowles recalled six reasons for doing so, most of which still resonate today:

- "The opportunity for the really able student to go beyond the normal offerings of the secondary school."
- "The opportunity for the well trained secondary school teacher to have a course of his own on the college level."
- The "quite unexpected effect" in many schools of achievement rising "in a secondary school class when four or five brighter students were taken out and put in another class." Far from holding back the slower pupils, Bowles declared that "removal of the group of brilliant individuals allowed those who had normal ability to speak up without fear of showing their inadequacy when compared with the brilliants [sic]."
- The necessity "of doing something for the bright student. (This was about the time when we were beginning to notice that secondary schools had been oriented toward the average student and that the brighties [sic] were being neglected.)"
- The stimulating effect of such programs on entire secondary school faculties.
- Higher education was expanding so fast that "it was going to be necessary to take innovative steps in the secondary schools of all kinds and varieties. At the time neither I, nor anyone else so far as I know, foresaw the tremendous effect that the Advanced Placement Program would have in raising standards of achievement in secondary school and indirectly in raising the minimum requirements for admission to the Ivy League colleges— requirements, that is, when stated in terms of standards of real achievement."[14]

In fall 1955, the College Board shouldered responsibility for the "continuation and expansion" of the nascent Advanced Placement program. Charles R. Keller was named to run it, and ETS was retained to handle exam development, administration, and scoring. The scoring scale had to be standardized across subjects, and several approaches were tried, including a fifteen-point version. To reach that total in US History, for example, Rothschild recalls, "Each exam was read three times. . . . The first time through, the reader could award up to five points for factual thoroughness and accuracy, the second time up to five points for the student's interpretation, and the final run-through up to five points for presentation. Soon the three different scores were lumped into one holistic score."[15]

Some colleges were loath to accept these results. As Keller later recalled, "College people were reluctant to believe that school teachers could do something as well as—or almost as well as—they could."[16] Slowly but surely, however, he and his fellow AP "missionaries" gained traction. It probably helped that Harvard signed up—and a number of parents and students began to demand that such opportunities come to their high schools, too. It also helped that college faculty could themselves see the course descriptions and—in the early days—students' actual exam papers along with their scores. Rothschild suggests, however, that "the best selling point for AP was probably the college performance of former AP students. In the first group to attend college in the fall of 1954, 32 percent finished in the top one-sixth of their class at the end of their freshman year, 65 percent were in the middle two-thirds, and only 3 percent were in the bottom one-sixth."[17]

A National Program

After the College Board took on the program, May 1956 saw the first nationally administered exams in eleven disciplines: US history, biology, chemistry, English, French, German, Latin IV, Latin V, mathematics, physics, and Spanish. 1,229 students enrolled in 104 high schools took 2,199 of those exams before sending their scores to 130 colleges.[18] European history was added the following year, but the program was so small in those days that all fifty-nine of those exams could be read in a single day by four examiners sitting on the "second floor of a firehouse" near the ETS office in Princeton.[19]

At the outset, Advanced Placement was explicitly intended for the strongest students at top high schools, those who "already had the luxury of being bound for prestigious colleges and universities, room to excel and an inducement to continue to work hard."[20] But while the lore surrounding the program's birth associates it mostly with eastern prep schools, in fact the "pioneer schools" were a mix of independent and public institutions, the latter mostly located in upper-middle-class suburbs of major cities in the East and Midwest. Evanston Township High School, for example, is situated in a wealthy northern suburb of Chicago, near a road sign that still boasts that this school was a "Founding Member, Advanced Placement Program." Today, that school is half minority and continues to rank among the nation's top secondary schools. Still, there's no denying that the early cohorts of AP high schools were among the more privileged. Rothschild recalled that they were "unabashedly elitist . . . those taking the exams in the early years were largely male, largely students from private prep schools and elite public high schools, and probably mostly Protestant."[21] David Dudley, who became the AP program's second head, wrote in 1958 that the program's "basic philosophy . . . is simply that all students are not created equal."[22]

By decade's end, the AP infant had entered a growth spurt. Dudley termed the program "a sound and long-range movement. It has been received well by educators because it answers a need, because it is conservative at the same time that it is new, and because it is a normal growth in the evolution of American education."[23] The number of exams taken grew by an average of 58 percent annually between 1954 and 1960. In May 1960, more than 10,000 students sat for 14,158 tests, almost twice as many as the previous year. AP veterans enrolled in 567 colleges that fall, and the future began to brighten. In 1961, former Harvard president—and eminent high school reformer—James B. Conant termed the program's growth one of "the most encouraging signs of real improvement in our educational system."[24]

Also helpful were the fruitful interactions and positive vibes associated with annual AP conferences, which turned out to be valuable but otherwise hard-to-find opportunities for high school teachers and college professors to meet and work together. As early as 1954, Edwin C. Douglas, who taught math at Connecticut's Taft School, described "a warm respect for the abilities of those at both levels of the education structure."[25] One participating school principal termed it a "most productive and satisfying occurrence."[26]

Positive feelings also accompanied the exam-reading process, which in the early years was decentralized or "cottage style," with readers meeting in different places according to subject: Historians gathered at Williams College, chemists at Kenyon, biologists at Wabash, and so forth. But their numbers, too, kept growing. By June 1957, more than seven hundred school and college instructors and one hundred administrators were gathering to appraise students' exam papers.[27]

As is the case today, not everyone was smitten by AP. Charles Keller cited one college official who declared: "It is doubtful that anyone at the College is convinced that this is a step in the right direction; they would rather see stronger prep courses for those that can take them rather than encroachment on college work by high schools."[28] Rothschild noted:

> In these early years . . . many colleges demanded a higher level of performance from their advanced placement applicants than they did of their own first-year students. For instance, a number of colleges awarded "contingent credit" to AP students who earned a score of 3. If they received a

grade of B or better in an advanced course in the same field, the credit was theirs; if they received less than a B, they were out of luck. . . . Edward T. Wilcox, AP director at Harvard in the early years of the program, later recounted horror stories about some Harvard professors who began their upper-level classes by identifying the advanced placement students and then tossing them out, to the amusement of the non-AP students who remained.[29]

Wilcox was the dean who gave author Finn the option in 1962 of skipping his freshman year. At the time—note the later changes sketched in chapter 10—Harvard's policy was to offer "sophomore standing" to any entering student who displayed scores of 3 or better on at least three AP exams. By 1975, 137 colleges in thirty-nine states followed similar practices, yielding what was sometimes termed the "AP year."[30]

Not every student seized that opportunity, however. It was big news in *The Crimson* in 1959 when, for the first time, several Harvard matriculants declined to enter as sophomores.[31] Nor was foregoing the freshman year the right move for all who were eligible. As Wilcox noted, Harvard required undergraduates to declare their majors at the start of sophomore year, meaning that anyone who skipped the freshman experience had better know at the outset what he wanted to study because he wouldn't have two semesters in which to browse, explore unfamiliar fields, meet faculty members, and talk with other students. By 1965, half of the 210 Harvard newbies who had the option of sophomore standing declined to exercise it.[32]

Acceleration and degree credit weren't the only appeal—or benefit—of Advanced Placement. Rothschild reports that many students were "content with the enrichment that the AP courses had provided" and "never applied for either AP credit or advancement in college."[33] Williams College admissions director Fred Copeland "was glad to report that at Williams as elsewhere there had been little demand for acceleration."[34]

Growing Pains

In 1963, 22,000 students from 1,700 schools took some 29,000 exams and went on to attend 765 colleges. Advanced Placement had become the "fastest growing" College Board program according to then program director Jack Arbolino.[35]

By the end of that decade, however, the growth rate was flattening. Just 1,200 more students took AP exams in 1973 than in 1969. Indeed, 1973 was the first (and only) year in AP's history when participation actually declined a bit. As Rothschild writes, "education was not immune to the social and political shocks of the late 1960s."[36] Many concerns that gave rise to college-student protests in that era were trickling into high schools, too, including wariness of anything viewed as elitist.[37] In 1969, AP was available in just 14 percent of US secondary schools and seemed out of step with the egalitarianism that marked this period.[38] Moreover, as civil rights struggles intensified, historian William Hochman observed that "because there have not been as many black students in AP courses, some people regard the program as touched with . . . 'institutional racism,' that is, the very structure of the program results in the unintended exclusion of blacks."[39] One researcher went so far as to conclude that "the social climate of the late 60s and early 70s caused a near collapse of AP."[40]

AP's struggles weren't the only sign of trouble in American education during that period. SAT scores were slipping. "Equity" rather than "achievement" was the foremost concern of policy makers, who strove to open educational opportunities for poor and minority youngsters as well as girls and children with disabilities. There was a tension—one that hasn't gone away and that we will encounter repeatedly in these pages—between proponents of wider democratization of educational opportunities and those preoccupied with higher standards and stronger achievement.

Financially, too, AP faced issues. Back in 1958, it had cost the College Board a deficit of $150,000. To make ends meet, exam fees were raised to $8 and a $5 registration fee was added, while two separate English exams (composition and literature) were merged to cut costs. Notwithstanding the growth in participation, Lacy reports that the AP program ran annual deficits throughout the 1960s. The situation was sufficiently dire that "there were discussions about ending the program."[41] In time, however, as Rothschild notes, "The financial problems which had threatened to sink AP had vanished, as growing numbers of students took and paid for the examinations. Soon the program was a source of monies for other College Board enterprises."[42]

Gradual growth resumed after 1973, and in May 1976 more than 75,000 youngsters sat for nearly 100,000 exams. Nearly 4,000 secondary schools were participating by then, and the catalog had expanded to eighteen courses, now including Music, Studio Art, and Art History.[43]

Even during—or perhaps because of—a time of intense concern with equity, Advanced Placement benefited from the participation of high-status schools and universities and from the energies of zealous, well-credentialed advocates. Many of their institutions were striving to open their doors to a broader spectrum of students (and, in the case of colleges, a broader spectrum of feeder schools) than they had historically served. It was a time of desegregation, of warring on poverty, and of purposeful efforts to widen opportunities for individuals and populations that historically hadn't had many. It made sense that elite universities, reaching out to "non-traditional" populations attending unfamiliar high schools in far-flung places, would seek evidence they could trust that candidates for admission were indeed up to their standards. Not knowing much about the content, quality of instruction, or rigor of high schools in, say, Memphis, Albuquerque, or Sacramento—except, perhaps, in their long-standing private academies, "country day" schools, and posh suburban schools—and unfamiliar with the judgments, candor, and integrity of their teachers and college advisors, a place like Yale or Duke or Williams might sensibly view applicants' AP scores as metrics that they understood and could rely on. SAT scores were good clues to individuals' potential, but AP was a way to gauge what they had actually learned and how successfully they had already grappled with college-level intellectual challenges. That such institutions also had the option of conferring credit on enrollees with respectable AP scores was a dual incentive—for the college to attract more diverse but high-achieving pupils and for students to enroll in a prestigious college that was prepared to recognize and reward their accomplishments.

In that environment, it also made sense for more high schools in more places to sign up for Advanced Placement as a way to raise their own status and reputations, equip their stronger students with academic credentials, boost them into good colleges, and perhaps save them time and money en route to a bachelor's degree. Nor did it hurt that high school teachers who relished—and were up to the challenge of—teaching high-ability students welcomed this new form of "honors" classrooms within a national endeavor that afforded stimulating professional opportunities as well as recognition and positive feedback for instructors. Some felt that it renewed and upgraded their chosen vocation. As AP teacher William Snyder remarked during the 1960s, "It has rejuvenated my entire teaching career. Anything you've been doing for a while gets stale. AP provides another path, a different avenue filled with adventure. For a teacher, it's like beginning again."[44]

For all the excitement and expansion, however, after two decades AP remained predominantly a boon for relatively privileged kids. Besides the elite institutions that launched the program, the new additions often numbered just one or two high schools in places like Fort Worth (Paschal High School) or Cincinnati (Walnut Hills). Other schools may have offered a couple of courses, but the full AP treatment was not widely available. Save for "magnet" programs meant to foster voluntary integration, the first few thousand schools to embrace AP were likely either to practice selective admissions to the school itself, selective entry for students into AP classrooms—or were simply located in affluent, usually white, neighborhoods, not on the far sides of many tracks.

In the next chapter, we watch AP tiptoe across those tracks.

Notes

1. Eric Rothschild, "Four Decades of the Advanced Placement Program," *History Teacher* 32, no. 2 (1999): 175–76.

2. Tim Lacy, "Examining AP: Access, Rigor, and Revenue in the History of the Advanced Placement Program," in *AP: A Critical Examination of the Advanced Placement Program*, ed. Phillip M. Sadler and others (Cambridge, MA: Harvard Education Press, 2010), 20–21.

3. Rothschild, "Four Decades," 176.

4. Fund for the Advancement of Education, *They Went to College Early* (New York: Fund for the Advancement of Education, 1957), vi.

5. Fund for the Advancement of Education, *They Went to College Early*, vii.

6. *General Education in School and College: A Committee Report by Members of the Faculties of Andover, Exeter, Lawrenceville, Harvard, Princeton, and Yale* (Cambridge, MA: Harvard University Press, 1952).

7. Rothschild, "Four Decades," 177.

8. *General Education in School and College*, 10, 13.

9. *General Education in School and College*, 111, 118.

10. Rothschild, "Four Decades," 178.

11. Rothschild, "Four Decades," 178, 202. The first participating schools were the Bronx High School of Science, New York; Central High School, Pennsylvania; Germantown Friends School, Pennsylvania; Evanston Township High School, Illinois; Horace Mann School, New York; Newton High School, Massachusetts; and Saint Louis Country Day School, Missouri.

12. Rothschild, "Four Decades," 179.

13. Frank H. Bowles, "Historical Notes on the Advanced Placement Program," December 13, 1965. These historical notes were provided to us by the College Board.

14. Bowles, "Historical Notes," 4–5.

15. Rothschild, "Four Decades," 181.

16. Charles R. Keller, quoted in Rothschild, "Four Decades," 181.

17. Charles R. Keller, quoted in Rothschild, "Four Decades," 182.

18. College Board, "Annual AP Program Participation, 1956–2018," accessed November 2, 2018. https://secure-media.collegeboard.org/digitalServices/pdf/research/2018/2018-Annual -Participation.pdf.

19. Andrew Mollison, "Surviving a Midlife Crisis: Advanced Placement Turns Fifty," *Education Next* 6, no. 1 (2006): 34.

20. Jack Schneider, *Excellence for All: How a New Breed of Reformers Is Transforming America's Public Schools* (Nashville: Vanderbilt University Press, 2009), 109.

21. Eric Rothschild, quoted in Mollison, "Surviving a Midlife Crisis," 34.

22. David Dudley, "The Advanced Placement Program," *NASSP Bulletin* 42, no. 242 (1958): 1.

23. Dudley, "Advanced Placement Program," 1.

24. James B. Conant, *Slums and Suburbs: A Commentary on Schools in Metropolitan Areas* (New York: McGraw-Hill, 1961), 92.

25. Edwin C. Douglas, "The Advanced Placement Program of the CEEB," *NASSP Bulletin* 43, no. 247 (1959): 95. Douglas was also chairman of the College Board's mathematics examining committee at the time.

26. Charles R. Keller, "The Advanced Placement Program Now Has a History," *NASSP Bulletin* 42, no. 242 (1958): 11.

27. Keller, "Advanced Placement Program Now Has a History," 11.

28. Charles R. Keller, "Piercing the Sheepskin Curtain: Reflections of the First Director," *College Board Review* 30, no. 2 (1956): 30.

29. Rothschild, "Four Decades," 183.

30. Sidney P. Marland Jr., "Advanced Placement: An Above-Average Opportunity," *NASSP Bulletin* 59, no. 391 (1975): 37.

31. Stephen F. Jencks, "Several Advanced Students Decline Sophomore Status," *Harvard Crimson*, October 1, 1959. https://www.thecrimson.com/article/1959/10/1/several-advanced-students-decline-sophomore-status/.

32. Harvard tuition at the time was $1,760 per annum, versus today's $43,280. Had it changed with the value of the dollar over the ensuing half century, the present charge would be just $13,622!

33. Rothschild, "Four Decades," 183.

34. Rothschild, "Four Decades," 183.

35. Jack N. Arbolino, "The Advance Placement Program," *NASSP Bulletin* 48, no. 291 (1964): 136.

36. Rothschild, "Four Decades," 185.

37. Lacy, "Examining AP," 32.

38. William R. Hochman, quoted in Rothschild, "Four Decades," 185.

39. William R. Hochman, quoted in Rothschild, "Four Decades," 185.

40. Jon C. Rehm, "Advanced Placement and American Education: A Foucauldian Analysis of the Advanced Placement Program of the College Board" (EdD diss., Florida International University, 2014), 27. https://digitalcommons.fiu.edu/etd/1530.

41. Lacy, "Examining AP," 33.

42. Rothschild, "Four Decades," 184.

43. College Board, "Annual AP Program Participation"; Rothschild, "Four Decades," 187.

44. William Snyder quoted in School District of Indian River County, "AP Program History," accessed November 2, 2018 (no longer available). https://www.indianriverschools.org/vbhs-pages/152-vbhs-ap/403-vbhs-ap-program-history.

2

Poor Kids Advance, Too

For its first two decades, as we have seen, the Advanced Placement program mostly served high-flying students in well-functioning high schools. For them, AP functioned both as a form of secondary-school "gifted and talented" supplement, affording academic challenges beyond the standard-issue curriculum, and as a way to jump-start their college education, whether by establishing credit on entry that sped their progress toward a degree, by enabling them to waive some requirements (compulsory math or history, for example, perhaps mandatory foreign language study), and/or by skipping the 101 course in an interesting subject and starting off at the 201 level.

In 1976, some 75,000 students took nearly 100,000 AP exams in nearly 4,000 schools. Those numbers more than doubled over the ensuing decade: to roughly 230,000 youngsters sitting for almost 320,000 exams in 1986, while the number of participating schools exceeded 7,000.[1]

By then, however, mutations were occurring in the AP genome. Advanced Placement was beginning to be seen as an adaptable tool that could be applied to the solution of several distinct education problems, beginning with the stiffening competition to enter selective colleges.[2] The percentage of freshman applicants accepted onto those campuses has shrunk for decades. At Harvard, the 1976 admission rate was 20 percent; five years later, it was down to 16 percent.[3] At Stanford, 34 percent of applicants were offered places in 1974, down to 16 percent by 1984.[4] Taking and passing AP exams—the more the better—was thought by more and more students, parents, high school counselors, and evidently also by many college admissions officers to boost one's chances of getting in. It was peerless evidence that students could handle rigorous, college-level academics.

Also heating up was competition for GPAs and class ranks. Beginning with a 1983 decision by the University of California Regents, schools started giving extra GPA points for grades in AP courses, and colleges took those amped-up averages and leapfrogged class ranks into consideration when deciding whom to admit. Various forms of this credit-weighting practice have spread across the land, and it indisputably leads more students to enroll in AP classes—as well as in International Baccalaureate (IB), dual-credit, and honors courses—so as to boost their standing among fellow applicants and their admissions prospects at selective campuses. Gaining that transcript and class rank advantage doesn't even hinge on one's AP exam score, merely on the grade that one's teacher bestows on one's classwork.

During the same period, the United States was awakening to its "at risk" educational status: students not learning nearly enough and expectations pegged too low. "Official" notification came in 1983 with *A Nation at Risk*, the alarm sounded by the National Commission on Excellence in Education, but warning signs could be glimpsed earlier.[5] (The College Board itself concealed one such sign for years: SAT scores started dropping in 1965 but the test's owner didn't point that out until 1975.)

It seemed logical that Advanced Placement might help to arrest this decline, as it embodied more demanding academic standards and rigorous expectations, a higher bar worth pushing more schools to teach toward, and more students to aspire to. Because performance on it was externally evaluated, it was tamper-proof in the sense that kindly teachers or misguided equal-opportunity policies could not conceal weak performance. And unlike SAT scores, which at the time were said to gauge only students' aptitude for college, AP results attested to actual academic accomplishment.

AP also fit into the renewed view that one way to tackle the problem of too-low achievement was to accelerate students. Former US education commissioner Ernest Boyer, then president of the Carnegie Foundation for the Advancement of Teaching, wrote in 1983 that instead of confining able students in standard high school courses, "secondary schools and colleges have a special obligation to break the bureaucratic barriers and develop flexible arrangements for students as they move from one level to another." Heading his list of such arrangements was Advanced Placement.[6]

Mission Shift

Historian Tim Lacy terms this period a time when "stability characterize[d] the AP program," but that's not exactly right.[7] For by the late 1970s an even more profound directional shift began with the gradual emergence of a second major AP mission: assisting able disadvantaged students to engage with and master college-level academic challenges during high school; boosting their confidence that they might in fact be "college material" even if family members and neighbors had never matriculated; and—as with their more privileged age-mates—holding out the possibility of exam scores that would elevate their admissions prospects and kick-start their progress toward degrees.

Deploying it as an opportunity enhancer for kids in need of better opportunities remains a robust education-reform strategy today, a tool grasped by philanthropic initiatives, government programs, nonprofit organizations, and schools focused on life transformation for such youngsters. Indeed, many of them rest their "theory of change" on the purposeful use of AP.

Besides the proactive impulse to turn it into a booster rocket that might propel disadvantaged kids to higher levels, there was angst—owing to its origins as a program for elites—that AP ought not widen gaps. As historian Jack Schneider writes, "At the beginning of the 1960s . . . AP was in a sense exacerbating inequality." This needed to change—and began to change—as more education reformers and policy makers recognized that "all students . . . particularly those in underserved communities long denied educational equity, deserved a challenging high school education and an opportunity for a university degree." Nothing happened overnight but, "by the mid-1970s, a number of education leaders and school reformers began to view AP as a lever for school reform in underserved communities, particularly as a means of helping students move into post-secondary institutions."[8]

The first major declaration of AP's capacity to play this additional role came in 1975 when College Board president Sidney P. Marland Jr., himself a former US commissioner of education and school superintendent in cities from Winnetka to Pittsburgh, wrote that Advanced Placement was "a very effective instrument for serving gifted but socially disadvantaged students," and he noted that "pride in the program often helps urban school leaders change negative stereotypes held by some parents and segments of the public."[9] Further proof of this was shortly to be supplied.

"Stand and Deliver"

The highest-profile example of AP-as-booster-rocket came in the early 1980s at Garfield High School, located in an impoverished immigrant section of East Los Angeles and personified by the legendary math teacher Jaime Escalante, who in turn was immortalized in the 1988 film *Stand and Deliver* and in Jay Mathews's fine biography of the same year, *Escalante: The Best Teacher in America*.

The Escalante story, as recounted in both book and movie, vividly depicted how AP could boost the educational and life prospects of poor Hispanic youngsters from an inner-city high school, and for a time the school where that happened occupied a singular place in American education.[10] As Mathews reported in the *Washington Post*, "In 1987, 26 percent of all Mexican-American students in the country who passed the AP Calculus exams attended a single high school: Garfield. That meant that hundreds of thousands of overlooked students could probably do as well if they got what Escalante was giving out. But what was that?"[11]

An immigrant from Bolivia, Escalante had arrived at Garfield in 1974. It was a sorely troubled school, awash in low achievement, gangs and fights, lax expectations, and hundreds of dropouts. In other words, it was not very different from many other US high schools serving disadvantaged and immigrant youngsters—and in many respects it showed the effects of the dominant direction of US education policy of the previous two decades: An equity-obsessed, resource-based focus on including everyone but not pushing poor and minority students very hard, lest they grow discouraged, lose confidence, erode self-esteem, and leave school.

Escalante saw big problems with that approach, which was so different from the kind of education he had practiced (and personally experienced) in Latin America. He sensed that his low-income Latino pupils could—and would—achieve far more if their sights were raised, if they were both pushed and encouraged to reach beyond their self-perceived (and school-fostered) limits, and if they were prodded and incentivized to work much harder. He had a few allies among the Garfield teachers, and in the late 1970s the school experimented with small AP and honors programs. Escalante launched his first AP Calculus class in 1978–79—and two of the first five pupils who made it as far as the exam earned passing scores. In the following years, he refined his pedagogy and recruited more kids into his classes. He improvised classroom props and staged candy-apple sales and car washes to raise the cash to pay the students' exam fees. By May 1981, all but one of his fifteen test-takers achieved scores of 3 or better. (One even scored 5, a first for Escalante.) This progress continued and gradually accelerated under Garfield's new principal, a Latino educator (and former army lieutenant) named Henry Gradillas, who took the school's helm in 1981. He saw that it was well and good to have a small AP program for a handful of students, but Garfield had some three thousand pupils, many of whom sorely needed an educational kick in the pants. Something more ambitious—and capacious—was called for.

Gradillas launched a magnet program in math and computer science, seeing it as both a way to attract hundreds of college-bound students to his school and as "a great opportunity to start pulling up the kids in the regular Garfield program." Then, with Escalante, he fastened onto Advanced Placement, declaring (in his own memoir years later) that "AP was the perfect program for some of our bright kids whose talents had not been identified in tests. Any student with the *ganas* and the appropriate academic prerequisites could take AP classes."[12]

In his book, Gradillas offered a superb explanation of AP's capacity to leverage change in a school like Garfield, complete with tactics to make that happen:

> The beauty of AP is that it puts a school's students up against the best students in the United States. It also brings people together. In regular classes, there are always complaints from students and their parents about teacher-made tests. Someone always finds them unfair and there are always kids and parents who want to bargain for higher grades. The system sometimes makes students and teachers adversaries. With AP, parents, students, teachers and administrators are all on the same side. Rather than being the "enemy" who is punishing the student with poor grades or tests that are too hard, the teacher is the coach working with the students to help them meet the goal of passing the AP exam. If there must be an "enemy," it is the Educational Testing Service. . . .
>
> We did all that we could to decrease the number of roadblocks to AP enrollment. . . . At one time, only students with A averages were allowed in AP. We found a lot of bright, formerly mediocre students who had seen the light and were really ready for AP, even if their transcripts indicated that they were not, so we dropped that requirement. We dropped the requirement that parents give written permission before kids could enroll in AP classes. . . . When a student enrolled in an AP class, we demanded

a serious commitment. The contract demanded that all students actually take the test. . . . The test makes the AP what it is, and we would not allow kids to avoid it. Fundraisers helped to pay the costs.

In 1985 we started having rallies for our AP participants. . . . AP success at Garfield was a great example of Escalante's model of pulling kids up. When barrio kids saw their cousins and neighbors graduating from high school with at least a semester's worth of college credit, and they saw them going to schools like MIT, Yale, Stanford and USC on full scholarships, and they realized that those kids were a lot like they are, they wanted a piece of the action.[13]

The psychological insight in that statement—that "barrio kids" who saw others like themselves succeeding in AP, then in college, would realize that they, too, might join those ranks—aligns perfectly with some of today's most energetic and creative deployers of Advanced Placement as an opportunity enhancer, people like Reid Saaris and the Equal Opportunity Schools program that he started (see more in chapter 6).[14]

Just as important is Gradillas's observation that revving the curriculum also toned up the whole school and engaged parents:

Nothing changed Garfield more than the change of curriculum. Nothing involved parents more. At first it was because the kids complained. . . . After the parents came to see the fruits of Garfield's curricular change, we got steadily less complaints and more support as time went by. Gang activity and drug use decreased and attendance improved as kids realized that challenging courses were leading them to the light at the end of the tunnel.[15]

The attention-grabbing episode that made Garfield—and Escalante—famous came in 1982: His students did so well on the AP Calculus exam that ETS monitors suspected cheating. After a huge ruckus, almost all the kids retook the test in August—and everyone who retook it passed. Because of the national notoriety that surrounded this saga, complete with legal maneuvers and allegations of anti-Hispanic discrimination by snooty eastern institutions, Escalante and his students were sudden celebrities. The hit movie surely helped, as did Escalante's public embrace by Education Secretary William J. Bennett and Presidents Ronald Reagan and George H. W. Bush.[16]

Garfield's own AP program grew rapidly while Escalante and Gradillas remained at the school. By 1988, only six schools in the country prepared more students for the AP Calculus test than Garfield, and AP enthusiasm had spread to other subjects. Garfield pupils from sixteen AP classes took 443 exams in 1988 and earned 266 qualifying scores. Some philanthropic dollars started to flow in Garfield's direction.[17]

This impressive example of AP success in a school full of poor, immigrant kids radiated from Los Angeles across the country and was coupled with reverberations from *A Nation at Risk* and mounting evidence from other sources that high expectations and truly effective schools could work wonders for young people in general and disadvantaged youngsters in particular.[18] AP was by no means the sole source of such expectations, but Garfield showed that it could serve this purpose—and serve it successfully.

After Escalante and Gradillas moved on to other schools, Garfield's AP program staggered. Such building-level reforms can prove fragile, heavily dependent on heroic work—both in the classroom and in leadership roles—by particular individuals, as well as examples of how hard it is to transform a school's culture in a lasting way. But Garfield ultimately sustained a sizable AP program, and many students continued to earn qualifying scores, even as the school struggled with demographic shifts, overcrowding, and more.[19] As recently as 2018, it ranked 2,252 on Jay Mathews's national "Challenge Index," a list of high schools that fare well on criteria based largely on AP participation—not a bad showing for a school where almost 90 percent of students are low income and many are newcomers to American education.[20]

The Garfield experience affected Mathews, too. The school's stunning performance in calculus in 1987, he recalled three decades later, was "a moment that changed my life. . . . My focus since then has been to explore how this was done and identify those schools working hardest to challenge students from all backgrounds with courses such as AP and International Baccalaureate."[21]

In addition to articles and regular columns in the *Washington Post* and, for many years, *Newsweek* magazine, Mathews would go on (in 1998) to devise his influential annual rating—and ranking—of the nation's "most challenging high schools." This would have a big impact in our ratings-and-rankings-obsessed country, with ever-stiffening admission to elite colleges and with more families gaining the right and the means to choose their children's schools. Since Mathews devised his "Challenge Index" and *U.S. News* began doing something similar for high schools in 2007, schools and districts that took their rankings seriously clearly needed to expand their AP (and IB) programs. And because Mathews counted tests taken, not scores achieved, schools had no incentive to limit participation to their strongest students. Nor did Mathews want them to. Besides selling newspapers and magazines, he was knowingly prodding more high schools to become more like Garfield by welcoming into AP classes more young people who might not have been as welcome if the school focused exclusively on qualifying scores. He has, in his way, contributed to the democratizing of AP and to the scrapping of gates, prerequisites, and teacher recommendations that historically limited access to these advanced courses in many schools and districts. (We explain his—and *U.S. News*'s—rating systems in more detail in the next chapter.)

Besides expanding their AP course offerings and student participation as a way to boost their schools' rankings in an increasingly competitive education environment, some enterprising principals found—as had Gradillas—that they could deploy AP as a lever for curricular and pedagogical reforms. As one math teacher noted to Mathews in 1987, "the advantage of AP is that it strengthens the curriculum immediately." At her school, launching AP Calculus for seniors forced teachers to deliver sufficient doses of trigonometry and analytic geometry in eleventh grade and advanced algebra in tenth, which forced the ninth and eighth grades to provide full courses in geometry and beginning algebra.[22]

AP also helped principals hold onto their best teachers. The curriculum was challenging, the kids were eager, smart, and generally well-behaved, and it was stimulating to teach them. Why leave for another school?

It isn't easy, though, to install and make a success of a challenging program like Advanced Placement in a school that had little or no prior experience with it, and it's far harder in schools like Garfield, places full of poor kids who face many pressures, threats, and temptations, institutions that must often give other needs—safety, health and nutrition, attendance, remediation, basic achievement—higher priority than augmenting their curricular offerings for successful pupils.

In such a circumstance—as we'll see again when we look at AP expansion efforts in Fort Worth and New York City—the school team faces much heavy lifting. Attitudes and expectations need to be altered. Teachers need additional preparation, and students need extra instruction—and, often, different approaches to instruction. Textbooks and other curricular materials must be obtained. Principals must persevere, which generally calls for stable leadership over multiple years. Qualified teachers must hang in there, too, all of which is hard to make happen in schools long marked by turnover at every level. And even when the adult infrastructure is in place, the kids must still be dealt with. Students who had not previously seen themselves as plausible prospects for AP—or college—or who hadn't felt welcome in AP classrooms, must often be cajoled through the classroom door. Parents, too, must be helped to understand how all this extra studying, homework, and

pressure can pay off for their kids, and that college-oriented programs like
AP aren't just for middle-class youngsters. It may cost money, too—exam
fees, maybe additional textbooks, and such, as well as foregone income if
studious teens aren't able to spend as much time earning money to help with
their own and their families' budgets.

In short, it's one thing for highbrow committees and education officials
to conclude that Advanced Placement can help more students from different
circumstances. It's quite another to create the school and classroom environment that fosters success. Superstar educators like Escalante and Gradillas
show that this is possible—but there are never enough superstars to spearhead a thriving program in thousands of schools.

Seeds of Change

On the heels of the Garfield example, the national AP population began to
diversify, as the participation of minority youngsters expanded faster than
the program as a whole, particularly toward the end of the 1980s. By 1988
(as some kids and teachers were viewing *Stand and Deliver* in theaters),
19.5 percent of AP exam-takers nationwide were minorities (including Asian
Americans). This went up to 26.3 percent in 1994 with participation by black
and Hispanic students reaching 11.6 percent. Because they comprised nearly
29 percent of the nation's high school population that year, they were still
sorely underrepresented, but a big, important change was underway both
for them and for the program itself.[23]

State legislators began to pass laws that encouraged AP participation and
expanded access to it. South Carolina enacted legislation in 1984 requiring
all of its high schools to offer AP courses and all of its public colleges to accept
scores of 3 or better. By 1994, Florida, Georgia, Indiana, Kentucky, North
Carolina, Minnesota, South Carolina, and the District of Columbia were
paying part or all of their students' exam fees. (Texas followed in 1995. We
return to that story in chapter 4.)[24]

These years also saw the College Board adding more subjects to the
AP catalog, as the number of options rose from eighteen to twenty-eight
between 1976 and 1996. Some of the new classes were accessible to younger
high school students without a lot of prerequisites, and some appeared less
daunting than physics and calculus. Spanish launched in 1977, Studio Art:
Drawing in 1980, Computer Science in 1984, US Government and Politics
in 1987, Microeconomics and Macroeconomics in 1989, followed by Psychology in 1992.

By 1996, some 540,000 students were taking part in AP, a near sextupling over two decades. Nor was it entirely domestic: In 1981, just 2,700 exams were taken overseas. By 1994, that number had risen to 16,700—and students from forty-nine countries were taking part.[25] And as student numbers rose, so did the number of exams taken per participant: from 1.3 in 1976 to 1.6 two decades later.[26] Yet those exams were also getting pricier: Fees went up from $20 in 1975 to $72 by 1995.[27]

The College Board made a promotional film in 1984 to entice still more students and schools into the program,[28] and by the mid-1990s nearly 12,000 secondary schools—almost half the schools in the country—were engaged. As Eric Rothschild writes, during this period, "Advanced Placement became a national program to a degree which even its most fervent supporters in the early years could not have imagined."[29]

What was to follow, however, would prove yet more dramatic. In the next chapter, we bring the AP saga into the twenty-first century.

Notes

1. College Board, "Annual AP Program Participation, 1956–2018," accessed November 2, 2018. https://secure-media.collegeboard.org/digitalServices/pdf/research/2018/2018-Annual -Participation.pdf.

2. Spark Admissions, "Admissions Rate Changes at Yale, Stanford, and Princeton since 1980," accessed October 20, 2015. https://www.sparkadmissions.com/blog/college-admissions-trends /admissions-rate-changes-yale-stanford-princeton.

3. M. Brett Gladstone, "Officials Pleased with New Admissions," *Harvard Crimson*, April 17, 1976. https://www.thecrimson.com/article/1976/4/17/officials-pleased-with-new-admissions -pmonday/; Pamela Paul, "Being a Legacy Has Its Burden," *New York Times*, November 4, 2011. https://www.nytimes.com/2011/11/06/education/edlife/being-a-legacy-has-its-burden.html.

4. George Anders, "What If Stanford Admitted 31 Percent? A Journey Back to the 1970s," *Forbes*, April 3, 2015. https://www.forbes.com/sites/georgeanders/2015/04/03/what-if-stanford -admitted-31-a-journey-back-to-the-1970s; "You Really Are 'Great,'" *Stanford Daily*, September 20, 1984, 9. https://stanforddailyarchive.com/cgi-bin/imageserver/imageserver.pl?oid =stanford19840920-01&getpdf=true.

5. Chester E. Finn, Jr., "A Call for Quality Education: We Must Recommit Our Schools to Excellence," *Life*, March 1981, 82–102; Annegret Harnischfeger and David E. Wiley, *Achievement Test Score Decline: Do We Need to Worry?* (Saint Louis, MO: Cemrel, 1976); Chester E. Finn, Jr., "School's Out," *Forbes*, March 3, 2010. https://www.forbes.com/2010/03/02/diane-ravitch -education-schools-opinions-book-reviews-chester-e-finn-jr.html.

6. Ernest L. Boyer, *High School: A Report on Secondary Education in America* (New York: Harper and Row, 1983), 255.

7. Tim Lacy, "Examining AP: Access, Rigor, and Revenue in the History of the Advanced Placement Program," in *AP: A Critical Examination of the Advanced Placement Program*, ed. Phillip M. Sadler and others (Cambridge, MA: Harvard Education Press, 2010), 35.

8. Jack Schneider, "Privilege, Equity, and the Advanced Placement Program: Tug of War," *Journal of Curriculum Studies* 41, no. 6 (2009): 8.

9. Sidney P. Marland Jr., "Advanced Placement: An Above-Average Opportunity," *NASSP Bulletin* 59, no. 391 (1975): 38.

10. Throughout this book, we use the terms *Hispanic*, *Latino*, and *Hispanic/Latino* interchangeably.

11. Jay Mathews, "Jaime Escalante Didn't Just Stand and Deliver: He Changed U.S. Schools Forever," *Washington Post*, April 4, 2010. https://focusdc.org/jaime-escalante-didnt-just-stand-and-deliver-he-changed-us-schools-forever.

12. Henry Gradillas and Jerry Jesness, *Standing and Delivering: What the Movie Didn't Tell* (Lanham, MD: Rowman and Littlefield Education, 2010), 47.

13. Gradillas and Jesness, *Standing and Delivering*, 47–48.

14. Gradillas and Jesness, *Standing and Delivering*, 48.

15. Gradillas and Jesness, *Standing and Delivering*, 48–49.

16. Ron La Brecque, "Something More Than Calculus," *New York Times*, November 6, 1988. https://www.nytimes.com/1988/11/06/education/something-more-than-calculus.html.

17. La Brecque, "Something More than Calculus."

18. See, for example, Ron Edmonds, "Effective Schools for the Urban Poor," *Educational Leadership* 37, no. 1 (1979): 15–24.

19. Stu Adler, "Garfield High Math Program," *Los Angeles Times*, November 8, 1992. http://articles.latimes.com/1992-11-08/opinion/op-191_1_garfield-high-math-program-advanced placement-calculus.

20. Mathews's 2018 rankings can be found at "Jay Mathews Challenge Index High School Rankings 2018," accessed February 3, 2019. https://jaymathewschallengeindex.com.

21. Jay Mathews, "America's Most Challenging High Schools: A 30-Year Project That Keeps Growing," *Washington Post*, May 5, 2017. https://www.washingtonpost.com/local/education/jays-americas-most-challenging-high-schools-main-column/2017/05/03/eebf0288-2617-11e7-a1b3-faff0034e2de_story.html?utm_term=.37501bef6fb8.

22. Jay Mathews, "Tests Help 'Ordinary' Schools Leap Ahead," *Washington Post*, May 14, 1987, accessed March 28, 2018. https://www.washingtonpost.com/archive/politics/1987/05/14/tests-help-ordinary-schools-leap-ahead/88ff94fb-e2d6-4592-9e30-1b81d5c15155/?utm_term=.557f1bdd2415.

23. Eric Rothschild, "Four Decades of the Advanced Placement Program," *History Teacher* 32, no. 2 (1999): 196–97; United States Census Bureau, "Table A-1: School Enrollment of the Population 3 Years Old and Over, by Level and Control of School, Race, and Hispanic Origin: October 1955 to 2016," August 23, 2017. https://www.census.gov/data/tables/time-series/demo/school-enrollment/cps-historical-time-series.html.

24. South Carolina Department of Education, "AP," accessed November 2, 2018. https://ed.sc.gov/data/test-scores/national-assessments/ap/; Rothschild, "Four Decades," 195.

25. College Board data, quoted in Rothschild, "Four Decades," 193.

26. College Board, "Annual AP Program Participation."

27. Lacy, "Examining AP," 35.

28. *A Chance to Excel*, film produced by Stefan Moore (New York: College Entrance Exam Board, 1984).

29. Rothschild, "Four Decades," 189.

3

Growth Industry

AP's recent decades are notable for the program's stunning growth on multiple dimensions. Many more schools, students, and subjects joined in, and they did so at accelerating rates. The number of exams taken in May breached the million mark in 1998, doubled just seven years later, and exceeded five million for the first time in 2018. In this chapter, we chart these developments (primarily across the twenty years from 1997 through 2017) and take up lingering challenges of access, equity, and their knotty intersection with outcomes.

Schools

Globally, the number of schools offering AP exams to their students rose by 84 percent between 1997 and 2017, reaching 22,612 by 2018. The program is still more than 90 percent US-based, however.[1] Confining ourselves to public high schools only, we estimate that 71 percent of them enabled their students to take AP exams in 2017—up from 52 percent in 1997, numbers verified by the College Board (figure 3.1). If, however, we also consider schools that combine elementary and secondary grades—an institutional category that more than doubled since 1997 to about 6,800 today—as potential candidates to offer AP, then the 2017 school participation rate was about 54 percent, still way up from 44 percent in 1997.[2] Additionally, we estimate that half of US private high schools offer AP exams, which means they comprise about a quarter of all participating American high schools.[3]

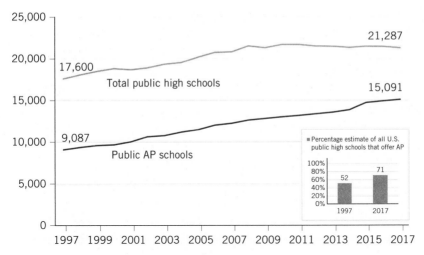

FIGURE 3.1. US public high schools administering AP exams, 1997–2017.
"AP schools" are defined by the College Board as schools offering AP exams to at least some
students, whether on campus or elsewhere. Schools with off-campus testing were first included in
2015, so some of the recent increase in school numbers may be due to this definitional change.
Sources: College Board and NCES

Among the schools that administer AP exams, about 80 percent also
teach College Board–sanctioned AP courses. Some 14,000 public and private schools offered such courses in the United States in 2007–8, rising to
about 16,300 by 2017–18.[4] Because a student need not take a Board-approved
course in order to take an AP exam, schools have some flexibility to work
with students who want to take the exams but—for whatever reason—may
not be able to take the pertinent AP-sanctioned courses at the school itself.
It also allows some schools to shun College Board course frameworks and
syllabus approvals that they find restrictive or ill-suited to their curricula yet
still enable their pupils to take the exams and potentially benefit from their
results. (See further discussion in chapter 10.)

Courses, Students, and Exams

When AP began in the 1950s, it consisted of ten courses and exams. In 2018,
there were thirty-eight (see table A.1 in appendix II). The list is dynamic (more
on this in chapter 9) as courses get revamped and occasionally dropped as
well as added. Between 1997 and 2017, nine entirely new AP courses were
launched, three were removed, and three were relabeled, divided, or consolidated.[5] Latin, for example, originally consisted of both Latin-Vergil and

Latin Literature, but the latter was dropped in 2009, and the remaining course was revised (now simply "AP Latin") in 2012. World History joined the catalog in 2002 and has already received two revisions (the latest of which stirred unexpected controversy, discussed in chapter 11). The most recent addition, Computer Science Principles, was a huge hit when introduced in 2017.

The number of students (globally) who took at least one AP exam in 2017 (2.7 million) was nearly five times the 1997 number. The impressive rise in total exams taken results both from wider school and student participation and from another bump in exams taken per participating student: from an average of 1.6 in 1997 to 1.8 in 2017.[6]

Of exam-takers, 89 percent attended public schools in 2017, also up (from 82 percent) since 1997. It's not that private school participation shrank; rather, the public sector part grew faster. During those two decades, the number of public school pupils taking AP exams nearly quintupled while their private school peers "merely" tripled. Note, too, that private schools are generally smaller, which is why they may comprise a quarter of participating schools yet house just 11 percent of participating students

Lacking more precise private school data, we compared public school students sitting for AP exams with eleventh and twelfth grade enrollments, as those have traditionally been when most AP exams are taken. We see that enrollments in those grades declined over the past decade, yet AP participation continued to rise, both in numbers of students and—more strikingly—in numbers of AP exams taken (see figure 3.2).

AP is no longer confined to the latter half of high school, however. A major source of the recent uptick in exam taking is the program's deepening reach into the freshman and sophomore years. In 1997, just 7.5 percent of examinees were ninth and tenth graders, but that more than tripled by 2017 to 26.4 percent (see figure A.1 in appendix II). Also striking: AP exam taking is now more widespread among juniors than seniors.

Students at different stages of their education tend to tap into different parts of the program. For example, 64 percent of all AP exams taken by ninth graders in 2017 were in Human Geography. Of all the European History and World History exams given that year, the vast majority were taken by tenth graders (65 and 79 percent respectively). Physics, Calculus, and English Literature, on the other hand, belong almost entirely to eleventh and twelfth graders, as these are typically upper-level courses with prerequisites and often represent the pinnacle in their disciplines during high school. Yet grade level has little to do with qualifying scores. The pass rate

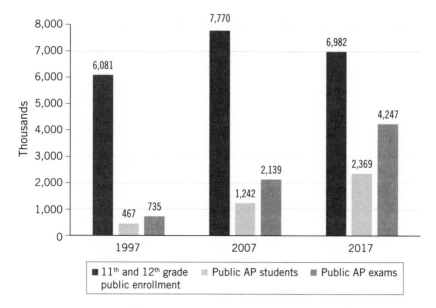

FIGURE 3.2. 11th–12th grade public school enrollments, public AP students, and AP exams taken in US public schools, 1997, 2007, and 2017.

11th and 12th grade enrollment data come from Applied Educational Research, Inc. (AERI) and are cited by the College Board. While these data show a decline between 2007 and 2017, other sources yield slightly different results. The US Census Bureau shows that total public high school enrollment fell from 15.6 million in 2006–7 to 15.3 million in 2016–17, while NCES reports 15.08 million in 2006–7, rising slightly to 15.11 million in 2016–17.

Sources: Applied Educational Research, Inc., College Board, US Census Bureau, and NCES

of underclassmen on AP exams in 2017 was almost identical to the rates of eleventh and twelfth graders.

Although AP offers more than three dozen course options, just half a dozen of these account for nearly half of all exams taken in 2017: English Language, US History, English Literature, US Government, Calculus AB, and Psychology. Black and Hispanic students are less likely to take STEM exams than their white and Asian peers, and Asian students are less likely to take English and social studies exams, but most such differences are small. The exception is Latino students, who take the two Spanish exams at significantly higher rates than their peers (13 percent of all exams that they take, compared with 3 percent for other students).[7]

As for pass rates (that is, exam scores of 3 or better), the strongest showings are found in the arts (74 percent), world languages (84 percent), and the new "Capstone" courses (82 percent).[8] Among the high-volume subjects, success rates range widely. Compare, for example, three subjects with similar exam shares: Statistics, Human Geography, and Spanish Language. The pass rate for Spanish eclipses the other two (88 percent, versus 54 percent for Statistics and 49 percent for Human Geography), but again that's largely driven by Hispanic students. No other student group takes as much of, or does as well on, any other exam.

Drivers of Growth

At least five factors have fueled the Advanced Placement program's expansion in recent years.

RATINGS AND RANKINGS

The use of AP participation (and sometimes exam results) to rate and rank high schools has impelled more of them to increase their student numbers so as to boost their standings, much as the metrics employed by *U.S. News* in its high-visibility college rankings have altered the incentives and behavior of many postsecondary institutions.

Veteran education journalist Jay Mathews is more than a chronicler of AP and an Escalante biographer (see chapter 2). He emerged as an AP booster rocket when he began using exam participation as a key metric in his high school rating system, known as the "Challenge Index," now more than two decades old. (Formerly appearing in *Newsweek* and the *Washington Post*, it's now published by Mathews himself.) This has proven a strong spur to AP expansion and perhaps also to mission shift, though growth was well underway pre-Mathews. *U.S. News* began to rank high schools in 2007 and also incorporates AP into its algorithms.

Mathews's "Challenge Index" takes the total number of Advanced Placement, International Baccalaureate, and Cambridge tests given at a school each year and divides by the number of seniors who graduated that year.[9] With a few exceptions, public high schools with at least as many exams as graduates in a given year get onto the national list. In 2018, only about 2,500 U.S. high schools reached this threshold.[10]

U.S. News employs a four-step algorithm for ranking high schools. The first three are based on state proficiency tests (in reading and math), the performance of underserved minorities, and graduation rates. The final step, termed the "College Readiness Index" (CRI), is based on AP participation (25 percent) and exam performance (75 percent). The former considers the number of twelfth grade students who took at least one AP test before graduating divided by the school's total twelfth grade enrollment. The latter is the number of twelfth graders who *passed* at least one AP exam (with scores of 3 or higher) before graduating, again divided by the senior-class enrollment.[11]

Influential as they are, both metrics also have critics. Mathews's list has been faulted for ignoring exam performance when rating schools, although he responds that AP participation itself has value for students, that schools otherwise tend to manipulate their rankings by allowing only top students into AP. For its part, *U.S. News* is criticized for using old data (its 2018 rankings were based on 2016 numbers) and for comparing successful AP examinees with total senior enrollment rather than with seniors who took an AP exam.[12]

As in higher education, showcasing and rewarding institutions for their performance on specific metrics can create perverse incentives. High schools may inveigle kids into taking AP classes and exams for which they're ill-prepared. Teachers may be deployed to teach those classes who are poorly grounded in the subject matter, may not be accustomed to educating high performers, or may shun the heavy lifting needed to do this well. This particular incentive structure also tends to disadvantage small and rural high schools that can't afford much AP—or it may reshape a school's priorities in ways that shortchange other needs, such as drawing resources from career-oriented education for kids who would benefit from it. We also see a mixed effect when one counts exams taken rather than those passed, as this puts the onus on just getting kids into the exam rooms, not on their performance. (Mathews has a point, however, that simply participating in an advanced class may benefit students, especially those from disadvantaged backgrounds.)

RISING EXPECTATIONS

A host of reasons besides enhanced ratings may induce schools and districts to add more AP courses and encourage more kids to take them. They may want to challenge their students intellectually, tone up their curricula, hold on to their best teachers, attract and retain more middle-class families, draw more sophisticated employers to the area, and respond to demands from parents of gifted kids.[13] Further nudging in this direction has come from the country's broad effort to elevate education achievement, a lasting consequence of *A Nation at Risk*; from heightened attention to America's slipshod performance on international assessments and its own National Assessment of Educational Progress; from professors' complaints about ill-prepared students and employers' grumps about poorly skilled workers; from concerns among governors about their states' stagnant economies (and the role of education therein); and from the many officials and commentators alarmed by the country's faltering competitiveness in the world economy.

Washington encouraged AP growth, too. By 1993, the US Department of Education was using Advanced Placement data in its annual *Condition of Education* report, which tended to validate those data as a bona fide quality marker for the education system. In 2000, the federal Office for Civil Rights also began tracking AP participation and reporting it as part of its periodic equity surveys.

From 1998 through 2016, Uncle Sam operated several modest-sized programs of discretionary grants to states and districts to subsidize access to AP courses for disadvantaged youngsters, and to help with their exam fees. Changes arrived in 2017, however, as the Every Student Succeeds Act (ESSA) consolidated AP dollars along with many other categorical programs into a block grant, leaving in state and local hands the future deployment of funds to support AP access—and highlighting the tension between a policy shift that may make sense in terms of federalism and the targeted nationwide attainment of a specific objective.[14] But (with much College Board encouragement) AP is faring reasonably well: By early 2019, twenty-seven states and DC had moved to provide financial support to low-income students to take the exams.[15]

THE PURSUIT OF EQUITY

The country's mounting concern about equalizing opportunity for poor and minority youngsters and getting more of them into and through college inevitably drew greater attention to AP's potential contribution. The program already existed—and had a track record—as a high-status, widely understood and relatively portable mechanism that could introduce more students to college-level academic work, prove to them (and their teachers and parents) that they could succeed with such work, boost their prospects for getting into college, and perhaps launch them toward the credits needed for a degree. The College Board welcomed AP expansion in this direction and organizations such as the National Math and Science Initiative (NMSI), Equal Opportunity Schools (EOS), and Mass Insight Education and Research (MassInsight) have worked hard to cause all those things to happen for more students in more schools and districts.[16] Our later discussion of NMSI's efforts in Fort Worth (chapter 4), EOS's work in Maryland (chapter 6), and the exertions of both in New York City (chapter 5), illustrates both the great potential and the sizable challenges associated with this initiative. But there's no doubt that it has contributed in a big way—and still does—to AP's recent growth.

THE COLLEGE ADMISSION RAT RACE

Stiffening competition to enter top colleges and more scrambling by kids to advantage themselves in the admissions process also continued to pump air into the AP balloon. Stanford's acceptance rate is now below 5 percent.[17] In 1997, Texas lawmakers moved to grant automatic admission to state universities (including its flagship campuses) to any student graduating in the top tenth of his/her high school class, which put a premium on the extra GPA points that typically accompany one's grades in AP and other advanced courses (discussed further in chapters 4 and 10). Introduction of the "Common Application" in 1998 made it easier and cheaper for high school seniors to apply to more colleges, which further depressed acceptance rates at selective schools while amplifying the value of a sterling transcript full of "challenging" courses as well as a maxed-out grade point average.

COLLEGE BOARD EFFORTS

The forceful marketing and lobbying activities of the College Board itself added yet more oomph. AP is a big deal for the Board and many of its member institutions. Growing it does good for kids, to be sure, but it also helps the organization do well. We estimate that fees from AP tests and instructional materials make up about 47 percent of the College Board's total revenue (which means they brought in some $446 million in 2016),[18] more than it now receives from the rest of its vast catalog of assessments, including the high-visibility SAT.[19]

Unsurprisingly, almost all of the Board's own research on the outcomes of AP has been positive. (Its in-house analysts have generated or commissioned at least 150 studies over the past two decades.) AP's competitors have nothing comparable when it comes to R&D firepower, nor do they have the College Board's sophisticated marketing and public-information systems, its networks of state and federal lobbyists, or its deep penetration among high school counselors and teachers as well as college-minded students and their families. (We discuss the research literature on AP, by both College Board and outside analysts, in greater depth in appendix I.)

Inequalities

As Advanced Placement has expanded, it has done so unevenly, giving rise to multiple issues of fairness. We now turn to these.

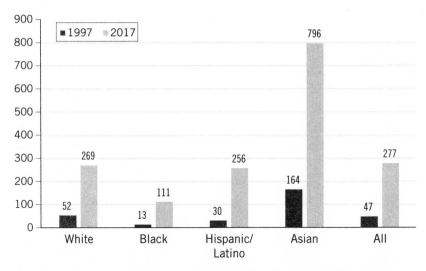

FIGURE 3.3. AP exams taken per 1,000 US public high school students, by race/ethnicity, 1997 and 2017.
College Board data are public school data for numbers of AP exams taken by race/ethnicity in 1997 and 2017. Census data are based on numbers of public high schoolers by race/ethnicity shown in fall 1996 and fall 2016. "All" refers to all students, including other races/ethnicities that are not shown here but delineated by the College Board and US Census Bureau.
Sources: College Board, 2017, and the US Census Bureau, 2016

DEMOGRAPHICS

AP participation varies widely by student group. Comparing exam taking per thousand high school pupils (see figure 3.3), we see bars of very different heights, depending on students' race and ethnicity, though all have lengthened impressively since 1997. Obvious discrepancies remain, yet some gaps have narrowed as participation has grown at differing rates: Black students, for example, took AP at about 24 percent the rate of white students in 1997, rising to 41 percent in 2017, even as white participation quintupled. Hispanic pupils participated in 1997 at just over half the rate of white students, but two decades later their rates were nearly equal.

LOCATION, LOCATION, LOCATION

It matters where a student lives. When we look at exams taken per thousand eleventh and twelfth graders in 2017, states differ greatly. Wealthy, densely populated coastal states such as Maryland, Florida, and California have lots of Advanced Placement (see table A.2 in appendix II), while kids in the bottom ten states take AP exams at about a third the rate of the top ten.

Intrastate differences abound, too, with AP access a particular problem for rural students.[20] According to one study, just 23 percent of rural seniors in 2015 had taken an AP exam during high school versus 36 and 37 percent, respectively, among urban and suburban seniors. As participation has risen across the country, the gaps between rural and urban/suburban schools have narrowed somewhat, but they remain stubborn, owing to issues of school size, infrastructure, human capital, economics, and pupil transportation. Such gaps reappear in exam scores, too: 53 percent of rural graduates in 2015 who had taken AP exams had racked up at least one qualifying score during high school, versus 58 percent of urban and 67 percent of suburban students.[21]

We also see inequality in AP course offerings between low- and high-income districts.[22] Although almost every state now offers incentives to increase access to AP coursework, mostly for disadvantaged students and their schools, via such strategies as subsidizing exam fees, paying for teacher training, or inserting it into their state accountability metric, middle-class schools and the populations that attend them have increased their AP participation even faster.[23]

Course offerings diverge within districts, too. In Washington, DC, for example, Woodrow Wilson High School in the city's prosperous northwest taught forty-one separate sections of twenty-seven different AP subjects in 2018–19. At Anacostia High School in the city's impoverished southeast, just seven sections in seven subjects were taught that year.[24]

For students in schools with scant AP offerings of their own, online options may help. In 2018, more than a thousand providers of online or virtual courses in the United States were accredited by the College Board, including some that operate entirely through the ether and others that beam their offerings into brick-and-mortar schools. Approved providers can use the Advanced Placement name so long as they take part in the AP Course Audit process (see chapter 9).[25] These include well-known entities such as APEX Learning and the Florida Virtual School, but quality varies and offerings skew toward popular courses such as English and US History rather than subjects like Music Theory. Costs also vary, ranging from free (EdX, governed by MIT and Harvard, offers no-cost online AP courses) or low-cost (many states now offer subsidized online options) to hundreds of dollars per student (an APEX course costs $700, plus textbooks and other materials).

For the nation's seven thousand plus rural school districts, online AP resources can be a particular boon. For example, if the only available teacher in a small high school is not qualified to teach an AP course, he or she could "facilitate" students' use of the online version, monitoring their progress, explaining sticky issues, and providing tutoring to the perplexed. Such experiments are already happening in Maine, for instance, where a state-funded online AP program (in partnership with the University of Maine at Fort Kent) supplies courses that are given with the assistance of adult "mentors" in the schools.[26] Similar initiatives have sprung up in Colorado, Iowa, and elsewhere.[27]

However an AP course gets into a school, further inequities may still arise there. Student awareness—and demand—is uneven, as is middle-school preparation. Access to such courses remains "gated" in a number of places, meaning that favorable teacher recommendations or GPAs are required even to enter the class. Several studies have illumined the dynamics that impede access for minority students in particular.[28] There may, for example, be few AP teachers of color to encourage the participation of same-race pupils. Other teachers may seek to limit participation in their classes to youngsters they expect to ace the exams. A Fordham Institute survey of more than a thousand AP teachers in 2009 found some 63 percent who felt that more, not less, screening was needed for students seeking to enter AP classes.[29]

OUTCOMES

As participation has ballooned, so, too, has the number of qualifying scores (3 or higher) on AP exams. Globally, that figure rose from nearly six hundred thousand in 1997 to over three million in 2018. Figure 3.4 displays the growth among US students. Lurking within these whopping numbers, however, are some important dilemmas, beginning with a gradual decline in the passing rate.

That the percentage of qualifying scores has fallen suggests that the College Board is maintaining rigor as it liberalizes access to AP, not easing expectations or inflating grades. But national isn't the whole story, as student success also varies dramatically by state. One in three Massachusetts seniors in 2018 graduated from public schools having passed at least one AP exam, five times the proportion in Mississippi (see table A.3 in appendix II). Here, too, the greatest success rates can be found in wealthy coastal states, the least in poorer, southern, and western states.

By and large, spikes in the number of qualifying scores have been accompanied by sinking pass rates (see table A.4 in appendix II). For example, the number of qualifying scores earned in Nevada grew at over twice the national rate between 1997 and 2017, while the state's pass rate dropped by nearly ten points. But it's not an iron law: During those same two decades, Washington

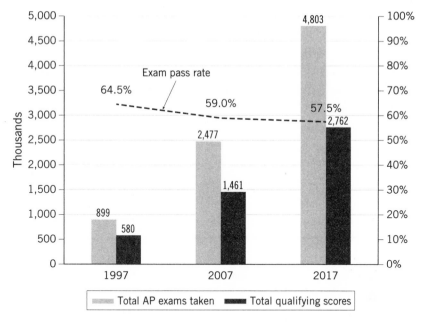

FIGURE 3.4. AP exams taken and qualifying scores earned in the United States, 1997, 2007, and 2017.

"Exam pass rate" refers to the total number of qualifying scores in a year divided by the total number of exams taken. This is shown for US schools, both public and private.
Source: College Board

State's qualifying scores grew by almost twice the national rate while its pass rate rose by over five percentage points.[30]

Turning to the racial picture, we encounter truly complicated—and in ways paradoxical—developments. The good news is that, when gauged by sheer numbers, every student group is getting more qualifying scores (see figure 3.5). Black public school students, for example, earned over eight times more qualifying scores in 2017 than in 1997, and Hispanic/Latino students earned nearly twelve times more.

Another key marker of progress on the equity front is the percentage of students who earn at least one AP qualifying score before graduating. The share of US public school graduates to hit that target rose from 15 percent (460,000 students) in 2008 to 23 percent (750,000 students) a decade later—a large and important change.[31] In other words, nearly a quarter of all young Americans who complete high school are now emerging with at least one qualifying score on an Advanced Placement exam. Nor did that rising tide just lift white and Asian youngsters. For black students, the rate doubled

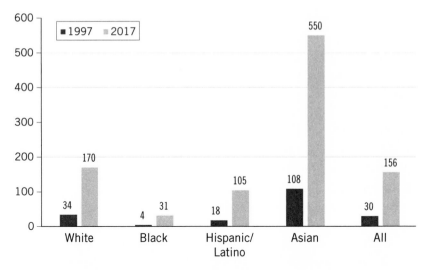

FIGURE 3.5. AP qualifying scores earned per 1,000 US public high school students, by race/ethnicity, 1997 and 2017.

College Board data are numbers of AP qualifying scores earned in public schools by race/ethnicity in 1997 and 2017. Census data are estimated numbers of public high school pupils by race/ethnicity in fall 1996 and fall 2016. "All" refers to all students, including other races/ethnicities that are not shown here but delineated by the College Board and US Census Bureau.
Sources: College Board and US Census Bureau

from 4 percent in 2008 to 8 percent in 2018, while for Latinos, it rose from 14 percent to an impressive 26 percent, thus surpassing both the national average and the percentage of successful white graduates that year.[32]

Combined, the number of black and Latino youngsters with at least one qualifying score under their belts rose from 80,000 in the graduating class of 2008 to nearly 210,000 in 2018, boosting their share of all such students from 17 to 28 percent over the same period. Also evident is an upward trend in the participation of low-income youngsters, from 17 percent of all exam-takers in 2008 to 31 percent in 2018.[33] Hoorah, say we.

The not-so-good news is that pass rates have fallen faster among black and Latino youngsters than in the student population as a whole (see figure A.2 in appendix II). Indeed, it appears that their sagging performance levels have been the main driver of the overall national decline. We see that, as the number of AP exams taken by Hispanic/Latino youngsters rose sixteen-fold from 1997 to 2017, their success rate on those exams sank from 59 to 41 percent—and to 34 percent when results on Spanish exams are excluded. We see a similar pattern for black students, even as the pass rate among white students barely budged—and actually rose for Asian youngsters.

The juxtaposition of drooping pass rates with soaring numbers of quali-fying scores poses the dilemma: Is it better to have a high rate of success among participating minority youngsters or to boost the number of quali-fying scores for these students, even if the latter means that many more of those who enter this deepening pool cannot swim across it?

The declining rate of success among the growing number of minority youngsters who sit for AP exams contributes to the much-lamented "excel-lence gap" (as it has been termed by scholars such as Jonathan Plucker and organizations like the Jack Kent Cooke Foundation and the National Associa-tion for Gifted Children). This poses a real challenge for policy makers who see advanced coursework like AP as a lever for lifting the overall educational attainment and mobility prospects of disadvantaged students.[34]

A different excellence gap can be seen within AP's five-point scoring scale. Of all exams taken in the United States by black students, 42 percent resulted in scores of 1 in 2017, versus 31 percent for Hispanic youngsters, 12 percent for white students, and 11 percent for Asian students. Among all exams taken, the portion resulting in scores of 1 or 2 rose from 36 to 42 percent between 1997 and 2017, but it ended that period at 58 percent for Hispanic students and 70 percent for black pupils. At the other end of the scale, scores of 4 and 5 exceed what the College Board deems "qualifying" and make an ever-larger difference in determining whether one's AP score will actually yield college credit, particularly in elite private institutions (discussed further in chapter 10). But at this lofty level we again find wide gaps: 45 percent of exams taken by Asian students in 2017 yielded 4's or 5's, as did 36 percent for white students, 21 percent for Hispanic students, and 12 percent for black students.

As discussed further in chapter 12, we're persuaded that getting a larger number of poor and minority youngsters into the ranks of AP successes is a worthy goal and one that's gradually being achieved, even as their passing rate sinks. We're also partly persuaded, along with many teachers and prin-cipals (and Jay Mathews), that participating in advanced courses has some value in itself, particularly when instructors observe stronger performance by their students during the course of a year and from one year to the next—improvements that may be matched by exam scores that rise from 1 to 2 and then perhaps to "qualifying" as a young person proceeds through high school. Getting a 2 shows that a student learned something. While it won't translate into recognition or acceleration in college, the skills, knowledge, and practice that it confers may well burnish one's performance in college courses. That's certainly the view of many instructors, attested to by former AP pupils who return to visit them. But for a program that has long set the bar at 3, and in a country where high-status colleges are demanding 4's and 5's, there's obviously a big unsolved problem when so many young people, particularly low-income kids and students of color, are scoring 1's and 2's.

The State of AP in 2018

As we've shown, the Advanced Placement program is the largest it's ever been. In 2018, some 2.8 million students enrolled in nearly 23,000 high schools around the world took more than five million AP exams in thirty-eight subjects. Just over three million of those exams yielded scores of 3 or higher. But the program continues to evolve as an education reform strategy, as a business proposition for the College Board, and as a complex response to diverse pressures from participants (students, teachers, schools, readers), critics, competitors, and the ecosystem in which it exists.

The program is well led, generally well regarded, and well placed to overcome many of these challenges, as it has done for more than half a century. Recent additions to the course catalog illustrate its adaptability. Computer Science Principles, which arrived in 2017, is partly a response to the ballooning computer industry and its career opportunities, partly a purposeful effort to draw more girls and minorities into STEM subjects, partly a curricular evolution from the Java programming focus of the early AP computer course (which also endures) to a broader understanding of the many aspects of computer science and its multiple applications. As more states add computer science (or "computing") to their K–12 curricula and high school graduation requirements, AP's move proved hugely popular, increasing the number of students taking a computer-related exam by 135 percent over two years since its introduction, including many more young women, black, Latino, and rural students.[35]

AP's new Capstone courses respond to several kinds of demand, including college faculty (and admissions officers) who were seeing too many students matriculate without the requisite research skills, unable to think across disciplines, or to write sustained papers at a sophisticated level. Capstone also addresses competition from the International Baccalaureate (IB) program with its emphasis on "deeper learning," and educators who have been shifting their curricula and pedagogy from "learn a lot about a subject" to "understand more about less." After an abortive effort to team up with Cambridge Assessment's "Global Perspectives" program, the College Board decided to go it alone and proceeded to develop and pilot Capstone's twin courses (called "Seminar" and "Research") and their elaborate teacher training and student evaluation systems, then slowly rolled them out as it built the number of instructors who could help teachers learn how to manage these challenging—and very different—new courses. The number of students participating in Capstone reached 41,000 in 2018.[36]

Also newly introduced (fall 2018) is a rebooted Pre-AP program for ninth graders, consisting of eight courses in the four core subjects (English, math, history, science) plus the arts, all aiming to build the content knowledge and skills that young people will need to succeed in AP and other college-level coursework.[37] Previous efforts to lay the groundwork for AP success were mostly ad hoc. The new program aims to help align curricula through middle and high school. As we will see in subsequent chapters, a key—and obvious—prerequisite for success in AP (and other college-level) high school coursework is what some call front-loading: constructing a solid academic foundation in the earlier grades. Back when coursework such as AP was aimed at fortunate youngsters emerging from good schools and already well prepared to profit from it, the College Board didn't have to pay much attention to strengthening that foundation. Now, however, with a swelling population of more diverse students coming into AP classrooms from very different circumstances, it's necessary to pay explicit attention to foundation building, by the College Board and by school systems and policy makers (and philanthropists and education reformers) bent not just on throwing open the classroom doors but also on maximizing the odds that kids passing through those doors will succeed there.

Beginning in the next chapter, we swoop down to examine how these national trends and challenges are playing out in actual places and schools, a journey that will take us from Texas and New York City to the suburbs of Ohio and Maryland, then into the newer territory of charter schools.

Notes

1. Global College Board data on AP since 1997, used throughout this chapter, can be found at College Board, "AP Data Overview," accessed February 13, 2018. https://research.collegeboard.org/programs/ap/data.

2. Here we compare public school data from the National Center for Education Statistics (NCES) from 1996–97 to 2016–17 with College Board data for the number of US public schools offering AP over the same period. NCES data are available at US Department of Education, National Center for Education Statistics, "Table 216.10: Public Elementary and Secondary Schools, By Level of School: Selected Years, 1967–68 through 2015–16." August 2017. https://nces.ed.gov/programs/digest/d17/tables/dt17_216.10.asp?current=yes. (Data for 2016–17 were obtained from NCES in advance of public release. In all cases, we exclude "junior high schools.")

3. Private school data reported here, limited to schools that offer twelfth grade, are based on the 2015–16 NCES dataset: Stephen P. Broughman and others, *Characteristics of Private Schools in the United States: Results from the 2015–16 Private School Universe Survey First Look* (Washington,

DC: US Department of Education, National Center for Education Statistics, 2017), 19, 20. https://nces.ed.gov/pubs2017/2017073.pdf. We compare this with the total number of AP nonpublic schools in the United States in 2016, as tabulated by the College Board. Note that those data may include some home schools and charter schools. For clarity, we use *private* to describe all *nonpublic* College Board data.

4. See College Board, "AP Course Ledger," accessed January 28, 2019. https://apcourseaudit.inflexion.org/ledger/. Here, the College Board counts the number of public and nonpublic AP course providers in the United States. We then compare this with the number of US schools that administer AP exams to their students, on campus or elsewhere. The ledger also includes accredited online AP course providers in the United States.

5. Italian is counted as a newly added exam during this time, although after its introduction in 2006 it was dropped in 2010 and 2011 before being reinstated in 2012.

6. This is the total number of AP exams taken globally divided by the total number of AP students.

7. Throughout this chapter and those that follow, we focus on the four largest participating student races/ethnicities delineated by College Board data in 2017: Asian; black; Hispanic/Latino; and white. When referring to data by racial/ethnic group, we omit the 6.4 percent of AP exam-takers who, in 2017, fit none of those four categories, but we include them in total numbers. The College Board has periodically changed its handling and terminology of students now termed Hispanic/Latino. As noted in chapter 2, we use the terms *Hispanic*, *Latino*, and *Hispanic/Latino* interchangeably.

8. We count AP "arts" subjects as Art History; Music Theory; Studio Art: 2-D Design; Studio Art: 3-D Design; and Studio Art: Drawing. "World languages" subjects are Chinese Language and Culture, French Language and Culture, German Language and Culture, Italian Language and Culture, Japanese Language and Culture, Latin, Spanish Language, and Spanish Literature and Culture. "Capstone" subjects consist of both Research and Seminar.

9. See chapter 8 for more discussion on the International Baccalaureate and Cambridge exams.

10. Mathews's 2018 rankings can be found at "Jay Mathews Challenge Index High School Rankings 2018," accessed January 29, 2019. https://jaymathewschallengeindex.com.

11. In 2018, step four in the *U.S. News* algorithm included IB along with AP participation and performance (scores of 4 or above). Although used in previous years, IB data were absent from the 2017 rankings as the IB organization did not supply the requisite data to *U.S. News*.

12. A school could dramatically increase its number of AP examinees and see the percentage that earn qualifying scores drop just as dramatically, but its *U.S. News* ranking would still rise if just a few more students (as a percentage of total senior enrollment) earned qualifying scores. Although such a metric rewards increases in the number of successful examinees, it can also mask increases in students who fail AP exams. We return to this dilemma later in this chapter.

13. See for example, Topeka High School in Kansas: Topeka Public Schools, "AP Exams," accessed November 5, 2018. https://www.topekapublicschools.net/Page/1327.

14. College Board, "Changes to AP Federal Funding under ESSA," accessed November 3, 2018. https://professionals.collegeboard.org/testing/states-local-governments/new-education-policies/essa-federal-funding-ap; *Non-Regulatory Guidance: Student Support and Academic Achievement Grants* (Washington, DC: US Department of Education, Office of Elementary and Secondary Education, 2016), 9. https://www2.ed.gov/policy/elsec/leg/essa/essassaegrantguid10212016.pdf.

15. The Board estimates that students in these states received an average subsidy of $37 per exam in 2018 in addition to the subsidies that it provides (detailed below). College Board, "AP Program Results: Class of 2018, Expanding AP Access," accessed February 7, 2019. https://reports.collegeboard.org/ap-program-results/expanding-ap-access.

16. Other like-minded organizations are listed on NMSI's website. National Math and Science Initiative, "Program Partners," accessed February 14, 2019. https://www.nms.org/Get-Involved/Partners.aspx.

17. Elliot Kaufman, "For a Stanford Applicant, Perseverance Pays Off," *Wall Street Journal*, April 7, 2016. https://www.wsj.com/articles/for-a-stanford-applicant-perseverance-pays-off -1491520784.

18. ProPublica, "College Entrance Exam Board: Full Text of Form 990 for Fiscal Year Ending Dec. 2016," accessed November 5, 2018. https://projects.propublica.org/nonprofits/organizations /131623965/201713009349301216/IRS990.

19. In 2018, each AP exam cost $94. Other fees are paid by (or on behalf of) students who retake an exam (another $94); send their score report to additional universities ($15 each after the first free report); withhold an unfavorable score from their report ($10 per score); or have the multiple-choice portion of their exam rescored by hand ($30). Partly offsetting such costs, the College Board provides certain discounts, such as a $32 exam-fee reduction for students with financial need. Such reductions totaled over $144 million between 2012 and 2017. See more at College Board, "Changes to AP Federal Funding under ESSA," accessed February 8, 2019. https:// professionals.collegeboard.org/testing/states-local-governments/new-education-policies/essa -federal-funding-ap.

20. Douglas J. Gagnon and Marybeth J. Mattingly, "Advanced Placement and Rural Schools: Access, Success, and Exploring Alternatives," *Journal of Advanced Academics* 27, no. 4 (2016): 266– 84; Christina Theokas and Reid Saaris, *Finding America's Missing AP and IB Students* (Washington, DC: The Education Trust, 2013). https://edtrust.org/wp-content/uploads/2013/10/Missing _Students.pdf; Nat Malkus, *The AP Peak: Public Schools Offering Advanced Placement, 2000–12* (Washington, DC: American Enterprise Institute, 2016). http://www.aei.org/wp-content/uploads /2016/01/The-AP-Peak.pdf.

21. Sharmila Mann and others, *Advanced Placement Access and Success: How Do Rural Schools Stack Up?* (Denver: Education Commission of the States, 2017), 6. https://www.ecs.org/wp-content /uploads/Advanced-Placement-Access-and-Success-How-do-rural-schools-stack-up.pdf.

22. Dylan Conger, Mark C. Long, and Patrice Iatarola, "Explaining Race, Poverty, and Gender Disparities in Advanced Course-Taking," *Journal of Policy Analysis and Management* 28, no. 4 (2009): 555–76; Kristin Klopfenstein, "The Advanced Placement Expansion of the 1990s: How Did Traditionally Underserved Students Fare?" *Education Policy Analysis Archives* 12, no. 68 (2004): 1–13; Suneal Kolluri, "Advanced Placement: The Dual Challenge of Equal Access and Effectiveness," *Review of Educational Research* 88, no. 5 (2018): 671–711.

23. See, for example, Kolluri, "Advanced Placement," 689; Education Commission of the States, "50-State Comparison: Advanced Placement Policies," May 11, 2016. https://www.ecs.org /advanced-placement-policies/.

24. College Board, "AP Course Ledger: Woodrow Wilson High School," accessed January 28, 2019. https://apcourseaudit.inflexion.org/ledger/school.php?a=NzA2NA==&b=MA==; College Board, "AP Course Ledger: Anacostia High School," accessed January 28, 2019. https:// apcourseaudit.inflexion.org/ledger/school.php?a=Njk3MA==&b=MA==. Per district policy, high schools are supposed to offer at least eight AP courses.

25. See AP Course Ledger data for 2018–19. For this estimate, we searched for providers with "online" and/or "virtual" in their names. These include brick-and-mortar schools that give at least one accredited AP course online via an external partner.

26. University of Maine at Fort Kent, Community Education, "AP4ALL," accessed January 31, 2018. https://communityed.umfk.edu/about/rural_u/ap4all/. See also Jennifer Schiess and Andy Rotherham, *Big Country: How Variations in High School Graduation Plans Impact Rural Students* (Boise: Rural Opportunities Consortium of Idaho, 2015).

27. Jackie Mader, "Can Online Learning Level the AP Playing Field for Rural Kids?" *Hechinger Report*, March 6, 2018. https://hechingerreport.org/can-online-learning-level-ap-playing -field-rural-kids/; Alexandra Pannoni, "Rural High Schools Get Teens into Advanced Placement

Courses," *U.S. News and World Report*, February 27, 2017. https://www.usnews.com/high-schools /blogs/high-school-notes/articles/2017-02-27/rural-high-schools-get-teens-into-advanced -placement-courses.

28. Kolluri, "Advanced Placement"; Kristin Klopfenstein, "Advanced Placement: Do Minorities Have Equal Opportunity?" *Economics of Education Review* 23, no. 2 (2004): 115–31; Jeannie Oakes and Gretchen Guiton,"Matchmaking: The Dynamics of High School Tracking Decisions," *American Educational Research Journal* 32, no. 1 (1995): 3–33.

29. Steve Farkas and Ann Duffett, *Growing Pains in the Advanced Placement Program: Do Tough Trade-Offs Lie Ahead?* (Washington, DC: Thomas B. Fordham Institute, 2009), 13.

30. Four other states surpassed the national growth rate in numbers of qualifying scores earned between 1997 and 2017 and simultaneously raised their pass rates: Kentucky, Indiana, Idaho, and Alabama. But none was as successful as Washington State (see table A.4 in appendix II).

31. College Board, "AP Program Results: Class of 2018," accessed February 7, 2019. https:// reports.collegeboard.org/ap-program-results/class-2018-data.

32. College Board, "AP Program Results: Class of 2018." We also compared AP data from the Class of 2018 with the Class of 2008, available from *The 5th Annual AP Report to the Nation* (New York: College Board, 2009). http://media.collegeboard.com/digitalServices/pdf/ap/rtn/5th -annual-ap-report-to-the-nation-2009.pdf.

33. College Board, "AP Program Results: Class of 2018."

34. See (among others) Jonathan A. Plucker and Scott J. Peters, *Excellence Gaps in Education: Expanding Opportunities for Talented Students* (Cambridge, MA: Harvard Education Press, 2016); Jonathan Plucker and others, *Equal Talents, Unequal Opportunities: A Report Card on State Support for Academically Talented Low-Income Students*, 2nd ed. (Lansdowne, VA: Jack Kent Cooke Foundation, 2018). https://www.jkcf.org/wp-content/uploads/2018/06/FINAL_2018_JKCF_- _Equal_Talents_Unequal_Opportunities_-_Web_version.pdf; Joshua S. Wyner, John M. Bridgeland, and John J. Dilulio Jr., *Achievement Trap: How America Is Failing Millions of High Achieving Students from Lower-Income Families* (Lansdowne, VA: Jack Kent Cooke Foundation; Washington, DC: Civic Enterprises, 2007). https://www.jkcf.org/wp-content/uploads/2018/06/Achievement _Trap.pdf; Paula Olszewski-Kubilius and Jane Clarenbach, *Unlocking Emergent Talent: Supporting High Achievement of Low-Income, High-Ability Students* (Washington, DC: National Association for Gifted Children, 2012). http://www.nagc.org/sites/default/files/key%20reports/Unlocking%20 Emergent%20Talent%20%28final%29.pdf.

35. College Board, "Student Participation and Performance in Advanced Placement Rise in Tandem," press release, February 7, 2019. https://www.collegeboard.org/releases/2018/student -participation-and-performance-in-ap-rise-in-tandem. The addition—and the marketing—of it was supported by the National Science Foundation and encouraged by Silicon Valley and sundry nonprofit groups, including Code.org, an industry-based organization that seeks to expand access to computer science in schools and to increase participation by women and minorities. https://code .org/.

36. College Board, "AP Program Results: Class of 2018, AP Capstone Expansion," accessed February 7, 2019. https://reports.collegeboard.org/ap-program-results/ap-capstone-expansion.

37. College Board, "Pre-AP Courses," accessed November 5, 2018. https://preap.collegeboard .org/courses.

PART II

On the Ground in 2018

4

The Lone Star Challenge

No place in America offers a larger or more vivid example of AP's recent history, its widening mission, and the challenges of carrying out that mission than Texas. The Lone Star State illustrates the complex interplay of traditional Advanced Placement success in upscale schools; ambitious efforts to extend it to more disadvantaged youngsters; robust, AP-centric charter schools; and an exceptionally bumptious and varied array of dual-credit alternatives. Here (and again in chapters 7 and 8) we delve into the Texas AP saga and some of the remarkable actors that have propelled it.

As in most of the nation, Advanced Placement participation has surged in Texas for four straight decades, and the upward slope has recently steepened. While the 1970s added about eighty-five students annually to the state's AP rolls, since 2010 the yearly increase has averaged fifteen thousand.[1] Between 1997 and 2017, the number of AP students in Texas public schools grew twice as fast as in the country as a whole, and far faster than the state's eleventh and twelfth grade public-school enrollment, even as that number also soared (see figure 4.1).[2] In 2018, Texas saw nearly 320,000 pupils (in both public and private schools) take almost 600,000 AP exams, second only to California, and accounting for 11 percent of worldwide participants. The number of exams per pupil rose, too, spurred by governmental and philanthropic moves to grow the program (and cover testing fees) as well as intensifying college competition among high school students.

The number of participating high schools climbed, too. In 2017, about 1,800 Texas schools enrolled AP exam-takers. That includes 58 percent of

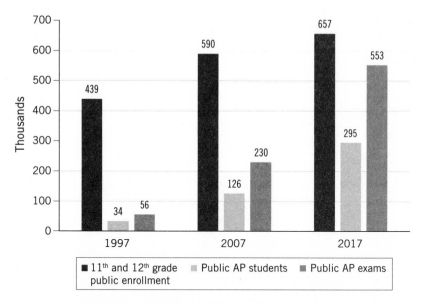

FIGURE 4.1. Total public 11th and 12th grade enrollment, public AP students, and exams taken, Texas, 1997, 2007, and 2017.
Enrollment data come from Applied Educational Research, Inc. (AERI) and are cited by the College Board. AP data come directly from the College Board.
Sources: Applied Educational Research, Inc. and College Board

public high schools in the state, up from 44 percent in 1997 (see figure A.3 in appendix II).[3] As is the pattern nationally, about four out of five schools where students take AP exams also teach College Board–approved AP courses.

Unsurprisingly, however, in a state this vast and diverse, Advanced Placement access depends greatly on where one lives, and those residing in Texas's many rural communities are at a distinct disadvantage. In 2016, 58 percent of rural high schools offered no AP courses (versus 18 percent of suburban and urban schools), and rural schools that host some AP courses can seldom offer many of them. Just 12 percent taught more than ten AP subjects in 2016, compared with 60 percent or more in the metro areas.[4] This squares with the national pattern noted in the previous chapter, as rural schools generally face multiple challenges, including inadequate infrastructure, human capital, transport, and—especially—small enrollments. It's important to bear this reality in mind as we travel deeper into the heart of Texas: Urban and suburban youngsters are far likelier to attend high schools that offer lots of AP.

Also in line with the national trend, AP growth in Texas has been starkly uneven among racial and ethnic groups. On the positive side, the number of exams taken by Hispanic students rose four times faster than among

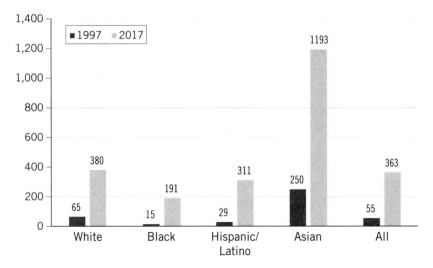

FIGURE 4.2. AP exams taken per 1,000 Texas public high school students, by race/ethnicity, 1997 and 2017.
College Board data show AP exams taken in public schools by race/ethnicity in May 1997 and 2017. Texas Education Agency data show public high school students by race/ethnicity in fall 1996 and fall 2016. "All" refers to all students, including other races/ethnicities that are not shown here but delineated by the College Board and the Texas Education Agency.
Sources: College Board and the Texas Education Agency

white pupils between 1997 and 2017. Among Asian and African American students, the rates of increase were twice and thrice that of whites, also reflecting profound shifts in Lone Star demographics. During those two decades, white students' share of public high school enrollment dropped from 49 to 30 percent, while the Hispanic share rose from 34 to 51 percent.[5]

Comparing exam taking per thousand high school pupils (figure 4.2), we again see big increases for black and Hispanic youngsters since 1997. On the worrisome side, however, black students still take AP at far lower rates than their peers, actually less in 2017 than the Asian rate of twenty years earlier. Even so, as we saw for the nation as a whole, participation gaps are narrowing; Hispanic students now take part in Advanced Placement at about 82 percent the rate of white students, up from 44 percent in 1997, and today's black students take AP exams at about half the rate of white students, up from 24 percent two decades earlier.

As AP participation soared in Texas, so, too, did the number of qualifying scores, up sevenfold in the two decades since 1997 (see figure A.4 in appendix II). Yet as we saw nationally, the passing rate declined, illustrating the now-familiar dilemma: Is it better to have a larger number of students earning qualifying scores or a higher rate of success among those who sit for the exams? While all groups' rates of qualifying scores dropped since 1997, the declines were steepest among Hispanic/Latino and black students (see figure A.5 in appendix II).

These disparities have been widely noted in the "excellence gap" literature—as well as in the two previous chapters—as have the enduring barriers that lead to unequal educational success for poor and minority youngsters. But that hasn't deterred Texas policy makers and civic leaders from striving to rectify matters. In many ways, AP's stunning growth in the Lone Star State over the past several decades is a tale of intensifying efforts to expand access to advanced learning opportunities for those very populations while also seeking to strengthen the state's human capital and future prosperity.

Driving Growth—and Diversity

By the early 1980s, forward-looking Texans recognized that their state's economic well-being could not forever rest on oil, gas, and cattle, and that it was time to make serious investments in science and technology. This led in fairly short order to major upgrades in the University of Texas's research capacity, multiple efforts to attract more tech-oriented firms (Texas Instruments was already there, as was Ross Perot's Electronic Data Systems), and an elaborately orchestrated bid to attract the Department of Energy's proposed Superconducting Super Collider.

Although many of the state's upscale suburban school systems—places like Highland Park, Plano, and Katy—had long offered their students enriched options such as Advanced Placement (as did most traditional independent schools), AP was all but absent from communities around the Super Collider's intended location in Waxahachie, south of Dallas. That deficiency would make it hard to attract the sophisticated scientific team that the project required, people who would be loath to move their families to a place that lacked high-powered education offerings for their children.

To address this problem, Dallas businessman, Republican stalwart, and veteran philanthropist Peter O'Donnell offered, via his family foundation, to help bring AP to nine high schools near the Super Collider site, five of which had no previous AP experience. In fact, as O'Donnell recounts in a recent memoir, in 1990 just 3 percent of eleventh and twelfth graders in the nine affected districts were even enrolled in AP classes. Half a decade later, thanks in large part to the incentives and encouragement of his philanthropy, those high schools surpassed state and national averages in AP course taking and exam passing, including gains by minority students and girls.[6]

In the end, Congress (for reasons of cost and politics) cancelled the entire Super Collider project, but O'Donnell's AP initiative had proven so successful, and he was so enamored of its potential to boost achievement, enhance equity, and widen the human capital pipeline, particularly in STEM subjects, that along with completing the nine-district pilot he went on, starting in 1994, to expand the AP Incentive Program into Dallas, initially with a five-year commitment to nine more high schools, schools this time that were overwhelmingly poor and minority.

This, too, went well. O'Donnell reports that "by the end of the fifth year, Dallas students were outperforming other students in Texas and the United States in AP math, science, and English in several categories, including male, female, African-American, and Hispanic/Latino students." The number of AP qualifying scores in participating high schools quintupled. "Dallas evaluators called it the most successful program the district ever had." Texas Instruments offered to add another school and to maintain the program after O'Donnell's largesse ended. Other foundations joined in and, in time, the AP Incentive Program reached every high school in the Dallas Independent School District.

By the turn of the millennium, AP expansion in Texas was following two intersecting paths. The one that went far beyond state borders involved ExxonMobil and led to the birth of the National Math and Science Initiative (NMSI). The other entailed purposeful efforts by philanthropists, education leaders, and policy makers to extend O'Donnell's pioneering work to other parts of the Lone Star State, including Austin and Fort Worth. We tread each path in turn.

Enter ExxonMobil and NMSI

By 2000, Peter O'Donnell had created a separate nonprofit outfit—Advanced Placement Strategies—to manage the burgeoning incentives program, take it statewide, and attract additional funders. Recruited to lead the new entity was Dallas's Gregg Fleisher, a successful veteran AP Calculus instructor in his own right.

Dallas was also home to the giant oil firm Exxon, which had a long-standing interest in education improvement. Indeed, this was a major focus of its corporate philanthropy—and the company's main charitable vehicle at the time was dubbed the Exxon Education Foundation.

When Rex Tillerson—more recently Donald Trump's first secretary of state—became head of the merged ExxonMobil Corporation in 2006, he was keen to create a sizable nonprofit legacy from his time at the helm of the massive energy company. He wanted it to advance math and science education in the United States, because of the country's urgent need for a better-educated population, especially in disadvantaged communities, and because the huge firm's own workforce needed a steady supply of technically competent people. He and his colleagues were also mindful of the blue-ribbon panel convened in 2005 by the National Academy of Sciences—O'Donnell was a member—that would issue a scathing report about America's declining STEM competence at the very time other countries were gaining strength in those fields.

Tillerson had no interest in starting from scratch, however. A data-driven executive in a data-driven company, he preferred to scale initiatives that had already shown success. He and his team turned for advice to Tom Luce, a prominent Dallas attorney and Texas education reformer, who was also a longtime friend of Peter O'Donnell's and who, in 2006, was concluding a stint in Washington with former Texas Governor George W. Bush and Education Secretary Margaret Spellings (another Texan).

Luce suggested that ExxonMobil launch a large-scale national program modeled on O'Donnell's Texas initiative, aimed at advancing math and science education by enlisting more high schools and young people, particularly those from poor and minority backgrounds, to participate in Advanced Placement. O'Donnell's project had accumulated impressive metrics showing that, with the help of extra resources and a focused program, it was indeed possible to boost AP participation and success in STEM subjects in high schools serving poor kids.

Tillerson liked that plan—provided that Tom Luce and Gregg Fleisher would come aboard to lead it and that other national foundations would help underwrite it. The Bill and Melinda Gates and Michael and Susan Dell Foundations signed on, as did Luce and Fleisher, and thus was born in 2007—the same year as the National Academy's "Rising Above the Gathering Storm" report—the National Math and Science Initiative (NMSI, pronounced "nims-ee").

ExxonMobil also undertook to expand the "UTeach" program, based at the University of Texas and designed to boost the number of well-prepared math and science teachers. This instructor-centered project complemented the student-oriented AP initiative—and both were STEM focused.

NMSI's AP program entails a three-year commitment to participating schools and districts and contains multiple elements that—program leaders are clear about this—must synchronize in order to yield the maximum impact. To join it, schools and communities must satisfy a number of preconditions, including local financial support ("skin in the game") and evidence of strong commitment, competent leadership, and a solid prospect that the program will continue after NMSI's exit. Absent a favorable environment for this multi-pronged program, says NMSI board chair (and former ExxonMobil executive) Ken Cohen, "You can miss the bulls-eye."[7]

For the past dozen years, NMSI has been the country's largest promoter of AP expansion. Leaders estimate that ExxonMobil's dollars have leveraged some $450 million in other philanthropy, an impressive figure that doesn't include substantial government funding as well as situations where NMSI is hired and paid directly by school districts or states.

Still focused primarily on STEM subjects (science, technology, engineering, math) plus English, and concentrating on high schools with many disadvantaged students and little previous AP activity, NMSI has so far worked in some 1,200 high schools in thirty-four states.[8] With Fleisher at or near the helm until 2018, its core model resembles the original O'Donnell initiative: multi-part teacher training (including online curricular resources, support from AP experts, and course-specific training), and financial incentives for teachers and kids who succeed on AP exams (as well as subsidized exam fees, textbooks, and other materials). NMSI continues diligently to organize "super Saturday" study sessions—extra instruction, tutoring, exam prep—for students, and it works with school and district leaders to implant a durable Advanced Placement culture, including help with performance analysis and shared goal setting, while facilitating access to academic and program experts.[9]

Where philanthropic dollars—usually a blend of national and local—can be mustered, NMSI functions as "donor" of its program and can pretty much dictate terms and conditions, including being fussy about which districts and schools are serious about the program and can satisfy its preconditions.[10] This costs NMSI backers approximately half a million dollars per school over the course of a three-year engagement, which works out to a couple of hundred dollars per student per year. That may be thought a bargain so long as it yields both success while NMSI is there and a lasting commitment to keep it going. It may also be judged a high price to pay if results are slim and transitory.

As NMSI has accumulated a generally impressive record of boosting AP participation and qualifying scores in core subjects, particularly for poor and minority youngsters, it has spun off state-level affiliates in half a dozen jurisdictions, has teamed up with other nonprofit STEM boosters, and has been engaged by a number of school systems—now including New York City, its largest-ever client—to bring its college-readiness and teacher-training services to town.[11] When functioning as a vendor rather than donor, however, as we see in the next chapter, NMSI has less control over its intervention model.

NMSI's mission is to make AP's potentially valuable education resource available to more disadvantaged youngsters, to introduce it into more of the high schools that they mostly attend, and to create the conditions for them to succeed in those demanding classrooms and thereafter in college. According to NMSI leaders, however, the greatest payoff isn't the credit that may result from a qualifying score. It's that the program, when successful, elevates the quality of teaching in a school, raises expectations for teachers and students alike, and changes the institutional culture. In other words, it's as much an education-reform strategy as a get-these-kids-college-credit program. "The goal," says board chair Cohen, "is to turn out science-literate people." This benefits society, he emphasizes, while also assisting firms like ExxonMobil.

Doing this well, as we repeatedly show in these pages, is a daunting challenge, but by no means hopeless. When labor economist C. Kirabo Jackson evaluated O'Donnell's AP Strategies program in 2007, he found—in addition to boosting AP participation and exam success rates, especially among minority youngsters—"a 30 percent increase in the number of students scoring above 1100 on the SAT or above 24 on the ACT, and an 8 percent increase in the number of students at a high school who enroll in a college or university in Texas."[12] He also saw climatic changes in participating high schools, noting, for example, that "all the guidance counselors with whom I spoke mentioned a shift in student and teacher attitudes toward AP courses. Following encouragement from counselors and teachers, students now view AP courses as difficult ones that anyone can take, rather than being only for the very brightest of students."[13]

A growing body of research appears to support NMSI's methods. Its College Readiness program has been shown to positively affect student enrollment in STEM-related AP courses and subsequent success on these exams, as well as student participation in AP generally.[14] Further studies by Jackson reported positive NMSI effects on AP course enrollment, SAT/ACT scores, college matriculation, college persistence, college GPAs, and even labor market outcomes.[15] In Colorado and Indiana, NMSI initiatives boosted the chances of students taking AP exams in math and science.[16] Elsewhere, positive effects could be found on AP participation and test success, particularly among female and minority students.[17]

As we shall see, however, the immense challenge of changing the culture of a school—creating an environment in which disadvantaged youngsters feel welcome in AP classes and well-prepared teachers are eager to instruct them—is ever present. NMSI's program appears most effective when schools treat AP as an engine for change and where teacher and leadership buy-in is strong. When those elements are shaky, success is more elusive.

Marching across Texas

Impressed by the rate of AP take-up and success in the would-be Super Collider region and in Dallas, and adroitly lobbied by O'Donnell and others, Texas lawmakers moved to enact a public-sector counterpart. That program launched in 1995 with the support of then governor George W. Bush and grew swiftly, such that within five years the number of young Texans earning qualifying scores on AP exams more than doubled. Under the state initiative, much like the O'Donnell program, eleventh and twelfth graders received cash awards if they scored 3 or higher. Teachers of AP and pre-AP courses received training plus modest pay boosts as well as bonuses when their pupils achieved qualifying scores. The focus, once again, was underserved student populations in schools that previously had little or no AP action.[18]

O'Donnell's privately funded program also continued apace. Buoyed by its Dallas venture, AP Strategies sought additional locations within the state. By 2002, it was working with high schools in four smaller communities and eyeing the capital city of Austin, which was plagued by a near-schizophrenic school system—successful on the prosperous west side of Interstate 35 but dismal on the disadvantaged and heavily minority east side. The same woes that attracted NMSI to Austin, however, also—in the form of nasty, racialized politics—led to pushback and delay, so the O'Donnell/Fleisher team turned instead to nearby Pflugerville, a relatively prosperous Austin suburb. Its school system enjoyed strong leadership and solid middle schools, so AP Strategies spent 2003 to 2007 more than doubling the number of AP exams taken and tripling the number of qualifying scores earned in STEM subjects and English across Pflugerville's three high schools.

When the program was finally able to launch in Austin's more challenging urban environment, the going got harder. Beginning in 2007 as part of a wider turnaround initiative by Superintendent Pascal Forgione (with the help of the Dell Foundation in its hometown), AP Strategies targeted seven of the district's most troubled high schools. Gains were minimal over three years, however, and Forgione left midway through, to be replaced by a superintendent with different priorities. The city was also experiencing a surfeit of education changes at the time, and teachers complained of reform fatigue.[19] Some observers recall the AP Strategies initiative as akin to giving a drowning man a new swimsuit: Austin's weakest schools were in such parlous condition that this program was never going to gain much traction. A second and similar intervention in 2010, this time by Dell and NMSI, was confined to three low-performing high schools and has produced respectable gains in them.

Austin illustrates the difficulty of growing AP (or much else) in a district overwhelmed by leadership turnover, multiple reform initiatives, teacher apathy or resistance, and political infighting. Today, however, things look somewhat brighter. In 2017, 61 percent of Austin's AP test takers earned qualifying scores versus 46 percent statewide.[20] The district drew praise from the Texas Education Agency.[21] Yet this impressive citywide passing rate masks continuing disparities in AP performance across Austin's seventeen high schools.

NMSI Comes to Fort Worth

Although resolutely headquartered in Dallas where it began, not until the fall of 2013 did NMSI venture into nearby Fort Worth. The fifth biggest city in Texas, often overshadowed by its higher-profile neighbor on the other side of the giant airport, shares many familiar urban challenges but also has some distinctive ones. Tarrant County, which surrounds Fort Worth, contains twenty different school districts, many of which have boundaries that snake in and out of the city limits. Fort Worth Independent School District (FWISD), which is the largest and spans most of the urban core, is an exceptionally challenging environment in which to launch an ambitious education reform. Of its students, 85 percent are Hispanic or African American and three-quarters are low income. Fewer than 10 percent of its graduating seniors reached 1100 on the SAT or 24 on the ACT in 2016. (The statewide figure was 22.5 percent.)[22] That number sank to a bleak 2.3 percent for black students and 5.2 percent for Latinos. Fort Worth is far removed from the serene environs of Advanced Placement's earliest adopters, but it's emblematic of many places where AP expansion is on the agenda today.

In 2013, NMSI board chair Tom Luce and several local philanthropies, spearheaded by the Sid W. Richardson Foundation, teamed up with then superintendent Walter Dansby to try to bring more Advanced Placement into five of the eighteen high schools in FWISD.[23]

Theretofore, this 85,000-pupil district had thriving AP courses in multiple subjects in just one venue: predominantly middle-class R. L. Paschal High School, where a dynamic math teacher named John Hamilton had worked for decades to promote this option. Paschal also boasted a solid record of student success on AP exams. Elsewhere in Fort Worth, Advanced Placement offerings were sparse and generally "gated," meaning that only students approved by teachers were encouraged to take those classes. In practice, this meant large segments of the district's surging minority populations never had much of a shot and, when they did, teachers sometimes deflected kids they thought might not fare well on the exams from even sitting for them. (At the time, exam taking was optional and families had to pay the fees.) In retrospect, past and present district officials acknowledge that this system was discriminatory, and Dansby and his former team are proud of—besides bringing NMSI to town—changing the rules such that every high school would offer at least some AP classes and entry into those courses would be open to all willing pupils, with the stipulation that everyone taking such a class would sit for the exam—and the district would cover the fees.

Those changes alone would boost AP participation and depress the exam-passing rate as more students enrolled in these challenging courses and took the tests. Moreover, as Dansby and his colleagues acknowledge, it's one thing for district leaders to declare that more AP classes will be offered in more schools, and quite another to find, prepare, and retain top-notch teachers and principals, without whom such a declaration is apt to prove hollow.

Along with challenging demographics, governance and politics have long beset the Fort Worth school system, mingling complex and often-fraught race relations, patronage, favoritism, neighborhood envy, and more. Its recent leadership history has also been turbulent, with seven superintendents (or acting superintendents) since 2004.

Promoted to the top job in 2012 after a lengthy career in the district, Dansby was the first person of color to lead FWISD. Encouraged by his friend, former board president William Koehler, he instituted a series of academic and management changes—the AP policy reforms and NMSI initiative among them—and these upset a host of vested interests, including an entrenched patronage system whereby individual board members were accustomed to placing friends and relatives in jobs throughout the district (and pushing out those they found irksome!).

In June 2014, not quite a year after signing the first memorandum of understanding with NMSI, Dansby was himself pushed out—and Koehler by then was gone from the board—meaning that the leaders who brought NMSI to town would not be around to ensure faithful implementation of that ambitious project.[24]

Every high school in FWISD was invited to apply for it and all did, though with varying levels of ardor and readiness. Resources were finite, however, so NMSI and the district chose five schools, all heavily minority. The NMSI intervention was to last the usual three years and spanned the usual goals: increasing the number of students, particularly disadvantaged youngsters, who enrolled in STEM and English AP courses, and boosting the number who earned qualifying scores on these exams. A further ambition—also standard operating procedure for NMSI—was to leave behind a durable AP culture in participating schools.

Each school worked with NMSI to encourage open enrollment in AP classes, seeking to relax the culture of exclusivity and persuade reluctant students to take the plunge. The project furnished financial rewards to schools, teachers, and students who succeeded on AP exams and instituted systems of support and training for teachers. It supplied tutoring and extra study sessions for students and committed to sharing data with schools, administering program and performance reviews, and assisting school leaders in other ways.

The district, however, faced a full measure of implementation challenges. Along with an interim superintendent for more than a year, and attrition of key staffers in the central office, at least one of the NMSI high schools changed principals. The elementary and middle schools that feed into those high schools through what the district terms a "pyramid" structure experienced even more turnover. The upshot was that some education leaders who had sought the program weren't there to make it happen at the building level or at headquarters.

Teacher turnover has long vexed FWISD, too, particularly in its many schools serving disadvantaged pupils. That's an acute problem for any reform that hinges both on teacher buy-in and on extensive training and professional development for those who must put it into practice, and it's an even larger problem for rigorous, content-heavy initiatives such as AP, which prosper only when instructors have a solid grounding in the material that they're teaching. In a school system with many low-achieving youngsters entering high school from less-than-stellar middle schools, the fate of a challenging initiative of this kind also hinges on getting better curricular and pedagogical alignment into the feeder schools and thereby ushering more kids into ninth grade who are adequately prepared for the rigors ahead. Yet Fort Worth, like many urban districts, has wrestled with grade-to-grade and school-to-school misalignments as well as with pupil mobility that undermines the feeder structure itself.

Mixed Results

Combine all these elements and it's remarkable that NMSI's five-school initiative produced any gains. Organization leaders insist that these compare
decently to NMSI's results in similar environments, but it's also understandable why the district's hopeful but tough-minded funders were less than
thrilled. One source of their divergent perspectives is the familiar question
of which matters more: rising numbers of passing scores (and students with
passing scores) or declining pass rates. Entangled therein is the question of
whether the increases represent new kids or more AP among the same students who were already engaged in it.

It's indisputable that participation grew during NMSI's time in Fort Worth.
At all five schools, the number of pupils taking at least one AP exam in NMSI-
supported subjects jumped—from 937 individuals in the baseline year to
1,451 by year three. The number of exams taken in those subjects rose from
995 to 2,362 at its peak (see figure 4.3).[25] For the two schools where we have
a fourth year of data, exam numbers rose further after NMSI's exit. Students
also took more exams per participant, with that figure increasing from an
average of 1.1 exams (in math, English, or science) in the baseline year to 1.5
by year three.

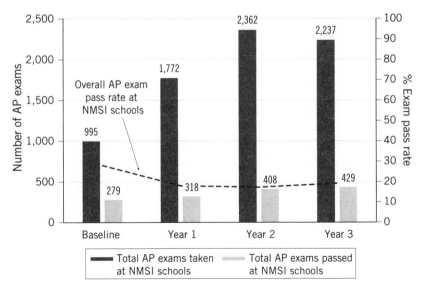

FIGURE 4.3. AP exams taken, passed, and qualifying score rate, at NMSI schools in FWISD.
Source: National Math and Science Initiative

There was also a gain—but far less impressive—in qualifying scores. Across the five NMSI schools, these went up from 279 in the base year to 429 in year three.

A legitimate concern among local funders is that increasing numbers of qualifying scores may have been substantially the result of abler students simply taking more exams in more subjects. Here, however, the data are inconclusive. In the year before NMSI's intervention, we see 1.4 qualifying scores per successful student, declining to 1.3 in year one but rebounding to 1.5 in years two and three. This suggests that, to some extent, successful students were taking more exams and doing well on them, and the funders' concerns appear to have some weight. But it's also the case that a total of 202 additional students (above baseline numbers) earned at least one qualifying score across the five schools over the course of NMSI's three-year intervention. Many of these may have been new AP students—exactly the kind that NMSI and the funders sought to target. And while such gains are modest for a district this big and an initiative this ambitious (and costly), we ought not discount the potential difference that it makes in the lives of individuals who, for the first time, find themselves passing Advanced Placement exams.[26]

In the end, though, it's not clear how much the visible gains in AP participation and success in Fort Worth were due to NMSI's labors there. The simultaneous policy changes made by the district surely made some difference, once it ordered all high schools to offer AP, to require those taking the courses to sit for the exams, and to cover their fees. Mindful of this, we compared the results of NMSI schools with non-NMSI schools during this period. We also looked separately at Paschal because of its sizable preexisting AP program.[27]

Here's what we found: From May 2014 through May 2017, Paschal increased its number of AP math, English, and science exams by 68 percent; NMSI's five schools increased by 80 percent; and the rest of the district increased by 107 percent.

During the same three-year period, Paschal boosted its number of qualifying scores by 13 percent, the NMSI schools raised theirs by 59 percent, and the rest of the district saw its pass rate go up by 75 percent. If we exclude Arlington Heights, which had a nontrivial AP program prior to NMSI's involvement, the other four NMSI schools increased their qualifying scores by 78 percent. These are not small or insignificant gains—but we also see that they coincided with, and perhaps were bested by, similar growth elsewhere in the district.

TABLE 4.1. Total number of additional qualifying scores earned, baseline exam pass rate, and average pass rate during NMSI intervention

Participating NMSI high school	Additional qualifying scores earned during three years of NMSI involvement	Baseline pass rate	Average pass rate during NMSI intervention
Green B. Trimble Technical	31	25%	13%
Northside	51	17%	10%
Amon Carter-Riverside	80	13%	15%
Arlington Heights	91	45%	29%
Southwest	65	22%	17%

Source: National Math and Science Initiative

Inevitably, the story grows even more complex at the building level. At all five of the NMSI high schools, the number of qualifying scores earned by students rose during NMSI's tenure, although by varying amounts. AP participation grew much more, the result being that the pass rate dropped at four schools, while inching upward at Carter-Riverside (see table 4.1).

These school-level disparities also mean that NMSI's (and the donors') return on investment ranged widely. On average, we estimate the cost of each additional qualifying score earned by students in NMSI high schools during the three-year initiative at about $9,500. At Carter-Riverside, however, that cost goes down to about $4,500 while at Trimble Tech it was nearly four times that figure.[28]

Ken Cohen terms NMSI's experience in Fort Worth a "mixed bag," with some schools proving relatively successful and others notably less so. It was always a heavy lift in a district plagued by staff churn, uncertain buy-in, and heavy-duty politics, so it's noteworthy that schools saw gains anyway, even as it remains unclear how many of those gains were caused by NMSI, considering everything else that was in flux.

NMSI has learned many lessons along the way—and not only in Fort Worth—particularly concerning the importance of sustained commitment at the school, district, and state levels as well as by key stakeholders and influencers. (They pulled out of Washington State, for example, when union opposition made it impossible to provide teacher incentives.[29]) They've racked up solid successes with the College Readiness Program in a number of places in and beyond Texas—North Dakota and Louisiana, for example[30]—but the ground must be fertile for NMSI's seeds to sprout and flourish until harvest time.

Aftermath

NMSI's direct involvement in Fort Worth ended in 2017, but AP remains. In 2018, 5,749 FWISD students sat for 10,566 exams (nearly two per participant) and 1,895 of them (almost one-third of exam-takers) earned at least one of 2,930 qualifying scores. Success remains elusive, however, for the minority pupils who make up the lion's share of the district's enrollment. At the time of writing, we could not obtain 2018 data by race, but Fort Worth's AP results in 2017 included scores of 1 for 62 percent of Hispanic exam-takers and 81 percent of black participants.

It's notable, too, that more than a third of all qualifying scores in FWISD still belong to students attending Paschal High School, which enrolls just 16 percent of the district's high school pupils.[31] Yet even in that generally successful (and much sought) school, we encountered signs that the AP program operates as a sort of enclave that's rarely entered by poor and minority youngsters. A parent of recent AP students at Paschal says the kids there "live so much in two separate worlds" while in school that "they almost never overlap in class, only in occasional elective courses like health or speech and athletics." Paschal students, we were advised, tend to "make assumptions about what classes kids are in based on race. They would assume that any white kids were in the AP classes and that non-white kids were in the 'regular' classes."

And that's half a decade after Walter Dansby initiated forceful steps to remove the (real and perceived) gates from AP in the district.

Current Fort Worth superintendent Kent Scribner told us that he values Advanced Placement for the challenge that it provides students, the experience that it affords them in wrestling with college-level coursework, and the potential benefit that it confers both in admissions and in degree credit. At the same time, he rues the difficulty of attracting, preparing, and retaining a sufficient cadre of teachers who master both AP's capacious content and the pedagogical challenge of imparting that content to young people who are willing to try it and probably have the requisite brainpower but arrive in class without the skills and knowledge needed to succeed there. It's much easier, he notes, to teach the "easy" kids—those who, besides being smart, have a solid academic background and ample home and peer support—than to supply students from tough circumstances with the requisite educational assets. And when both kinds of pupils turn up in the same classroom, it demands true prowess with this sort of differentiated yet high-level instruction.

Scribner sees equal value and possibly greater benefit for his students from dual-credit classes and early college high schools (both discussed in chapter 8). The district now has three of the latter, operated jointly with Tarrant County College (TCC), and the superintendent's enthusiasm for them and their career-oriented counterparts suggests that further growth in this model of enriched education will find favor during his tenure. With six campuses in the county, the college's recent expansion of all matter of dual credit has been extraordinary, mirroring its growing popularity across Texas. In fall 2017, 16 percent of TCC's total enrollment consisted of such students—8,493 of them from sixteen school districts—versus just sixty-two individuals back in in 2005.[32] One-fifth of them hailed from FWISD. There, the number of AP exam-takers is still more than thrice the population of dual-credit participants.[33] But dual credit is apt to grow faster under Scribner, who is also said to give higher priority to boosting low achievers than to maximizing options for high flyers, seeing the former as both more urgent and more cost effective.

The Fort Worth experience with NMSI (and the Texas experience more generally) illustrates the challenge of expanding AP to students who have not historically had much access to it or enjoyed great success with it. We return to Texas a few chapters hence to discuss the interplay of alternatives to AP in that state, notably its burgeoning dual credit offerings. In the next chapter, however, we move east to New York City and see how the nation's largest school district is tackling its own AP challenge, with NMSI again playing a prominent role.

Notes

1. AP data for Texas since 1997 can be found at College Board, "AP Data Overview," accessed November 5, 2018. https://research.collegeboard.org/programs/ap/data.

2. AP participation in Texas private schools also rose significantly, although "only" by 358 percent, versus the public-school increase of 766 percent.

3. Here we compare College Board counts of public schools offering AP exams with the Texas Education Agency's count of public schools that offered twelfth grade in 2016–17. TEA data were obtained by request in March 2018. Of nonpublic schools, 360 (or 22 percent of all Texas AP schools) enrolled at least one student who took at least one AP exam in 2017. We were unable to find a definitive count of private high schools in the state.

4. Jill Schott, "AP Access and Student Success," presentation given in Austin, Texas, Texas Education Agency, November 6, 2017. https://tea.texas.gov/WorkArea/DownloadAsset.aspx?id=51539618390.

5. Enrollment data from Texas Education Agency, "Enrollment Trends," accessed November 5, 2018. https://tea.texas.gov/Reports_and_Data/School_Performance/Accountability_Research/Enrollment_Trends/?LangType=1033.

6. Peter O'Donnell Jr. and Carolyn Barta, *Improving Education, Changing Lives: A Memoir to Encourage Philanthropy* (Austin, TX: Dolph Briscoe Center for American History, University of Texas at Austin, 2017), 50–51.

7. Personal conversation with Ken Cohen.

8. National Math and Science Initiative, "NMSI's College Readiness Program," accessed November 5, 2018. http://www.nms.org/getmedia/d462d9cc-e189–4be7–8c3d-d7301eb17bda/NMSI -CRP-Program-Schools-2008–2018.pdf.aspx.

9. NMSI's approach is described at National Math and Science Initiative, "College Readiness Program," accessed February 6, 2019. http://www.nms.org/Our-Approach/CRP.aspx.

10. See, for example, NMSI's partnership with Texas Instruments. "TI's 'Power of STEM Education' Grants Total $5.4 Million in 2016 to Improve STEM Learning and Teaching," Texas Instruments, press release, August 10, 2016. https://www.prnewswire.com/news-releases/tis-power -of-stem-education-grants-total-54-million-in-2016-to-improve-stem-learning-and-teaching -300310972.html.

11. National Math and Science Initiative, "Program Partners," accessed November 5, 2018. http://www.nms.org/Get-Involved/Partners.aspx.

12. C. Kirabo Jackson, "Cash for Test Scores: The Impact of the Texas Advanced Placement Incentive Program," *Education Next* 8, no. 4 (2008): 72.

13. Jackson, "Cash for Test Scores," 75.

14. D. J. Holtzman, "The Advanced Placement Teacher Training Incentive Program (APTIP): Estimating the Impact of an Incentive and Training Program on Students" (unpublished manuscript, Washington, DC, 2010). http://www.socialimpactexchange.org/sites/www.socialimpactexchange .org/files/Holtzman%20APTIP%20Evaluation_0.pdf.

15. C. Kirabo Jackson, "Do College-Preparatory Programs Improve Long-Term Outcomes?" *Economic Inquiry* 52, no. 1 (2014): 72–79; C. Kirabo Jackson, "A Little Now for a Lot Later: An Evaluation of a Texas Advanced Placement Incentive Program," *Journal of Human Resources* 45, no. 3 (2010): 591–639.

16. Dan Sherman and others, *Final Report of the Impacts of the National Math and Science Initiative's (NMSI's) College Readiness Program on High School Students' Outcomes* (Washington, DC: American Institutes of Research, 2017). https://files.eric.ed.gov/fulltext/ED577450.pdf.

17. Richard S. Brown and Kilchan Choi, *Measuring the Causal Effect of National Math and Science Initiative's College Readiness Program* (Los Angeles: University of California, Center for Research on Evaluation, Standards, and Student Testing, 2015). http://cresst.org/wp-content /uploads/R847.pdf.

18. Peter O'Donnell Jr., testimony concerning the protection of America's competitive edge, given on March 1, 2006 to the Committee on Health, Education, Labor, and Pensions, 109th Cong., 2nd sess., *Congressional Record.* http://www.nationalacademies.org/OCGA/109Session2 /testimonies/OCGA_151004.

19. Larry Cuban, *As Good as It Gets: What School Reform Brought to Austin* (Cambridge, MA: Harvard University Press, 2010), 80.

20. Karen Looby, *Advanced Placement (AP) Test Results: A District and Campus Summary, May 2017* (Austin, TX: Austin Independent School District, 2017). https://www.austinisd.org/sites /default/files/dre-surveys/rb/2017_AP_Results_May2017.pdf.

21. "Number of Texas Students Taking Advanced Placement Increases for Class of 2016," press release, Texas Education Agency, February 22, 2017. https://tea.texas.gov/About_TEA /News_and_Multimedia/News_Releases/2017/Number_of_Texas_students_taking_Advanced _Placement__increases_for_Class_of_2016/.

22. This represents the percentage of examinees who scored at or above the criterion score on either the SAT (1110 on the reading and math sections combined) or the ACT (composite score of at least 24). Campus, district, and state reports for 2015–16 that include this indicator can be found at Texas Education Agency, "2016–17 Texas Academic Performance Reports," accessed November 5, 2018. https://rptsvr1.tea.texas.gov/perfreport/tapr/2017/index.html.

23. Cohort 1 began with two schools in 2013–14 and continued through 2015–16; Cohort 2 began with three schools in 2014–15 and continued through 2016–17.

24. For more on this turbulent period, see Yamil Berard, "Dansby Resigns as Fort Worth School Superintendent," *Fort Worth Star Telegram*, June 2, 2014. https://www.star-telegram.com/news /local/community/fort-worth/article3860477.html; Tim Madigan and Yamil Berard, "Dansby, School Board: A Bitter Divorce," *Fort Worth Star Telegram*, June 10, 2014. https://www.star -telegram.com/news/local/community/fort-worth/article3861408.html.

25. "Participating students" means unique students who take at least one math, science, or English exam. Numbers may contain slight errors due to some data being concealed for student privacy. Data were combined for the two cohorts of schools, meaning the baseline years (2012–13 and 2013–14) were combined, year 1 (2013–14 and 2014–15) were combined, and so on. Baseline data for "unique students" showing participation and performance come from FWISD; all other data from NMSI.

26. With student-level data, one could determine which students took the additional exams and how they fared, but due to privacy considerations we did not have access to that information. It's also possible that some unique students are being duplicated year-on-year, as counts are per given year.

27. As NMSI worked with two schools between 2012–13 and 2015–16 and the other three between 2013–14 and 2016–17, some growth before 2014 may be missed, and growth shown after 2016 includes a year when the first two schools were no longer working with NMSI. By comparing four points in time, we aim to show trends between NMSI and non-NMSI schools during the time of peak NMSI involvement, but there may be minor errors due to the two nonsynchronous cohorts within that four-year period.

28. We reviewed memoranda of agreement between FWISD and NMSI for both school cohorts, yielding an estimated total cost for the three-year intervention at each school, which we divided by the number of qualifying scores earned.

29. Linda Shaw, "$13 Million Grant for AP Teachers Lost over Pay Dispute," *Seattle Times*, May 6, 2008. https://www.seattletimes.com/seattle-news/education/13-million-grant-for-ap -teachers-lost-over-pay-dispute/.

30. Charles Lussier, "ExxonMobil-Funded Program Credited with Expansion of AP at Capital Region High Schools," *The Advocate*, January 22, 2018. https://www.theadvocate.com/baton_rouge /news/education/article_8f7db22c-fef9-11e7-a155-aff10da7491f.html; Helmut Schmidt, "Teacher Training Initiative Aims to Boost AP Courses in ND," *Grand Forks Herald*, July 16, 2015. http:// www.grandforksherald.com/news/education/3798169-teacher-training-initiative-aims-boost-ap -courses-nd.

31. Authors' analysis of AP data from Fort Worth Independent School District.

32. *Dual Credit: TCCD's Partnership with Local ISDs* (Fort Worth, TX: Tarrant County College District, Office of Institutional Research, 2017), 3. https://www.tccd.edu/documents/about /research/institutional-intelligence-and-research/reports/internal/dual-credit-echs/2017-dual -credit-end-term.pdf; Statewide data on dual credit can be found at Texas Higher Education Board, "Dual Credit Data," accessed November 5, 2018. http://www.txhighereddata.org/index.cfm ?objectId=28CFDAD7-9721-1F85-364E1813799CE55B.

33. *Dual Credit: TCCD's Partnership with Local ISDs*, 11.

5

Growing AP in Gotham

New York State is home to America's third largest population of AP exam-takers—174,000 in 2018—trailing only Texas and California. Three in ten of the state's AP students take those tests in New York City.[1] In fact, in 2018 that city's Department of Education (DOE) housed more AP students than all but a dozen states. It's scarcely surprising that the challenge of effecting any major change in how Advanced Placement works in Gotham is gargantuan when placed alongside a city like Fort Worth.

Yet the story of AP in the Big Apple shares many of the same dynamics that we saw in Texas. Some high schools have taken part in the program forever, and some do it in a very big way. For example, Brooklyn Technical High School—a huge, selective-admission institution run by the DOE—offered 111 sections of twenty-nine different AP courses in 2018–19. Nonselective but middle-class Bayside High School in Queens offered as many courses, though "just" fifty-three classrooms' worth.[2]

At the same time, many of the city's four-hundred-plus high schools furnish their students with few or no AP options. As recently as 2015–16, more than a hundred offered no AP courses at all—and many of those schools are located in poor neighborhoods full of African American, Hispanic, and immigrant youngsters.[3]

Over the years, municipal leaders sought in various ways to rectify this obvious inequity, even as they undertook myriad other high school reforms, including devolving more authority to successful principals, splitting immense schools into smaller learning units, often with distinctive themes or specialties, and radically expanding the use of choice for matching students with those schools and programs.[4]

One such growth initiative came in September 2013, toward the end of Mayor Michael Bloomberg's last term, when the DOE joined forces with the College Board and the National Math and Science Initiative (NMSI) to launch an "AP Expansion" program meant to last three years and intended, said the agency:

> to start more than 120 new AP STEM-related courses in fifty-five New York City high schools, increasing the number of students studying science, technology, engineering and math. In its first year, approximately 2,500 students will obtain access to these courses for the first time, many who attend high schools in some of the city's most underserved neighborhoods and communities. Participating schools will have the option to implement AP courses in Biology, Calculus AB, Environmental Science, Statistics, English Literature and Composition, and U.S. History.[5]

Two years later, Mayor Bill de Blasio declared—as part of his own ambitious education initiatives—that Advanced Placement would be introduced into *every* high school that didn't already have it (or enough of it).[6] This venture, dubbed "AP for All," commenced in 2016, also in partnership with the College Board and NMSI, plus Seattle-based Equal Opportunity Schools (EOS).[7] (For more on NMSI and EOS, see chapters 4 and 6 respectively.)

We return below to those two citywide initiatives, including their early results and some lessons that may be drawn from their experience to date. First, though, we visit a small public high school that was incorporating AP into its curriculum for disadvantaged youngsters well before city hall pushed for more.

Urban Assembly School for Law and Justice

Sharing a building in downtown Brooklyn with two other small schools, the Urban Assembly School for Law and Justice opened in 2004 as part of Bloomberg's and former education chancellor Joel Klein's heroic move—aided by the Gates Foundation and other philanthropies—to create more intimate, safe, and functional learning environments for the city's high school students, most of whom had been attending massive institutions that lacked character, quality, and, often, discipline.[8]

The nonprofit Urban Assembly, which began in 1990 as a community development and antipoverty organization, teamed up with the DOE to create some of the first small schools and then operate them via a complex partnership arrangement with the city.[9] Today, it sponsors twenty-one such high schools in four of the five boroughs, accounting for some nine thousand students.[10] All are open enrollment, which distinguishes them from the many New York City high schools that select or screen prospective pupils, and most have particular themes or career foci. That includes the "School for Law and Justice," a.k.a. SLJ, which describes itself as a "college preparatory high school . . . committed to high standards and personal attention for all students . . . in an empowering environment that fosters intellectual independence and civic engagement." Its stated mission is to treat "law and justice" as "the lenses through which subject matter is viewed and academic skills are developed," which means it focuses more on social sciences and humanities than science and math. Its 460 students are almost all black and Latino, more than two-thirds qualify for federally subsidized meals, and three-quarters have parents who did not themselves complete college.

Although many SLJ pupils are disadvantaged, the school itself enjoys several advantages. A lot of its students come from relatively well-functioning families in which someone—an older sibling, aunt, or cousin—has been to college and can talk encouragingly about it. Many come from immigrant families with the classic newcomer's view of education as a path to upward mobility. There may not be much money at home but educational aspiration and success are not alien notions.

SLJ operates with relative independence, thanks to the buffering supplied by the Urban Assembly. The selection of its principal, for example, is essentially a joint decision, not something imposed from on high. The parts of the DOE bureaucracy that deal with Urban Assembly schools manage a fairly light touch—and the organization itself provides school leaders and staff with professional development, peer networking, and other supports. SLJ has benefited greatly from a succession of stand-out leaders, indeed its entire administrative team, plus a cadre of dedicated, top-notch teachers. Also exceptionally helpful is its Rolodex of influential and generous external partners, including a top-flight Wall Street law firm, as well as the school's notable success in raising private dollars with which to supplement its ample municipal budget.[11] These resources have paid for many extras, including a fanatically dedicated college-counseling team that works with students from day one to accustom them to the idea of attending college, preps them to succeed there, arranges campus visits, and directs them to other enabling activities after school, during summer, and more.

A key resource the school deploys to challenge its students with college-level academics is Advanced Placement, which has been part of the SLJ curriculum since 2008—the year of its first graduating class. Kids get no extra points on their GPAs for taking such courses. Instead, they enroll to challenge themselves, to earn college credit that may save them time and tuition ("more money in my own pocket" remarked one young man), because they want the "taste of college-level work" that AP supplies as well as the skills it can develop, and because they expect the presence of such courses on their transcripts to wow admissions officers. Even if they don't earn qualifying scores on the exams, those reviewing their applications will see that they tried—and, in so doing, took some ownership of their educations and perhaps their lives. A young woman we met who had scored only 1 on the AP Psychology exam the previous year was nonetheless glad that she had taken the course, because just surviving it—and the exam—built her confidence that she would be able to withstand the rigors of college.

Beginning with English Language and Microeconomics, SLJ's suite of AP courses has grown to include (in 2017–18) Environmental Science, Psychology, and US History. The school has also widened participation to engage underclassmen in AP. Qualified tenth and eleventh graders are now encouraged to partake, and the curriculum features deliberate progressions through a sequence of AP classes for those who can handle it. After a difficult start (2016 was the first year any SLJ underclassmen experienced AP, and many struggled), the school has positioned US History as a tenth-grade course, followed by Psychology in eleventh (for those who make it through history). The other three classes are reserved for seniors.

While most youngsters who seek out SLJ do so with some prior understanding of its college-prep focus, many arrive from middle school with dismal preparation for advanced academics: weak skills, skimpy knowledge, little to no experience with serious studying, note-taking, and so forth. As an open-enrollment school, SLJ takes all comers, though it strives to make clear in advance to prospective students (and their parents) what will be expected of them. As a stand-alone high school, it has no sway over what is and isn't taught or learned in New York's hundreds of middle schools that may feed graduates into it. Hence the remedial burden is weighty, the more so when the school's goal is to get kids into college-level coursework just a year or two after their slipshod (or worse) middle school experience.

The SLJ team engages in multiple strategies to overcome that bleak past and prepare its pupils for a bright academic future. Some are invisible to students, such as intensive course planning by teachers, facilitated by a school schedule that seldom exceeds four instructional periods a day and builds in time to collaborate with fellow teachers. Serious attention is paid to vertical and horizontal course alignment, and the whole team works to make ninth grade function as a "foundational year" during which all students work on study skills, note taking, structured writing, and other requisites for success in the academic challenges ahead.

Much is done for and with new AP pupils, too, beginning with "AP Camp" in late summer for those registered for any of SLJ's Advanced Placement courses. Even youngsters with previous AP experience are asked to return for an August week of coaching in skill building, peer editing, syllabus decoding, and more.

Once school starts, SLJ's "After School Learning Academy" houses an array of tutoring opportunities and review sessions plus traditional extracurricular activities. Students also have access to off-campus mentors, internships, field trips, and a host of summer opportunities. And every AP course has an extra weekly section that amounts to additional tutoring and small-group instruction in skills like note-taking—partial compensation for the acute time crunch faced by AP students (and teachers) in New York, where the school calendar provides far fewer—as many as twenty to thirty fewer—days of instruction ahead of the early May exams than are available in places like Texas.

The school faces a full measure of daunting challenges. Many kids arrive not only with skimpy study skills but also sloppy academic habits, such as not bothering to do homework. (During our visit to the AP Camp, perhaps one-third of them appeared not to have completed their overnight reading assignment.) Many also have family obligations and complications, after-school jobs, and other distractions.

Yet when all is said and done, a praiseworthy number of SLJ students are able not only to take Advanced Placement classes but also to rack up qualifying scores on the end-of-year exams. In May 2017, of the ninety pupils who sat for those exams, half earned at least one qualifying score, very close to the citywide average that year (52.3 percent).[12]

The following year, some 118 SLJ students—roughly a third of the school's tenth, eleventh, and twelfth graders (including about half the graduating class)—were enrolled in at least one AP course, and in May 2018 they tackled 178 exams. Those yielded a more-than-respectable fifty-eight qualifying scores, and an additional fifty-four scores of 2. In Microeconomics, more than half of the exams taken earned qualifying scores—an impressive accomplishment in its own right—and 27 percent of the class of 2018—more than the national ratio—emerged with at least one such score on their transcripts.[13]

This must be viewed as a major success story. Sure, it's light-years from the track records of the city's elite high schools, but SLJ takes all who apply, and an ever-growing fraction of its pupil population is benefiting both from the AP classroom experience and the rewards that accompany solid exam scores.[14] Particularly considering the school's demographics, these achievements cannot be overstated.

Indeed, what we see at this little school is about as strong an example as we are likely to find of the successful use of AP as part of a comprehensive building-level strategy to equip high school pupils from disadvantaged backgrounds and sketchy prior schooling with solid preparation for college along with the supports that get them into and—in most cases—through college.[15] As of June 2018, 92 percent of SLJ's class of 2017, 65 percent of SLJ's class of 2016, and 70 percent of the class of 2015, remained enrolled in college (whereas just 73 percent of US students who began college in 2015 were still there just one year later).[16] SLJ's college completion rate also compares well with the national average, even though the Brooklyn school has a far less advantaged population: 53 percent of its class of 2009 graduated from college within six years (versus 59 percent for the same cohort nationally).[17]

SLJ also shows both the benefits and hazards of undertaking this ambitious, multiheaded project within the confines of so small a school. Its intimate scale is a definite plus. With fewer than five hundred students, everyone knows everyone, the atmosphere is purposeful yet relaxed, behavior is good, nobody can hide, it's easy for teachers to team up for curriculum alignment and lesson coordination, and the adults working with a particular pupil—teachers, counselors, and administrators—can compare notes and develop joint action plans for that young person. (That the school's budget and schedule facilitate such gatherings is also a great plus.)

On the down side, small schools, even those with substantial resources, cannot offer many different AP courses and don't have much instructional bench strength. A single teacher is often responsible for an entire course, particularly the advanced kind. (Upper-level courses in STEM subjects are usually hardest to staff.) While it's possible to grow leaders from within—SLJ's current principal is a former assistant principal, part of a pattern of administrative continuity since the school opened—the departure of an AP Microeconomics teacher, for example, as happened in 2015–16, can mean that nobody left on the faculty has any experience with that course. Here, as elsewhere, it generally takes teachers a couple of years to hit their stride in handling both the subject matter and the students, and the learning curve is especially steep at a school like SLJ where kids enter AP classes with such divergent levels of preparation, background, and, sometimes, motivation.

SLJ has done better than most urban schools at holding onto teachers. It's safe, conveniently located, well led, and has a culture of serious purpose and accomplishment that appeals to talented and dedicated instructors, most of them on the youngish side. Even here, however, turnover happens, people get ill or pregnant or retire, other schools recruit them, and families relocate to the suburbs or move across the country. Even the best of small schools suffers from such wounds and often has trouble planning around them.

The other challenge confronting any small high school is its inability to offer a wide-ranging curriculum or full menu of extracurricular activities. It's not likely to teach multiple foreign languages, for example, and may not have enough students to justify a course in advanced physics or Asian history. While it may field a basketball team and robotics club, it probably doesn't have varsity soccer and may lack an orchestra. So long as the school is clear about its focus—as at SLJ—and doesn't pretend to cater to all interests, this problem is manageable, yet it will still frustrate a student whose interests change, who is ready for an advanced course in something else, or who decides to shift schools because of an overwhelming desire to play football—or the bassoon.

Despite these challenges, SLJ represents a stellar example of how effectively to leverage AP toward the betterment of underserved and minority youngsters, and it's done most of this on its own, led by an exceptional team, assisted by an energized college-counseling crew, resourced by generous friends as well as a sizable municipal budget, and sheltered by the Urban Assembly. But it has also shared in—and gained resources from—both of the two recent DOE-led initiatives to expand AP participation, which added substantial professional development—as much as seven days' worth—for teachers and school administrators, some further help for kids, and assistance in enlarging the school's suite of AP offerings. We now turn back to those two ambitious citywide initiatives.

Expanding AP at Scale

As we saw in Fort Worth in the previous chapter, top-down initiatives to introduce Advanced Placement into high schools that have scant prior experience with it are fraught with difficulty—and that was just in five schools. Although invariably well-intended—"let's extend the benefits of rigorous, college-level classes to lots more young people"—there are inevitable slips between such a goal and its realization. Policy and budget may be set by higher-ups at city hall, district headquarters, or the paneled precincts of prosperous philanthropies, yet almost all the implementation must be done by individual principals and teachers at the school and classroom levels. For that to go well, principals and teachers must embrace the mission, gain the requisite training, apply them- selves to unaccustomed and very demanding work, stick with it for multiple years, and simultaneously persuade innumerable colleagues and constituents (including kids and parents) that things are truly different. Indeed, they have to sell harder work, loftier expectations, and deferred gratification, and that's no easy pitch either to veteran instructors or to teenagers.

Instead of a smattering of advanced courses that are more or less restricted to the school's highest achieving and most motivated students and taught by the school's strongest and most motivated instructors, the climate has to change dramatically. Now there are more college-level courses, particularly (when NMSI is involved) in tough STEM subjects, and many more young people are being urged to sign up for them, including kids who hadn't previ- ously thought of themselves as college-bound, at least not for the kinds of colleges where entry is selective, where AP carries weight, and where GPA also matters. The workload in those classes is hard, the homework is heavy, the skills needed to do well—both in class and on that looming exam in May—are complex, one's prior preparation was likely weak, and following this path is apt to interfere with other necessary or cherished pursuits (earn- ing money, family duties, sports, socializing, and so on). The interference multiplies if one also attends the extra tutoring and study-skills sessions that accompany the classes—after school, lunchtime, even Saturdays—and that may prove necessary for one's success.

Teachers, too, have to work harder and very likely augment their own content knowledge and pedagogical skills, which is a big and perhaps unwel- come change for veteran instructors and a major undertaking for novices. They have to submit their course syllabi for College Board approval—and they probably fret about being held to account for their students' performance on the AP exams. Indeed, they're volunteering (or being persuaded) to take a sizable risk, because stepping into an AP classroom means exposing their performance to automatic measurement on a very public scale. Guidance counselors must change, too, rethinking entrenched patterns of organizing students' schedules and post-high-school advising and, because these are probably kids without much college lore in their families, counselors have to take unaccustomed pains to coax them into a college-going mentality, help them navigate the admissions and financial aid rapids, and advise them and their parents on college options. School leaders must take steps to ease those shifts and the glitches that always erupt, while cushioning the risks taken by teachers who agree to tackle AP classes and students who hesitantly venture into them. On top of which, the introduction of these courses into the school program causes disruptions in the master schedule, staff reassignments, and budgetary strains, such as additional lab equipment, different textbooks, custodial and security charges for the Saturday sessions, and extra salary and tuition costs for teachers to engage in professional development during the summer. Although the district—or philanthropists working with outside facilitators like NMSI or EOS—may cover the direct expenses for a few years, a school that persists with AP incurs a host of long-term obligations, costs, and priority shifts.

What this adds up to is a profound and—for it truly to succeed—enduring change in school culture, which is just about the hardest education reform of all.

The AP Expansion program that commenced in New York in 2013 resembled what NMSI had previously undertaken in many other places and was launching in Fort Worth around the same time. Because this was New York, however, the scale was far larger. The first round of AP Expansion comprised fifty-three high schools over three years (two schools dropped out from the original fifty-five and another recently closed), nearly eleven times the size of the Fort Worth project. A further twenty-four schools were added over the following two years, bringing the number that participated by the end of year three to seventy-seven. Audacious, yes, but perhaps doable so long as the schools were carefully chosen, the DOE stuck with it, and NMSI was able to continue injecting the requisite talent and resources.

Morton Orlov II spearheaded the expansion project for NMSI. A former lieutenant colonel in the army, he does not shrink from challenge. After retiring from the military in the early 2000s, Orlov cut his educator teeth as principal of Chelsea High School (in a high-poverty community just outside Boston) and later as president of the newly formed Massachusetts Math and Science Initiative, which undertook in the Bay State to replicate the success of NMSI's college readiness program in Dallas. His success in Massachusetts supplied evidence that the NMSI approach could work outside Texas and helped persuade the NMSI high command to shift Mort to New York in September 2013 to lead its efforts there, in which role he continued for more than five years.

He brought several lessons with him that illustrate NMSI's steepening learning curve as it reached beyond the Texas. First, he understood more clearly that education is a political act. In Texas, NMSI hadn't had to pay great attention to external stakeholders such as teacher unions, as it was supported by private dollars (and unions don't hold much sway in the Lone Star State). But after an expansion effort was thwarted by the teachers union in Washington State (over objections to teacher awards), Mort also saw how external support (via the late Senator Edward Kennedy) helped to overcome similar obstacles in Massachusetts, partly by treating such awards on a "don't ask, don't tell" basis and making clear that accepting one was a personal decision by the individual instructor.[18]

Mort also saw the value of "early wins." In Massachusetts, they had sought success in the three major cities, mindful that this would lubricate the program's statewide acceptance. Entering New York, he knew they needed some high-profile victories to justify continued faith in AP Expansion, especially as NMSI's initial contract was for a single year.[19]

Finally, he exited the Bay State with a clear understanding that student literacy is the bedrock on which other education successes rest. If kids can't read fluently and with understanding, they won't learn much else. So he pushed to make AP English Language mandatory in eleventh grade for participating Massachusetts schools, then tried to bring the same mandate to Gotham. Although English Language wasn't one of the six subjects that NMSI supported during its first year in the city, Mort got it added thereafter. He saw that schools that incorporated strong English Language courses were "punching above their weight" when the time came to tally AP successes.

At the outset, New York's AP Expansion schools could choose among Biology, Calculus AB, Environmental Science, Statistics, English Literature, and US History. During the initial year, nearly 2,500 students gained access to these courses for the first time.[20] NMSI provided several forms of teacher support, including four-day summer institutes, one-day curriculum workshops, mentors, and online curricular resources. There was also student support, including Saturday review sessions, online homework and test prep materials, and subsidized exam fees. At the building level, NMSI offered data analysis, academic and program experts, and administrative help.[21]

The expansion program yielded a solid increase in participation. In 2013, before it started, not a single student took an AP exam in thirteen of the first fifty-three high schools. In the other forty schools, 973 students sat for a total of 1,148 exams in the six subjects spanned by this project. By May 2016—that is, the third and final year of the initiative—two and a half times as many pupils

TABLE 5.1. Unique students to take at least one AP exam in NMSI-supported subjects and numbers earning at least one qualifying score, AP Expansion schools, first cohort, New York City, 2012–13 to 2016–17*

	2012–13 (base year)	2013–14	2014–15	2015–16	2016–17
Taking at least one AP exam	973	1,879	2,265	2,396	2,698
Earning at least one qualifying score	196	377	463	461	556

Source: New York City Department of Education

* "Unique students" shown in table 5.1 are unique in the year given, not from year to year. This means that some may be duplicated if they earned qualifying scores in more than one year.

(2,396) in these schools took nearly three times as many exams (3,249) in those subjects. Numbers continued to rise thereafter at these schools, to 2,698 students and 3,698 exams in 2017.[22] Exam performance also rose: from just 196 students with qualifying scores in NMSI-supported subjects in the baseline year to 461 in 2016 and 556 in 2017 (see table 5.1).

What to make of these numbers is complicated, however, as we saw in Fort Worth. In 2017, for example, more than 3,000 AP exams taken in those schools did *not* yield qualifying scores, and more than 2,000 exam-takers did not obtain a single such score. Although many students earned 2's, signaling that the classes did them some good, and many teachers could see progress during the year among their pupils, the actual pass rate remained underwhelming, fluctuating around 18 percent during the life of the program. Yet it's no small achievement to maintain the same passing rate as participation soars, and those who did pass almost certainly face a brighter future—in education and probably beyond—as a result of the program. Most of the participating high schools also sustained a more robust AP program after the three-year AP Expansion initiative morphed into AP for All (discussed below). Those who scored 2's, and perhaps some who scored 1's, are better prepared for further study, and the "intellectual muscle" built by this experience will serve them well.

As we also saw in Fort Worth, gains were unevenly distributed among the schools.[23] The top-performing third of the expansion schools saw impressive growth: 296 of their students sat for 361 exams in the base year, rising to 1,041 students taking 1,473 exams by 2016. Of all their students, eighty-five had earned 103 qualifying scores in 2013, rising to 179 students with 227 qualifying scores by 2016 and still more in 2017.

The bottom third of the AP Expansion schools started with similar baseline numbers but showed markedly less growth. In the base year, 316 of their students took 372 exams, edging up to 424 pupils and 517 exams by 2016, then sinking a bit in 2017. While forty-three students in those schools accounted for forty-eight qualifying scores in the base year, those numbers dropped to just thirty-four students and thirty-seven qualifying scores in 2016 (although 2017 brought a bit of revival). Cumulatively, between 2013 and 2017, numbers went up some, evidencing a measure of success—particularly in pupil participation—at even the least successful schools. Yet their gains were eclipsed by the best-performing schools and—for a host of reasons (such as teacher turnover, course churn, and more), reasons often beyond school leaders' control—their numbers proved more volatile from year to year.

This is not surprising. No large-scale reform across multiple schools shows equal success in all, particularly when tracked for just a few years. NMSI acknowledges that as many as a fifth of the first group of AP Expansion schools showed little or no true gain during its engagement with them. But for an ambitious, large-scale initiative like this—one that targeted urban schools with scant AP experience and conditions not especially conducive to AP success—it's impressive that (in NMSI's estimation) 80 percent of them saw participation and exam success tick upward.

It's not cheap, though. We estimate that the total price tag for the AP Expansion initiative was about $10 million between 2013 and 2016, which is roughly $47,000 annually per participating school. Mindful that 924 additional qualifying scores were earned from 2013–14 through 2015–16 (on top of the baseline number), we estimate that the city's price tag per additional qualifying score approached $11,000—a figure that would obviously shrink if scores of 2 and other signs of student accomplishment were factored in.[24]

AP for All

We can't be sure how much difference the mayoral changeover—Bill de Blasio entered city hall in January 2014—and replacement of the DOE chancellor made to the AP Expansion program, but there's no denying that the new team had other priorities. Hizzoner pledged to retain Bloomberg's emphasis on closing achievement gaps but chose very different means. Whereas the former administration focused on high-stakes accountability policies, an A–F school rating system, closure of subpar schools and considerable devolution of authority to successful principals, nearly all of which drew the unions' ire, the de Blasio cadres saw unions as allies and benefactors. They preferred to centralize decision making and management. They sought to turn around weak schools, not close them. They scrapped the school grading system and undertook to reduce learning gaps by expanding prekindergarten and, in time, Advanced Placement throughout the system.[25]

The new team was keen to push appealing programs and services into more communities and even keener to open up (or scrap) any activities that appeared exclusive or elitist. Moreover, the mayor swiftly came under pressure to show results.[26] He had to fend off multiple reform initiatives by Governor Andrew Cuomo, including proposals to expand charter schools, initiate voucher-like choice programs, place failing schools into receivership, and make it harder to get tenure, all of which were anathema to the teachers union.[27] He also found himself dueling with the city's well-connected and solidly performing charter-school sector, including the formidable Eva Moskowitz, founder of the Success Academy charter network. At the same time, he had to persuade legislators to renew mayoral control of the school system, which Bloomberg had obtained but which was scheduled to expire in June 2015.[28]

De Blasio was able to win just a one-year extension of that control and plainly needed to demonstrate greater success in the K–12 sphere. So in September 2015, he announced a half-dozen sizable reforms of his own, including "AP for All." His big address, titled "Equity and Excellence," painted a grim picture—"a tale of two cities in our schools"—and declared that "each and every child, in each and every classroom, deserves a future that isn't limited by their ZIP code."[29]

AP Expansion still had a year to run but was now overtaken by a far grander plan to deliver more Advanced Placement not just to the seventy-seven high schools on the previous list but throughout the country's largest city. Here was de Blasio's promise:

- Students at all four hundred high schools will have access to a full slate of at least five AP classes. Nearly 40,000 high school students are currently enrolled in schools serving grades 9–12 that do not offer any AP courses today.
- Cost: $51 million a year by FY2022 when fully phased in.
- Full implementation: New AP classes and prep classes starting in fall 2016, with 75 percent of students offered at least five AP classes by fall 2018 and implementation across all schools by fall 2021.[30]

To term this plan audacious is to understate the challenge that the mayor was placing on his Department of Education as well as the leaders and faculty of hundreds of schools. Although the College Board naturally pitched in, and the DOE enlisted both NMSI and EOS to help, this was bound to prove difficult.

Still, there was ample justification: Two months before the mayor's speech, the New School's Center for New York City Affairs reported that half the city's high schools had offered no AP science classes in 2013–14—the first year of AP Expansion—and more than half offered no AP math.[31] Orlov termed these schools "STEM deserts in the heart of Gotham."

During the first implementation year of AP for All (2016–17), NMSI worked with sixty-three high schools (four of them carried over from AP Expansion plus fifty-nine others, including thirty-five with no prior AP program),[32] again focusing on seven Advanced Placement courses, although this time—with NMSI again functioning as a vendor to the DOE rather than operator of a self-contained intervention program—they had to flex a bit when schools insisted on modifying the subject mix. Once more, NMSI's main work was helping schools build their AP programs by training teachers, providing curricular materials, advising school leaders, and supplying additional instruction to students who enrolled in the widened course offerings.[33]

By May 2017—as the first year ended—the initiative could already show some results. The previous year, 1,155 students took 1,406 AP exams at AP for All schools (excluding the four that had been part of AP Expansion). In 2017, those numbers more than doubled to 2,499 kids taking 3,126 exams. The number of young New Yorkers earning qualifying scores wasn't great, but it, too, was better than before: 173 students earned 205 qualifying scores in 2016, versus 277 successful pupils and 316 scores the following year.[34]

Equal Opportunity Schools worked with another twenty-four high schools in 2016–17 (and would add ten more the next year), focusing mainly on identifying poor and minority pupils who could succeed in AP courses but had not previously participated; developing ways to encourage those young people to join in; and creating systems whereby this process would repeat in future years.[35] The EOS schools typically already had some AP classes, but student participation had not reflected school demographics. EOS sought to eliminate such discrepancies and draw more disadvantaged pupils into AP. During its first year with AP for All, EOS joined with the schools to spot 1,400 "missing" students and enroll them in AP courses.

This is hard work wherever undertaken and harder still within New York's Byzantine, bureaucratic system. In fall 2017, author Finn talked with the principal of an AP for All school, one of five small, thematic high schools operating inside the huge, historic Erasmus Hall High School building in the Flatbush region of central Brooklyn.[36] All five had been part of AP Expansion and had recorded gains in AP course offerings, student participation, and qualifying scores by 2015–16. But the DOE's structures, governance, and personnel practices kept complicating matters—and those travails persisted as AP for All kicked in.

Because all five schools are small, it's hard for any one of them to support—with staff and enrollment—many AP classes and, because they're located under the same giant roof, it makes obvious sense to team up. (Orlov compared it to five small towns needing to share a single fire truck.) Yet there's been much turnover among principals in the past few years; they report to several different regional superintendents on the DOE organization chart; two of the schools start with sixth grade; and one is a "screened" (semi-selective) school, while the other four admit all comers. Under those circumstances, sustained collaboration is a big challenge or, as the principal we interviewed put it, "Getting to yes isn't easy" in multischool meetings where joint programming is on the table.

The leaders of that school are well disposed toward AP for All, however, and working hard to widen pupil (and teacher) participation. They see it as a valuable step toward making the school more college-focused and less sports-centric, even a way to attract more "nerds" from more neighborhoods—and the principal visits middle schools to recruit such kids. Still, we were told that it can take six to eight years to "build a culture of high achievement" in a school such as this, even when the leadership is stable and committed. To effect such a durable change, students must be able to observe others who have already followed the rigorous academic path and succeeded at it, including after graduation. Once such a culture exists, the principal observed, teachers can hear the new ninth graders, even those arriving from weak middle schools and troubled neighborhoods, talking about "which AP courses I am going to take." Yet, the principal still finds it necessary for teachers, counselors, and administrators to "coax and counsel many kids into trying college-level work," and AP isn't the only version of that. This school, like others on the Erasmus campus, participates in other DOE initiatives and has additional outside partners, including the "College Now" dual-credit option that the City University of New York is forcefully advancing.[37] Whichever path they choose, the principal is convinced that students benefit from having some college-level academic experience during high school, and returning alumni/ae attest to the ways that experience helped them when they reached college—even if they never eked out qualifying scores on the exams. Teachers we talked with had a similar view of the program. "If I can get a kid to a 2," said one veteran instructor, it will have done some good. It shows that "something happened."

Whether it's AP or NMSI, good leadership or something else, this small school has also made gains. It cannot yet boast many qualifying scores (though a hardworking calculus teacher, after several years of struggle, recently began to produce an impressive track record), but it's attracting more academically oriented students, and its graduation rate has risen "from the sixties to the eighties."

The principal voiced some concern, however, about "partner overload" in the district, that is, too many outside groups working simultaneously with schools on too many separate reform ventures, and how difficult this is to manage. Yet the school team regards Advanced Placement as a "solid centerpiece," a program "fully devoted to prepping kids for college but one that comes with specific metrics, not just vague information and exhortation."

Small schools like SLJ and this one at Erasmus aren't the only places where AP can make a difference. A full-size high school elsewhere in Brooklyn, which also took part in AP Expansion, had a pre-existing population of Advanced Placement students of the traditional kind. There the goal was to expand the pool, and during its first year in the program, the school more than doubled the number of AP exams its students took (from less than two hundred to more than four hundred) and raised the number of qualifying scores from less than forty to nearly seventy. Even more impressive, the number of exams taken by black and Hispanic students rose sevenfold and some—within just the first year—began to score 3 or better. At this school, the roster of individual kids to earn at least one qualifying score in NMSI-supported subjects came close to tripling between 2015 and 2017.

The Department of Education sees AP for All as part of its wider Excellence for All agenda, which also includes ambitious initiatives in preschool and algebra, plus citywide efforts to strengthen math and literacy instruction in elementary and middle schools. District leaders recognize the need for much stronger middle school preparation, as well as pre-AP coursework for students and professional development for teachers, so as to build a continuum of successful, subject-specific instruction that readies students for AP and other college-level coursework. In effect, they're working to incubate more schools, teachers, and pupils to succeed with AP for All.

That's much needed—and the city has quite a distance yet to travel. In the school we visited, a place where the principal said "most kids enter below standard," including some of Gotham's lowest achievers, so much catch-up is needed that it "takes three or more years to get them into one or more AP classes," which is why most of the AP course-taking there is by seniors.

Persevering with AP for All calls for a major attitude adjustment among veteran teachers who are accustomed to advanced classes open only to a school's strongest students. In a city with many such teachers in many high schools—and a powerful union that has often resisted top-down changes that complicate life for its members—attitudes may be the hardest thing to alter. That's compounded by the challenge of equipping them with the pedagogical skills and content knowledge needed to "scaffold" instruction for classes of up to thirty kids who bring such a range of preparation and, perhaps, ability and stick-to-itiveness as well as differing levels of outside support in their lives.

Outside support involves parents and families, of course, and the principal we interviewed was clear that succeeding with AP in a school like this one means changing that part of the culture, too. In partial contrast to SLJ, where kids arrive knowing that the school is college oriented and many can draw on some family college savvy, this little Flatbush school has been more about athletics than advanced academics, and fewer students hail from education-minded families. Parents need help to understand why college matters, why it's feasible for their kids, how AP can help blaze a trail there, and what it takes for their kids to succeed, including such unaccustomed add-ons as NMSI's Saturday tutoring sessions. "It takes a committed parent," noted the principal, "because it's very hard to wake up a teenager on Saturday morning."

At the time of our visit, the school offered five AP classes: Calculus AB, English Language, Biology, US Government, and Macroeconomics. Several other courses had been available in earlier years but—as at SLJ—shifting enrollments and teacher turnover make it hard for a small school to maintain a stable catalog. Even now, the principal remarked, some of the AP instruction in this school has to come from teachers who haven't had much specific preparation for it.

NMSI is a definite plus. Its battery of services includes training for (willing) teachers, extra instruction for (willing) students, and classroom supplies and equipment as well as cheerleading, number crunching, bureaucratic-interference-running, and other forms of support for school leaders from battle-scarred veterans like Mort Orlov. When functioning as "donor" rather than "vendor," NMSI also seeks to provide monetary awards to students who succeed on AP exams and to their teachers, but in New York the teacher part was never part of the plan—the union would not have tolerated it—and student awards were possible only when private dollars could be mustered (by Orlov) for that purpose, which proved workable for just one year.

The city has committed considerable treasure to AP for All: annual DOE funding for the program was slated to double from $12.5 million in 2017 to $25 million in 2018, then double again by 2020. That's a big raise from the estimated $10 million spent across three years of the AP Expansion program.[38] How rich will be the eventual return on that increased investment remains to be seen as the program grows. (It entered 2018–19 with a whopping 252 high schools on the list.) But the gains noted above in AP participation and passing scores during its first year are nothing to sneeze at. In all, reported the DOE, 36 percent of the city's 2018 graduates took at least one AP exam and 19 percent earned at least one qualifying score.[39]

As we have seen elsewhere, however, increased participation, particularly among disadvantaged youngsters, has meant lower passing rates in New York. For example, 35 percent more Hispanic students took AP exams in 2018 than in 2016, but the proportion passing at least one exam dipped from 47 to 43 percent.[40] Black students' participation also grew—by 15 percent—but their rate of qualifying scores also slipped slightly to a low 26 percent. By comparison, Asian and white students raised both their participation and passing rates.[41] It's wrong, though, to focus only on qualifying scores when a big, complex undertaking like this one is new, when schools, principals, and teachers are adjusting to it, and when many kids who don't reach that bar may yet gain from the rigor, content, and skill-building that are part of the AP experience. And it's important to note that pass rates dipped only slightly for black and Latino students, even as participation jumped. Still, it's impossible to ignore the very large number of youngsters, particularly low-income and minority students, who are entering those classrooms but not yet exiting with the exam-based credential that has long characterized the entire Advanced Placement venture.

We applaud the city's ambitious moves—under both Bloomberg and de Blasio—to deploy AP as a lever to lift students who otherwise may never set foot in such a classroom and who otherwise are probably not headed for much success in college if indeed they matriculate at all. That many more Gotham teens now benefit from AP is a testament to the work of both mayoral teams, even as de Blasio faces mounting criticism over the perceived missteps of a number of his ambitious reforms.[42]

But nobody should conclude that scaling something like Advanced Placement in a place like New York—or Fort Worth—is easy. Any such grand, top-down push can only work when matched by skill and commitment on the ground and when those qualities are sustained over multiple years. The success of schools like Law and Justice shows that it's possible for disadvantaged kids, given the right kinds of encouragement, support, curated curricula, and expert instruction, to buck national trends, but we also see clearly that such successes demand institutional infrastructure, professional expertise, steady hands on many tillers, a conducive climate, and much cumulative experience. One exceptionally steady hand—Mort Orlov's—was replaced by NMSI in early 2019, and it remains to be seen how well the AP for All initiative can sustain its promising start without him. We've also observed leadership turnover in the DOE—including yet another new chancellor starting in 2018—and signs of local politics that may slow the momentum.

Where the conditions for success aren't consistently present—as we also saw on the Erasmus campus—it cannot be taken for granted that additional mandates and increased resources alone will amount to much. The thousands of young people who gain from initiatives like AP Expansion and AP for All will surely fare better in the years ahead. But what will it take—and how long—to make anything comparable happen for tens of thousands more kids who look like them? And when another new mayor is elected, will these programs continue to prosper or will they get buried under the ever-shifting political sands of America's largest city?

Yet cities aren't the whole AP story. In the next chapter, we journey into suburbia, where Advanced Placement has flourished for decades but today faces new challenges and opportunities.

Notes

1. AP data for 2018 for New York City are available at NYC AP Results: 2018 (New York: New York City Department of Education, 2019). https://infohub.nyced.org/docs/default-source /default-document-library/2018-ap-results---for-web_20190226.pdf; AP data for New York State are available at College Board, "AP Data Overview," accessed February 4, 2019. https://research .collegeboard.org/programs/ap/data.

2. See College Board, "AP Course Ledger," accessed January 31, 2019. https://apcourseaudit .inflexion.org/ledger/.

3. "Chancellor Fariña Announces 63 High Schools to Offer New Advanced Placement Courses for 2016–17 through AP for All," press release, New York City Department of Education, June 13, 2016. https://www.schools.nyc.gov/about-us/news/announcements/contentdetails/2016/06/13 /chancellor-fariña-announces-63-high-schools-to-offer-new-advanced-placement-courses-for -2016-17-through-ap-for-all.

4. David M. Herszenhorn, "Revised Admission for High Schools," *New York Times*, October 3, 2003. https://www.nytimes.com/2003/10/03/nyregion/revised-admission-for-high-schools.html; Elizabeth A. Harris and Ford Fessenden, "The Broken Promises of Choice in New York City Schools," *New York Times*, May 5, 2017. https://www.nytimes.com/2017/05/05/nyregion/school-choice-new -york-city-high-school-admissions.html. As we see here, multiple reforms can collide. When it comes to offering substantial AP programs, for example, particularly in STEM fields, large high schools have advantages over small ones in terms of efficiency, critical mass, affordability, and sustainability.

5. "The NYC Department of Education, College Board and National Math and Science Initiative Collaborate to Launch the NYC Advanced Placement Expansion Initiative," press release, New York City Department of Education, September 30, 2013. https://www.scribd.com/document/172190629/Press-Release-NYCDOE.

6. "Equity and Excellence: Mayor de Blasio Announces Reforms to Raise Achievement across all Public Schools," press release, City of New York, Office of the Mayor, September 16, 2015. https://www1.nyc.gov/office-of-the-mayor/news/618-15/equity-excellence-mayor-de-blasio-reforms-raise-achievement-across-all-public.

7. New York City Department of Education, Office of Equity and Access, "AP for All," accessed November 6, 2018. https://oea.nyc/apforall/.

8. For more on New York City's small schools initiative, see MDRC, "New York City's Small Schools of Choice Evaluation: Project Overview," accessed November 6, 2018. https://www.mdrc.org/project/new-york-city-small-schools-choice-evaluation#overview. For more on the School for Law and Justice, see http://www.sljhs.org/.

9. The Urban Assembly, "About Us," accessed November 6, 2018. https://urbanassembly.org/about/about.

10. The Urban Assembly, "Schools," accessed November 6, 2018. https://urbanassembly.org/schools. In 2018, the Urban Assembly added its first charter school.

11. See more at The Urban Assembly School for Law and Justice, "Adams Street Foundation," accessed November 6, 2018. http://www.sljhs.org/asf-mission-and-history/. New York City now spends about $22,000 per student per year on its public schools. Selim Algar, "NY Spends More Money Per Student Than Any Other US State," *New York Post*, June 14, 2017. https://nypost.com/2017/06/14/ny-spends-more-money-per-student-than-any-other-us-state/.

12. See *NYC AP Results: 2018*. SLJ data were obtained directly from the school.

13. Authors' correspondence with staff at SLJ.

14. *U.S. News and World Report*, 2018 U.S. News Best High Schools Rankings, "Stuyvesant High School: Test Scores," accessed November 6, 2018. https://www.usnews.com/education/best-high-schools/new-york/districts/new-york-city-public-schools/stuyvesant-high-school-13092/test-scores; *U.S. News and World Report*, 2018 U.S. News Best High Schools Rankings, "Bronx High School of Science: Test Scores," accessed November 6, 2018. https://www.usnews.com/education/best-high-schools/new-york/districts/new-york-city-public-schools/bronx-high-school-of-science-13207/test-scores. Note, these 2018 rankings are based on 2016 data.

15. As we see in chapter 7, some sophisticated charter-school networks also do this exceptionally well, but most of them are able to start with students at much younger ages.

16. Authors' correspondence with staff at SLJ. National data are available at *Snapshot Report: First-Year Persistence and Retention* (Herndon, VA: National Student Clearinghouse Research Center, 2017). https://nscresearchcenter.org/wp-content/uploads/SnapshotReport28a.pdf.

17. Authors' correspondence with staff at SLJ.

18. NMSI didn't advertise that it would give bonuses to teachers whose students earned qualifying scores on the AP exams, and the union didn't fuss about them.

19. NMSI has had less control of program elements in New York because in New York it functions as a vendor, responding to the city's RFPs, rather than as a "donor."

20. "NYC Department of Education, College Board and National Math and Science Initiative Collaborate to Launch the NYC Advanced Placement Expansion Initiative," press release, College Board, September 30, 2013. https://www.collegeboard.org/releases/2013/nyc-department-education-college-board-and-national-math-and-science-initiative-collaborate-0.

21. Authors' correspondence with NMSI.

22. The supported subjects by then included English Language and Composition, making a total of seven. Data for the first cohort of AP Expansion schools come from the New York City Department of Education.

23. Data from the New York City Department of Education. "Top Performing" schools are defined as the sixteen AP Expansion schools that showed the greatest increases in exams taken between 2013 and 2017; "Bottom Third" schools are the fifteen AP Expansion schools with the smallest increases.

24. This estimate is based on an examination of multiple "Requests for Authorization" publicly available from the New York City Department of Education from 2013 to 2016. Year one of the expansion initiative cost about $2 million, year two about $3 million, year three about $4 million, and an amendment during this time added $1 million. We totaled those outlays and divided by the additional qualifying scores during the program's three years. "Requests for Authorization" are at New York City Department of Education, "Infohub," accessed June 1, 2018. https://infohub.nyced.org/.

25. Stephen Eide, "Ed Reform Rollback in New York City," *Education Next* 17, no. 1 (2017): 26. https://www.educationnext.org/files/ednext_xvii_1_eide.pdf; Kate Taylor, "Chancellor Carmen Fariña Changes New York City Schools' Course," *New York Times*, February 6, 2015. https://www.nytimes.com/2015/02/08/nyregion/chancellor-carmen-farina-changes-new-york-city-schools-course.html.

26. Patrick Wall, "Facing Pressure to Show Results, De Blasio Points to Changes at Some Renewal Schools," *Chalkbeat New York*, March 10, 2015. https://www.chalkbeat.org/posts/ny/2015/03/10/facing-pressure-to-show-results-de-blasio-touts-gains-at-some-renewal-schools/.

27. Tom Precious, "New York Governor Proposes Big Education Reforms in Annual Address," *Governing*, January 22, 2015. http://www.governing.com/topics/education/tns-new-york-andrew-cuomo-speech.html; Jillian Jorgensen, "De Blasio Pushes Back against Some Cuomo Education Reforms in Albany Testimony," *Observer*, February 25, 2015. https://observer.com/2015/02/de-blasio-pushes-back-against-some-cuomo-education-reforms-in-albany-testimony/.

28. Geoff Decker, "De Blasio Calls for Permanent Mayoral Control of Schools," *Chalkbeat New York*, February 25, 2015. https://www.chalkbeat.org/posts/ny/2015/02/25/de-blasio-calls-for-permanent-mayoral-control-in-testimony-on-state-budget/.

29. Kate Taylor, "De Blasio's Plan to Lift Poor Schools Comes with High Costs and Big Political Risks," *New York Times*, September 16, 2015. https://www.nytimes.com/2015/09/17/nyregion/de-blasios-plan-to-lift-poor-schools-comes-with-high-costs-and-big-political-risks.html.

30. "Equity and Excellence: Mayor de Blasio Announces Reforms to Raise Achievement across all Public Schools," press release, City of New York, Office of the Mayor, September 16, 2015. https://www1.nyc.gov/office-of-the-mayor/news/618-15/equity-excellence-mayor-de-blasio-reforms-raise-achievement-across-all-public.

31. Clara Hemphill, Nicole Mader, and Bruce Cory, *What's Wrong with Math and Science in NYC High Schools (And What to Do about It)* (New York: New School Center for New York City Affairs, 2015). https://static1.squarespace.com/static/53ee4f0be4b015b9c3690d84/t/55c413afe4b0a3278e55d9a7/1438913455694/Problems+with+Math+%26+Science+05.pdf.

32. One additional school, not counted here, withdrew early from the program.

33. In 2017–18, the city added five more courses to the program (Chemistry, US Government and Politics, Seminar, Psychology, and Spanish Language) and in 2018–19 added another five (Physics 1, World History, Human Geography, Art History, and Capstone Research). All but the last of those have been supported by NMSI.

34. New York City Department of Education, "AP for All."

35. A few schools enjoyed both NMSI and EOS treatments. The latter is described in the next chapter.

36. InsideSchools, "Erasmus Hall Educational Campus," accessed November 6, 2018. https://insideschools.org/school/00Z021.

37. City University of New York, "College Now," accessed November 6, 2018. http://www2.cuny.edu/academics/school-college-partnerships/college-now/.

38. Yolanda Smith, *Focus On: The Preliminary Budget* (New York: New York City Independent Budget Office, 2016). https://ibo.nyc.ny.us/iboreports/preliminary-budget-directs-over-$76 -million-in-2017-to-enhancing-educational-program-offerings-march-2016.pdf.

39. *NYC AP Results: 2018*; "Mayor de Blasio and Chancellor Carranza Announce Record-High 55,011 Students Taking Advanced Placement Exams," press release, New York City Department of Education, February 26, 2019. https://www1.nyc.gov/office-of-the-mayor/news/113-19/mayor -de-blasio-chancellor-carranza-record-high-55-011-students-taking-advanced#/0.

40. *NYC AP Results: 2018.*

41. *NYC AP Results: 2018*; Alex Zimmerman, "More New York City Students Are Taking AP Exams, Though Racial Gaps Persist," *Chalkbeat New York*, October 10, 2017. https://www .chalkbeat.org/posts/ny/2017/10/10/more-new-york-city-students-are-taking-ap-exams-though -racial-gaps-persist/.

42. Eliza Shapiro, "New York Knew Some Schools in Its $773 Million Plan Were Likely to Fail: It Kept Children in Them Anyway," *New York Times*, October 26, 2018. https://www.nytimes.com /2018/10/26/nyregion/deblasio-school-renewal-bill.html.

6

In Suburbia

Even as urban centers like Fort Worth and New York typify today's livelier venues for Advanced Placement expansion, the program has deep roots in the prosperous suburbs that abut them. Along with elite private schools, upscale suburban high schools were among the program's earliest adopters, and they remain natural habitats for a nationally benchmarked, high-status venture that gives strong students a head start on the college education that they're almost certainly going to get and perhaps an extra advantage in gaining admission to the universities they aspire to. Yet they're also ripe for attention as they struggle with equity and growth issues of their own.

AP has enlarged its footprint and extended its mission in recent decades, and many suburban districts have kept pace: adding to the list of courses that they offer and widening access to those classrooms; sending teachers for the requisite training; obtaining suitable instructional materials; deploying counselors to help kids pick the right classes and schedules, then assisting them with college applications; creating gifted-and-talented programs, accelerated math sequences, and pre-AP offerings in elementary and middle schools; subsidizing exam fees when needed; and enabling tens of thousands of eager (and often parent-driven) pupils to clamber aboard the Advanced Placement express.

A number of schools have also embraced the International Baccalaureate, but it's seldom deployed across entire districts, save for some small suburbs that have invested in systemwide IB programs.[1] Implementing IB is relatively expensive, bound by rules set in far-off Geneva, not necessarily aligned with state academic standards, and less familiar to many parents (discussed more in chapter 8).

Suburban districts are complicated places, however, and less homogeneous than they once were. Family aspirations aside, is college really the right destination for all their young people? Should advanced offerings be reserved for academic superstars or open to all who want them—and, if the latter, how to deal with the blowback from parents who complain that their own brilliant progeny are being slowed by the entry of less polished newcomers? Should youngsters who might not venture into AP classrooms on their own be pushed to sign up? What does an explosion of AP (and kindred) offerings mean for budgets, staffing assignments, and schedules? And—especially in big, demographically diverse places—are these offerings distributed evenhandedly or concentrated in schools with lots of student and parent (and perhaps teacher) demand? Where concentration—intentional or not—has been the practice, might pushing more AP courses into more high schools serving more different kinds of kids be a viable way to narrow gaps, further equity, and assist a wider swath of the population not only to aim toward college but also prepare to succeed there?

With those questions in mind, we visited two well-known yet very different suburban districts. Both are celebrated as education successes in their states and both boast long and impressive Advanced Placement track records. Both, however, face distinctive challenges as they seek to serve today's constituents. Their stories illustrate how AP is functioning in places that know it well yet continue to evolve with it.

Dublin City Schools (Ohio)

This exceptionally comfortable community of 48,000 people northwest of Columbus—90 percent white and Asian with a median household income of $125,000—has deployed Advanced Placement in its three bulging-at-the-seams high schools for as long as anyone can recall, and many of its students have done well with this opportunity.[2] Of 4,895 pupils enrolled in those schools during 2017–18, 1,787 took at least one AP exam and 1,249 earned a 3 or above (70 percent).[3] A high-priority district goal today is enabling every pupil who can handle it to experience at least one challenging academic course that covers college-level material and seeks college-level mastery. And they're making decent progress: 73 percent of Dublin's graduates in 2016 and 2017 had taken at least one AP class during high school, versus 22 percent in nearby Columbus City Schools.[4]

Dublin is accustomed to strong academic achievement. In recent years, it has boasted more National Merit semifinalists than any other Ohio district. But this well-run district isn't resting on its laurels. Besides AP, Dublin offers the International Baccalaureate program, and it collaborates with both Columbus State (community) College and Ohio State University on dual-credit offerings. More than a few of the high school pupils we met were partaking of all three at once—the secondary-school equivalent of grazing at a bounteous buffet.

For kids who aren't necessarily college-bound, at least not immediately, Dublin teams up with a nearby vocational center and a career-focused early-college high school that Honda helped launch in another Columbus suburb. And instead of opening a fourth high school to house its growing pupil population, the district recently purchased a centrally located commercial building that it's turning into a multiservice center aimed mostly at career-oriented offerings.

In a place like Dublin, awash in college-obsessed, high-achieving parents, it would be fatal to use the word "vocational" to describe what's going on in the former Verizon building. That would muddy the "driveway conversations" in which parents boast to one another about the four-year colleges their daughters and sons plan to attend. Yet many kids falter along the way, presenting the school system with perhaps its most urgent challenge. District leaders are keenly aware that, while almost everybody graduates from Dublin high schools and 90 percent enter college, just 60 percent earn college degrees. In other words, some 550 kids from a typical graduating class of 1,200 are not making very successful transitions into post-high-school life. This is obviously a disappointment for families, a seeming failure on the part of the school system, a waste of human capital, and a clear-and-present problem for the young people who are affected.

One source of this disturbing situation is the community's (and nation's) "college for all" fixation. While Dublin City Schools can't tell families that perhaps one or two of their kids shouldn't necessarily go to college, at least not the four-year kind, it can furnish tempting alternatives and real-world acquaintance with other possibilities. District leaders diplomatically phrase this as wanting every student to leave a Dublin high school with "a diploma and something else," whether that's college credit, an industry certification, an IB diploma, or whatever. Which means organizing the high school experience so it's not just a prescribed list of courses one must take, followed by graduation and matriculation, but something more purposeful, something constructed around a plan for the next phase of one's life coupled with relevant experience and acquisition whenever possible of useful credentials aligned with that plan.

For those who are properly bound for the bachelor's degree and perhaps beyond, the district is keen to supply more advanced courses, especially the kind that focus on analysis, research, independent thinking, and the quest for evidence, not just "learning." School leaders understand that succeeding in such courses during high school gives kids a vivid sense of what "college work" is like while equipping them with skills that will help them prosper inside the ivy gates.

Actually delivering such courses, however, entails a shift in pedagogy from the teacher's traditional "sage on stage" role and whole-class delivery to more project-style, groupwork and otherwise participatory learning by students. That's not an easy or welcome change for veteran teachers accustomed to success with the old way. But such a shift is consistent with the "new AP" as the College Board retools and adds courses, and it's notably compatible with the new "Capstone" courses.

Although Dublin City Schools gamely (and expensively) provide a smorgasbord of advanced courses, AP remains a mainstay. Mostly, however, this takes the form of one-off classes, not structured sequences. There's not been a lot of attention yet to purposeful "pre-AP" courses or to organizing the middle school curriculum to prepare kids for AP in high school. It is, however, possible for able middle schoolers to accelerate their progress through math, science, and sometimes English, making them eligible to enroll in more advanced courses when they reach high school.

Fifteen years ago, entry into AP classes was "gate controlled" in Dublin, meaning that if one lacked solid grades and a teacher endorsement, one couldn't just waltz into the Advanced Placement course of one's choice. This produced the usual population of AP course- and exam-takers, a predictable and finite number of them, and it yielded relatively high exam scores—although the number of participants was always sizable in Dublin, as in most communities with similar demographics.

More recently, Dublin, like much of the country, has liberalized access and encouraged more—and more different kinds of—pupils to tackle AP and other advanced classes. This arose from a round of "international benchmarking" of the district's curricular offerings as well as a philosophical shift to the view that student demand should drive more curricular decisions. Today, pretty much anyone who wants to take such a course is welcome to try it and, as mentioned, counselors urge almost every high school pupil to attempt at least one college-level class. Although teachers still recommend—or not—students for AP classes, such endorsements are no longer dispositive. After noting a non-recommendation, the guidance counselor might suggest to a youngster and his/her parents that perhaps it would be prudent to think twice about signing up for this particular course, especially if the kid has a heavy schedule of other classes, extracurriculars, outside jobs, family obligations, and such. But those who persist aren't denied access to AP classes. Dublin, in other words, is struggling to give all of its students a fair shot at college—and college success—even as it reckons with the fact that many of its college-bound graduates don't make it all the way to degrees and as it seeks to provide more career-oriented options for youngsters who perhaps ought not tread the traditional ivy-sheltered path.

As AP participation grew in Dublin, so did the menu of course offerings, expanding from the original trio of Calculus, English, and US Government to today's twelve to fifteen options. That's not nearly as many as some schools offer, but these high schools are not huge, and ordinarily at least a dozen students must seek an AP class in a given subject for the district to budget, schedule, and staff it that year. Because the district agreed also to furnish IB and dual credit, it can't afford to lay out the full AP array. Moreover, the three schools are semi-autonomous when it comes to specialized course offerings, and most of the newer AP classes that they proffer—a list that differs somewhat from school to school—arose from student demand, teacher interest, and departmental capacity. Thus, for example, we saw a superb AP Studio Art class in one school that has an exceptional art teacher, but that option isn't available in the other two schools.

Perhaps Dublin's single most interesting course—and the "gateway drug" to AP for most students—is an interdisciplinary American Studies course that's generally taken in tenth grade. This is a team-taught, double-period class that typically combines AP US History and honors English. Up to two-thirds of Dublin pupils sign up for this combo, which gets many accustomed to AP-level academics and exams while also giving tenth grade English a content focus, demanding a lot of study skills and advanced writing tasks, and furthering the goal of less didactic, more participatory classroom experiences.

Dublin has other imaginative course combinations, including a handful that blend AP and IB in the same room. That, however, is not so much a matter of intentional curricular design as a result of student numbers insufficient to justify two separate classes. When we asked a science instructor how he manages it, he explained that for most of the year he teaches the same content to both groups of students; during the last quarter, he differentiates between what his AP and IB pupils are doing. This sort of thing only works, of course, in the hands of versatile and dedicated teachers—and Dublin, being an appealing place in which to live and work, and with high schools that are well run, well behaved, and for the most part full of motivated pupils, manages to hire and retain more than its share of such people.

Indeed, the caliber of instruction that we observed in its classrooms was generally high, and principals are proud of their teachers' (and counselors') prowess and commitment. One illustration was a principal's remark that he strives to get his own faculty members approved to teach the dual-credit courses offered (in his building) by Columbus State, because those teachers often prove to be better instructors—at least for high school kids—than the "adjuncts" dispatched by the community college.[5]

We encountered mixed opinions among students, teachers, and administrators regarding the relative merits of AP, IB, and dual credit. The kids understand that a full-fledged IB diploma gets admiring recognition by universities around the planet but they also know that many US colleges are barely aware of it and that parents, grandparents, and future employers understand AP far better. Yet the young people mostly see IB courses as "easier" than AP—and dual credit as easier still. One difference is that IB courses typically span two school years, making them somewhat more leisurely and less obsessed with that early May exam. Another difference is that IB classes work at being "deep" rather than "broad," so while they may push students harder to think, they don't compel them to ingest as much "content."[6]

Some kids, however, said they favor the structured pacing and clarity of the AP syllabus, commenting that "you know when you know it" rather than leaving it open to interpretation and disputation.

DUBLIN'S HIGH SCHOOLS TODAY

Dublin Jerome

Dublin's newest high school—opened in 2004–5—is located in the swankiest part of town, giving rise to jokes that its strongest sports are tennis and golf. (It does, in fact, offer both of those, plus lacrosse.[7]) Scarcely any of its 1,500 students qualify for subsidized lunches and, while a quarter of them are minority, most of those are Asian. Essentially everyone meets state standards and graduates from high school, and Jerome ranked seventh in Ohio (and 288th nationally) on the *U.S. News* list in 2018, which is based largely on AP performance. Indeed, some 75 percent of Jerome twelfth graders do participate in AP at some point, and 86 percent of those earn qualifying scores.[8]

Dublin Coffman

Situated adjacent to district headquarters, Coffman is older, somewhat larger—almost 1,900 pupils—and not quite as upscale. Among the 11 percent of its pupils who qualify as disadvantaged, the visitor sees a smattering of brown and black faces, and 4 percent fail to graduate. Still, Coffman ranks 14th in Ohio (383rd nationally) on the *U.S. News* tally with an AP participation rate of 74 percent, and four-fifths of those who take the exams earn scores of 3 or better.

Dublin Scioto

Scioto is as close to "inner city" as Dublin gets. In fact, about a quarter of its students live within the city of Columbus. (How that came about deserves its own book.) The smallest of the district's high schools (about 1,200 pupils), it's also the most disadvantaged (almost 30 percent) and minority (37 percent—and from many different backgrounds, including recent immigrants). Yet Scioto ranks 33rd in Ohio (910th nationally) on the *U.S. News* tally, and its AP participation rate is a more-than-respectable 60 percent, with some 73 percent of those who take the exams earning qualifying scores, which is not far behind the other two schools.

TAKING STOCK

Recent testing decisions by Dublin City Schools are also apt to nudge more kids toward AP, as the district switched from ACT to SAT—Ohio requires one or the other. They made the shift in part because SAT comes with a suite of related tests, programs, and services, including what Dublin is treating as universal, district-paid PSAT testing in eighth grade, the results of which help with high school course placement, including the College Board's own "AP readiness" reports based on PSAT scores.[9]

Whether they gravitate to AP, IB, or dual credit (or the district's own honors classes), one consideration on the minds of many Dublin high schoolers is the extra transcript points that attach to one's grades in advanced courses. For many of the young people we met, the GPA effect of taking such courses loomed larger than the potential college credit. They seemed markedly more concerned with admission to college than with establishing credit after getting there. In any case, many are looking forward to the full four-year experience, and college costs are not a big concern for most Dublin families. But the schools to which lots of them apply—or will as seniors—take GPAs seriously, the more so when they're giant institutions like Ohio State (just down the road) that can't realistically engage in holistic admissions and therefore rely heavily on test scores, transcripts, and class rank.

When an enhanced GPA is a Dublin student's goal, more than gaining advanced skills, challenging oneself academically, or winning college credit that's both transferable among campuses and that vaults one over entry-level courses, dual credit is apt to look more attractive. It's a far surer thing—all one needs for credit is a good grade from one's instructor—and it's also less demanding in the here and now, at least when it takes the form of a conventional community college course. Even when taken within the high school, dual-credit classes typically meet on a college schedule, that is, just two or three times a week.

The main reasons for a Dublin pupil to stick with AP (or IB) rather than dual credit are a combination of status and credit transferability. District administrators hint that they view Ohio's College Credit Plus program as aimed primarily at disadvantaged youngsters, and their body language suggests that, if districts weren't required by law to participate in it, they might not. At present, Dublin high schools offer just a few dual-credit classes. This may change if student demand is strong, but status also matters to parents— they know AP and perhaps also IB as nationally recognized, high-status credentials—and they and their kids may well be eyeing private or out-of-state colleges where they can't count on credit being granted on the basis of an Ohio community college class.

Which means the Advanced Placement program almost certainly has a large role to play in Dublin City Schools for the foreseeable future. Yet district leaders acknowledge that, while their high schools are generally strong, they haven't been doing very well at closing gaps among pupil groups, their college-completion rate (as already noted) doesn't begin to match their matriculation rate, and their pupils don't do as well on the state's "growth" measures as on simple gauges of achievement. This pattern is common in posh suburbs but it's unflattering to their public schools, for it is widely understood in the education field that growth—sometimes termed "value added"—is a better indicator of schools' actual effectiveness in boosting pupil skills and knowledge, whereas raw achievement tends to correlate with family background. So Dublin still has plenty of work to do, and AP is destined to play a substantial part in the work ahead.

Montgomery County Public Schools (Maryland) and Equal Opportunity Schools

Maryland's largest school system—enrolling some 163,000 pupils in 2018[10]—is generally high performing and highly regarded. Its high school enrollment of 50,500 is over ten times that of Dublin, Ohio, indeed a bit greater than Dublin's total population.

Montgomery County is a sprawling suburb of Washington, DC, that's home to many well-educated and well-connected professionals who seek—and will practically kill to obtain—a first-rate public education for their children. The system is fairly well funded—some $16,500 per pupil in 2018[11]—and offers many programs, special services, and extra opportunities. In 2018, its top three high schools also led the state on the *U.S. News* rankings. The class of 2018 had a composite SAT score of 1167 (versus 1066 statewide and 1049 nationally) and an average composite ACT score of 25.1 (compared with 22.5 for Maryland and 20.8 for the United States).[12]

For as long as anyone can remember, however, the Montgomery County Public Schools (MCPS) have contained two distinct realities. A large swath of the district—boasting such familiar names as Chevy Chase, Potomac, and Bethesda—is well off, degree heavy, mostly white and Asian, and very high achieving. The sources of that achievement include robust Advanced Placement programs in schools from which nearly all graduates go on to four-year colleges. In 2017, seven of the district's twenty-five high schools saw more AP exams taken than they had students in all four grades, averaging almost 1.3 exams per high school pupil—and more than 82 percent of those exams yielded qualifying scores.[13] That's an enormous participation level and an awesome passing rate.

Yet the rest of Montgomery County—indeed, *most* of the county—looks very different, and so do its schools. Communities with names like Wheaton, Silver Spring, Briggs Chaney, and Brookville contain plenty of poverty and lots of black and brown faces, including many immigrant families.[14] Caused by shifting demographics and residential patterns over several decades, it means that people whose impressions of Montgomery County were formed earlier may not fully grasp how changed it now is.

The eighteen high schools located in that "other" county averaged barely half an AP exam per student and managed a pass rate of 59 percent. The five lowest performers among them clocked just twenty-six exams per hundred pupils with a pass rate of 45 percent—a stunning contrast with the high flyers a few miles away.

Parts of Montgomery County resemble an urban school system with 150 languages spoken, and more than one-third of pupils qualifying for subsidized lunches.[15] All this—plus thousands of youngsters who reside in sprawling new developments that are neither poor nor rich but too raw to have much character, culture, or tradition—makes its way into those eighteen high schools. Many are decent-enough places, neither stellar nor troubled, the sort of middling schools that rarely get much attention for either their successes or their travails—Superintendent Jack Smith terms them "neglected"—while a handful are (as educators tend delicately to put it) "more challenged."

Just as there are fewer programs for gifted students in the elementary and middle schools of "the other county"—a situation that Smith is forcefully addressing—most of its eighteen high schools haven't had nearly as robust AP programs as in the seven already noted. Insofar as AP classes are available, the kids coming into them tend to have parents with some college education, are likelier to be white or Asian, and are less apt to have their lunches underwritten by the US Department of Agriculture.

Although a procession of recent MCPS superintendents strove in various ways to equalize resources across the county, to integrate schools racially (including much busing), and to boost achievement in the poorer neighborhoods and schools, most of that attention focused—this was the No Child Left Behind era—on bringing low achievers up to proficiency. Not much heed was given to the "excellence gap," which meant that smart poor kids tended to be shortchanged by MCPS, much as they have been across American education.[16] Less-than-proficient pupils took priority, as did narrowing the achievement gaps that separated poor and minority youngsters from their better-off peers. Children who were disadvantaged by virtue of poverty, language, ill-educated parents, or race but nevertheless managed to reach the proficiency bar were not seen as an urgent problem for the district, even when such kids were capable of achieving far more.

Jack Smith had paid attention to excellence-gap issues before he became MCPS's newest superintendent in 2016, and he brought that concern with him. As he pored over data and visited schools, he saw vividly how lopsided were the county's high-end achievement demographics, how much human potential was thereby wasted, and how important it was to find strategies by which to bring more advanced learning opportunities to more of the district's poor-but-able pupils.

"We can't have some who achieve at the highest levels and some who don't achieve," Smith declared soon after arriving, "We can't have some who walk into accelerated programs in college and many who find themselves in remedial college or working in the lowest wage jobs in our society and they cannot get living-wage jobs. We cannot tolerate it any longer."[17]

Smith likes to quote the Home Depot slogan, "You can do it. We can help." With manifest sincerity, he says he wants every kid in far-flung—more than five hundred square miles—MCPS to be challenged, to go as far as they can, including many more youngsters making their way into advanced classes. But it's not just getting them through the door that matters. Even more important, Smith says, is helping those young people feel that they *belong* in such classes and assisting them to gain enough self-awareness and confidence to succeed there.

He set out on several fronts to move this immense system—with its truly huge bureaucracy and its long-time-in-harness, well paid, and generally very liberal elected school board—to do more for those kids.

At the secondary level, he's no fan of à la carte dual credit, nor wild about associate's degrees in "general studies," but sees merit in versions that can equip high school students with actual credentials or degrees in fields with bona fide career opportunities. (He cited cybersecurity as an example.) MCPS has teamed up with Montgomery College to operate several career-oriented "early college" and "middle college" programs, focused in areas like engineering, information technology, and preparation for teaching math.[18] Mostly, though, Smith seems confident that the district can itself supply whatever accelerated and college-level academic work its students need—and (as in Dublin) he must be sensitive to union issues that arise when students are taught by college instructors rather than members of the district's bargaining unit.

Instead, Smith's chief strategy for narrowing the excellence gap at this level is to boost AP and IB participation in the eighteen schools that hadn't had much of it or opened it to enough of their students. Toward this end, and with help from Maryland's "Lead Higher" initiative, he enlisted Seattle-based Equal Opportunity Schools (EOS) to change the modus operandi in those schools.[19] Akin in its core mission to—though different in approach from—the National Math and Science Initiative (see chapter 4), EOS works with high schools across the land to identify more minority youngsters who could likely succeed in AP (and IB) courses and to implant attitudes and practices in those schools that will lead to big increases in those numbers both in the near term and over the long haul.[20]

At a cost to the county of about $17,000 per school (not including state or other support),[21] MCPS contracted with EOS to work with four of its "other eighteen" high schools beginning in 2016–17, adding six more in 2017–18, and the final eight in 2018–19. Smith's goal is for each school to have two years of intensive collaboration with EOS, which is twice as much as EOS supplies in most other places.

In Smith's view, this is more than an AP/IB expansion effort. It's also a broad high school reform strategy: changing adult mind-sets regarding what kids are capable of and how to help them achieve their utmost. That way it becomes an enduring change in schools, not a temporary fix. And the superintendent regards this not just as boosting numbers but also lifting psychological barriers: getting kids to believe they belong in such classes, getting teachers to believe that more different kinds of kids can succeed there, and persuading the entire school team that it's their responsibility to ensure that these young people make it.

Such an ambitious reform should commence well before high school, of course. Smith and his lieutenants understand that boosting more kids into high-level learning options in the upper grades requires a cascade of other changes starting in kindergarten (or before), and the district is altering its curriculum, staff development, and much more, to try to effect the needed alignment, well aware of how complicated all that becomes.

As for the schools' capacity to handle larger AP/IB enrollments and classes, MCPS is making parallel moves on the human resources front, including shifting back to December the following year's student course selection, school schedules, and identification of staff needs, thereby making it easier to recruit talent to teach those classes—and to retain instructors who might otherwise be lured by competing districts.

Ample staff development is needed, too, because advanced courses don't succeed unless those teaching them possess the requisite knowledge, pedagogical (and psychological) skills, and passion to make this work. In the EOS schools, the district pays for summer training institutes and mounts its own sessions for school teams on topics like "growth mind-set" and "trusted adults."[22] Because of an all-encompassing union contract, district leaders don't have a free rein on the HR front, but they're generally able to dismiss or move teachers who refuse to flex with a school's changing instructional needs.

EOS is acutely data-intensive, mining a school's existing information and casting a wide net for other evidence of pupil potential, while also surveying students and teachers on their attitudes and aspirations. In the EOS experience, a young person's motivation to embark on a challenging class predicts success there better than test scores or previous grades—and such motivation can be stimulated by adult encouragement, peers, and a heightened sense that yes, "I may actually belong there."

Like Jack Smith, EOS views that sense of belonging as hugely conse-
quential, which is why its operatives strive both for swift acceptance by the
school's adults of a more inclusive attitude toward who should enter advanced
courses and for a swift front-loading of nontraditional students. They've
learned that minority youngsters are apt to shun those courses on grounds
that they won't feel comfortable in such a classroom if, when they peer in,
they see only a sprinkling of "kids like them."

All the data and survey results are fed through sophisticated EOS
algorithms—and smart human brains—in search of young people who had not
participated in AP/IB courses but could likely succeed there. Just as important
is altering adult behaviors, such as how advisors and teachers help students
select courses and how instructors respond when unfamiliar kids walk into
their classrooms, so as to create a culture of equity rather than preference.
Only then will the "access gap" and in time the "excellence gap" be narrowed.

While NMSI works with a school over several years (and at considerable
cost) to train more teachers, expand the building's AP capacity, give extra
instruction to students, and—where resources and politics allow it—offer cash
rewards for qualifying scores to both pupils and teachers, EOS generally
seeks underutilized instructional capacity and ways of rearranging a school's
extant resources to augment that capacity. Its representatives work intensively
with a school's leaders and teachers to locate "missing" students (of whom
they estimate the United States contains three-quarters of a million), kids who
are "currently stuck just across the hall from the education they need and
deserve,"[23] and to install the systems and—it is hoped—shift the culture.

The goal is to equalize participation in advanced courses—EOS is agnostic
as between AP and International Baccalaureate (where founder Reid Saaris
once taught himself)—and they're not especially concerned with which subjects the kids sign up for or whether they earn qualifying scores on the exams.
Unlike NMSI, which focuses on STEM fields and on passing the May exams,
the EOS team is pretty confident that participation itself—provided that one
sticks with the class and gets a passing grade from the teacher—confers both
cognitive benefit and a boost in self-confidence and future aspiration as well
as increased likelihood of entering and faring well in college.

The MCPS expansion initiative launched swiftly. As Smith wrote his board
in September 2017:

> In one year, every participating high school in the district added more
> than one hundred low-income students and students of color to their
> AP/IB programs. Across the four pilot high schools, the number of

students of color and low-income students in AP/IB classes increased by 40 percent. . . . As we move forward with this work, we intend to increase access by closing the equity gaps in ten MCPS high schools, working with EOS partners and school staff to identify approximately 1,400 underrepresented students across the ten schools by spring 2018.[24]

EOS typically spends its first year recruiting kids into the following year's AP and IB classrooms. It is only during their second year (for MCPS cohort one, that meant 2017–18) that EOS would expect to see the fruits of those endeavors, not just in terms of more kids sitting in advanced courses, but also faring well there and perhaps passing the exams, too. The program is so new in Montgomery County that we don't have a lot of hard data. We do know, however, that at the end of 2017–18, the number of AP and IB exams taken at the first four high schools rose by 41 percent (4,872 to 6,887) above the baseline year (2015–16). And these numbers rose fastest for black (52 percent), Hispanic (64 percent), and low-income students (68 percent), compared with Asian (39 percent) and white (27 percent) pupils.[25]

The number of qualifying scores (3 or above in AP, 4 or higher in IB) rose too, by 26 percent (2,860 to 3,595) for all students in the four schools during this time. Again, the rates of increase were most robust for Hispanic (32 percent), black (34 percent), and low-income (43 percent) kids, compared with Asian (30 percent) and white (20 percent) students.

Such gains naturally encouraged Saaris and Smith, as did progress in lowering the within-year attrition rate (students who start but then drop an advanced class). At the same time, however, here as in most places, the impressive increase in AP/IB participation was joined by a decline in the overall exam pass rate, which went down from 59 to 52 percent in the four schools. Hispanic students dropped from 52 to 42 percent. EOS insists, not without reason, that this is a predictable consequence of opening the doors to many more first-time AP students, and they estimate that 85 percent of the growth in AP exam taking from 2016 to 2018 came from first-time examtakers. As we saw in New York City, a relatively modest drop in overall passing rates can be viewed as a kind of success when the participation of nontraditional youngsters is rising so rapidly. Given more time, EOS says, these newcomers will become more accustomed to this kind of rigor, their instructors will have more experience teaching them, and pass rates will tend to stabilize.

The solid rise in AP and IB participation and in the absolute number of passing scores contributed to Montgomery County's decision to add two more cohorts of high schools and to keep EOS working in the first four schools for another year. Early signs from the second cohort were encouraging, too, as those six high schools witnessed nearly one thousand more students signing up for AP and IB courses in 2018–19, again with the largest gains among their minority pupils.[26]

A TALE OF TWO SCHOOLS

Northwest High School

Located in fast-growing Germantown, fast-growing Northwest High School is demographically diverse and has a reasonably solid history of Advanced Placement participation and passing scores but now—with a dynamic principal, the superintendent's encouragement, and EOS's help—is bent on growing that program and drawing more (and more different kinds of) students into it.

Northwest offers no IB program but a number of pupils take dual-enrollment courses at nearby Montgomery College and—in conjunction with the same institution—it houses one of the district's rare "middle college" programs, this one focused on engineering careers.

Montgomery College itself makes creative use of AP exams to validate some of the dual-enrollment classes taken by Northwest students. When these are taught by high school teachers, the college treats the exam as a quality-control mechanism. A student seeking college credit for such a class must get a qualifying score on the AP exam as evidence of having completed college-level work.[27]

Although MCPS doesn't automatically pay for AP exams, it grants fee waivers for kids who seek the help. Nor are students who enroll in AP courses obligated to take the exam, but "if you don't sign up for it you'll hear from your counselor."

Expansion of AP at Northwest has brought growing pains, as the school suddenly had to accommodate hundreds more students in those classes, which it did by adding more sections. Teachers who weren't already teaching AP were reluctant to do so, which forced the principal to scramble to recruit a cadre of new (sometimes beginner) teachers to staff those classrooms. But the EOS recruitment push did not, for the most part, cause Northwest's already-sizable (thirty-pupil) classes to grow larger.

A number of students who volunteered (or were persuaded) to register for AP classes also—inevitably—turned out to be ill-prepared for academic work at that level. Teachers reported slipshod study skills, inept note taking, weak reading comprehension, and sometimes a lack of diligence. Getting those kids up to speed has been a struggle for instructors, and we heard grumbles from a few veterans who were accustomed to AP classrooms full of eager, well-prepared "traditional" pupils. New teachers, on the other hand, seemed calmly to accept the added challenge, perhaps because they had nothing to contrast it with.

EOS focuses on getting kids into advanced courses in eleventh and twelfth grade, so they concentrate their outreach efforts on tenth graders. They also tend to think more of single classes than of course sequences. But Northwest already had many of its abler students embarking on an AP sequence as early as ninth grade, typically in social studies (for example, US Government as freshmen, US History as sophomores, World History in the junior year, possibly Psychology as seniors). Smoothly melding that pattern with the EOS approach took some doing and highlighted the need for more attention to readiness for more students. How, for example, to ensure that students entering AP English Language in eleventh grade were adequately prepared by their ninth and tenth grade English teachers? How to develop more pre-AP classes? How to work more effectively on vertical curriculum alignment with the middle schools that feed pupils into Northwest?

The teachers with whom we met felt that participation in courses like these is a plus for kids whether or not they get a lofty exam score. Some, however, were frustrated by the pedagogical challenge of differentiating instruction within their more diverse AP classes—several implied that they're having to "dumb it down"—and by the presence in their classrooms of kids who don't appear fully committed to doing the work. School leaders, on the other hand, waved off this problem by naming instructors who—they said—work 24/7 to get their variegated populations of AP students to succeed both in class and on the exam.

Springbrook High School

The streets around Springbrook High in outer Silver Spring look like a well-established if tattered suburb, but this school comes closer than Northwest to "inner city" demographics—almost 80 percent black and Latino, almost half eligible for subsidized lunches—and historically has had some of the county's lowest AP participation and passing scores. It also has a reasonably robust International Baccalaureate program that has traditionally attracted the school's stronger students, at least in the humanities. (Kids focused on math and science tend to favor AP as a more rigorous path into the STEM realm.)

The EOS initiative at Springbrook feeds kids into both AP and IB, and it's not always a smooth transition. Observing several classes, we saw a number of inattentive students and watched heroic efforts by teachers to engage their pupils. As at Northwest, AP teachers here insist that they're not wedded to exam scores but are willing to settle for participation and hope their pupils will at least get 2's in May. Also like their peers at Northwest, teachers at Springbrook remarked on their uncertainty as to how best to handle kids who enroll in AP classes but don't do the work and don't keep up. Once again, however, this concern was voiced more by veteran teachers than by new instructors who hadn't previously experienced the "traditional AP demographic" in their classrooms.

The students we spoke to—who appeared to come more from that traditional population than new EOS recruits—seemed fully cognizant of the challenge (and importance) of keeping up with the work but also signaled that they could get the help they need either from teachers ("we have almost a second class at lunch time") or from peers. The kids are accustomed to working together because here, as at Northwest, teachers emphasize group activity in AP classes, believing that this boosts pupil motivation and participation.

School leaders voiced pride both that the EOS program had successfully attracted many more kids into Springbrook's AP and IB classes and also that the newbies were sticking with it. One teacher suggested that the EOS recruits felt really special when encouraged to sign up for AP/IB and didn't want to lose that feeling by dropping the class, even when they found it hard.

WILL IT WORK?

There's good reason to expect Smith's ambitious AP/IB expansion initiative to bear some fruit, so long as the district sticks with it. Early returns were promising. As we have seen, AP and IB participation at targeted high schools rose in 2018, especially among black, Hispanic, and low-income kids and lesser but still encouraging gains in passing scores were notched in the first cohort of schools. Yet challenges remain. As in other places that have launched ambitious AP expansions, participation is rising far faster than qualifying scores. There can be many reasons for this, including weak preparation among students and inexperience among teachers. As opportunities for more kids to take more such classes open up in more schools, more AP teachers are needed and more principals and district hierarchs have to muster the commitment to make the requisite changes and see them through.

But this district is off to a solid start. For all its unwieldy size, this is a well-led system with much talent and bench strength in its staff. That makes MCPS the kind of place that EOS seeks out: one with the capacity to embed and sustain an initiative like this. As one of the most appealing—and generally well paid—places for educators to work in one of the country's most alluring metro areas, the schools of Montgomery County are also a talent magnet, and that magnet is powerful enough to hold onto most of those it attracts. With total enrollments rising, there are more teaching jobs every year (which mitigates potential union opposition) and, despite the competitive teacher job market around the Washington Beltway, MCPS has done well at attracting well-educated people to its instructional and administrative ranks. District leaders are nimble enough to shift their hiring calendars and strategies to stay ahead of the HR game. Smith also noted that expanding AP and IB in the county's less privileged schools creates welcome career opportunities for youngish teachers who are keen to take on such courses, else they'd have to wait for veteran instructors to retire from schools where such classes have long been entrenched.

EOS is a sophisticated and experienced partner organization; school budgets are relatively robust; and the fact that the venture is cloaked in the rhetoric and spirit of equity rather than elitism plays well in liberal Montgomery County.[28] Yet making lasting changes in a school's culture—especially that of a big, complicated high school—is a major crusade. There's inevitable sluggishness on the part of counselors accustomed to handling course placements and student schedules in a certain way and from administrators who must alter staffing assignments. Teachers are apt to worry that introducing more of "those kids" into their classrooms will swell pupil numbers to unworkable levels, will cause their lofty passing rates to fall, thus making them look less effective, and may force them to slow the pace of instruction and perhaps falter in preparing their students for rigorous external tests. Teachers also know that working with a room full of kids at different levels of preparedness, background, and motivation is far harder than teaching a homogeneous group of practiced overachievers.

Politics are also unpredictable. Parents of those veteran overachievers tend to grump to principals and school board members when Ashley's and Brandon's accelerated classes take in lots of different kids. Although equity is the name of the game for EOS as well as MCPS, district leaders dare not alienate the upper-middle-class part of the county that makes the most noise, pulls the most strings, and pays much of the bill. What's more, equity concerns can readily shift back to worrying about low achievers rather than potential highflyers, particularly if achievement gaps should widen or graduation rates falter.

Leadership matters, too. Although MCPS had several energetic reformers at its helm before Smith arrived, boosting AP and IB participation (and other gifted-student opportunities) in "the other county" wasn't on their agendas—and there's no way to be sure that it will remain high on his successors' agendas. (Smith is sixty years old and may or may not seek another post—but his predecessor was eased out by the school board after a single four-year term.) Initiatives such as this can wither, or simply sink into routines, especially when external partners such as EOS turn their eyes elsewhere, unless those in charge of the school system keep pushing on their own. EOS itself may also be in flux, as visionary founder Reid Saaris stepped down from the CEO role in early 2019, and it's not yet known who will succeed him or how smooth will be the transition in working arrangements with partner districts like MCPS.

Nor is it easy for even the strongest and most dynamic of school-system leaders to push all of the collateral changes in a giant organization that are ultimately needed for ambitious reforms like this to bear maximum fruit—such as better aligning the curriculum between target high schools and their feeder schools (and *their* feeder elementary schools), keeping this initiative compatible with the state's ever-changing graduation requirements and testing practices, finding the right balance among AP, IB, dual credit, and the schools' own honors classes, and locating sufficient funds in the vast budget to keep this program progressing even as other demands and constituencies press hard.

In sum, Montgomery County has rich soil in which to plant this initiative—but it's not immune to drought, flood, and locusts. What we see there, as in much smaller and more homogeneous Dublin, Ohio, is a solid history of success with AP among the schools and populations that have historically sought out such opportunities, along with big challenges—and exciting opportunities—that surface when leaders ask tough questions about who else in their districts might benefit from similar programs but haven't had much access to (or encouragement to participate in) them. Dublin is striving to find ways—in part via AP and other advanced courses—to prepare more of its college-bound pupils to succeed within the ivy gates while also creating solid options for kids who might be better served in other destinations. Montgomery County finds itself today with thousands of youngsters who could and should be on a path to success in college but have not previously found the academic opportunities, personal supports, and culture of encouragement that would place and keep them on such paths. Successfully implementing an AP expansion effort is a promising response to those challenges, but doing it right—and sustaining it over the long run—demands vision, courage, and expert leadership.

In today's America, however, there's more to public education than district-operated schools in cities and suburbs. In the following chapter, we delve into AP's growing presence in the country's fast-growing crop of public charter schools.

Notes

1. Close to the Twin Cities, for example, several well-to-do Minnesota suburbs make IB offerings accessible to all their pupils. *Rigorous Course Taking Advanced Placement, International Baccalaureate, Concurrent Enrollment and Postsecondary Enrollment Options Programs* (Minneapolis: Minnesota Department of Education, 2017), 8–9. https://www.leg.state.mn.us/docs/2017/mandated/170691.pdf.

2. Data USA, "Dublin, OH," accessed November 8, 2018. https://datausa.io/profile/geo/dublin-oh/; United States Census Bureau, "Quick Facts: Dublin City, Ohio," July 1, 2017. https://www.census.gov/quickfacts/fact/table/dublincityohio/PST045217#PST045217.

3. Ohio public and nonpublic school enrollment data found at Ohio Department of Education, "Enrollment Data," July 12, 2018. http://education.ohio.gov/Topics/Data/Frequently-Requested-Data/Enrollment-Data. AP data for Dublin City Schools were supplied by the district.

4. Ohio Department of Education, "Ohio School Report Cards," accessed February 1, 2019. https://reportcard.education.ohio.gov/.

5. Union considerations are also at play. When a course is taught by a college instructor, it reduces the high school faculty's course load. If this is repeated multiple times, the district will need fewer teachers. The union is understandably anxious about this—as is the college faculty union in the reciprocal case in which a college course is handled by a high school instructor.

6. A further wrinkle is that IB courses come in two levels of difficulty—"standard" and "higher"—while AP has just one level (see more on IB in chapter 8).

7. More conventional sports such as basketball, track, and baseball are also offered.

8. Robert Morse, "How *U.S. News* Calculated the 2018 Best High Schools Rankings," *U.S. News and World Report*, February 1, 2019. https://www.usnews.com/education/best-high-schools/articles/how-us-news-calculated-the-rankings. See chapter 3 for an explanation of the *U.S. News* school-ranking algorithm.

9. Dublin officials—and parents—also welcome the College Board's recent affiliation with the Khan Academy as a mechanism for boosting SAT scores. Richard Chang, "College Board and Khan Academy Partner on AP Courses, Test Prep," *The Journal*, July 3, 2017. https://thejournal.com/articles/2017/07/31/college-board-and-khan-academy-partner-on-ap-courses-test-prep.aspx.

10. Montgomery County Public Schools, "Montgomery County Public Schools at a Glance: School Year 2018–2019," accessed February 1, 2019. https://www.montgomeryschoolsmd.org/uploadedFiles/about/homepage/At%20a%20Glance%20%2001.24.19.pdf.

11. Robin Clark Ellenberg, "2018 School Funding per Student County-by-County," *Conduit Street* (blog), *Maryland Association of Counties*, February 21, 2018. https://conduitstreet.mdcounties.org/2018/02/21/chart-compares-school-funding-per-student-county-by-county/.

12. "School Notes: Educational Foundation Launches Dine with Dignity Campaign," *Bethesda Beat* (blog), *Bethesda Magazine*, November 5, 2018. https://bethesdamagazine.com/bethesda-beat/schools/school-notes-educational-foundation-launches-dine-with-dignity-campaign/; Caitlynn Peetz, "MCPS Students Score Nearly Five Points Higher Than National Average on ACT," *Bethesda Beat* (blog), *Bethesda Magazine*, October 24, 2018. https://bethesdamagazine.com/bethesda-beat/schools/mcps-students-score-nearly-five-points-higher-than-national-average-on-act/; "Maryland SAT Scores Take a Leap Forward for the Class or 2018," press release, Maryland State

Department of Education, October 25, 2018. https://news.maryland.gov/msde/maryland-sat
-scores-take-a-leap-forward-for-the-class-of-2018/; *Average ACT Scores by State Graduating Class 2018* (Iowa City, IA: ACT, 2018). https://www.act.org/content/dam/act/unsecured/documents
/cccr2018/Average-Scores-by-State.pdf.

13. Authors' analysis of data provided by Montgomery County Public Schools. In 2018, an eighth school joined the ranks of those that saw more AP exams taken than they had students in all four grades.

14. Bill Turque, "Affluent Montgomery County Has Pockets of Poverty, Mostly in the East," *Washington Post*, September 6, 2014. https://www.washingtonpost.com/.

15. Montgomery County Public Schools, "Montgomery County"; Maryland State Department of Education, "2017–18 Maryland Title I Schools," August 2, 2018. http://www.marylandpublicschools
.org/about/Documents/DSFSS/TitleI/titleIschools/Title_I_ListofSchools_20172018.pdf.

16. Chester E. Finn, Jr. and Brandon L. Wright, *Failing Our Brightest Kids: The Global Challenge of Educating High-Ability Students* (Cambridge, MA: Harvard Education Press, 2015).

17. Donna St. George, "Superintendent Says Narrowing Academic Achievement Gap Is 'A Moral Imperative,'" *Washington Post*, July 26, 2016. https://www.washingtonpost.com/local
/education/superintendent-says-narrowing-academic-achievement-gap-is-a-moral-imperative
/2016/07/26/4aff3e0a-529c-11e6-b7de-dfe509430c39_story.html?utm_term=.319aa101ffcd.

18. Montgomery County Public Schools, "Dual Enrollment: MCPS and Montgomery College (MC) Partnership," accessed November 6, 2018. https://www.montgomeryschoolsmd.org
/curriculum/partnerships/dual-enrollment.aspx.

19. Karen B. Salmon, "Update: Lead Higher Initiative," board memo to Maryland State Board of Education, July 18, 2017. http://www.marylandpublicschools.org/stateboard/Documents/07182017
/TabJ-LeadHigher.pdf.

20. Equal Opportunity Schools, "Approach," accessed November 6, 2018. https://eoschools
.org/approach/.

21. Salmon, "Update: Lead Higher."

22. EOS has found that students are likelier to tackle a challenging course if encouraged by an adult in the school whom they like and trust. That "trusted adult" may be an administrator, teacher, or coach, not necessarily a guidance counselor.

23. Authors' correspondence with Reid Saaris, CEO of Equal Opportunity Schools.

24. Jack R. Smith, "Learning, Accountability, and Results: Equal Opportunity Schools," board memo to Montgomery County Public Schools Board of Education, September 12, 2017.

25. Data from Montgomery County Public Schools. "Low-income" is based on MCPS's designation of students as eligible for free and reduced-price meals.

26. We won't see the first exam results for this second cohort until late 2019.

27. Where the college staffs the course—whether classes meet in the high school or on the nearby campus—instructor judgment is all that's required for credit.

28. Donna St. George, "Boundary Struggles: A Maryland School System Looks for More Diversity," *Washington Post*, September 15, 2018. https://www.washingtonpost.com/.

7

Advancing Charter Schools

Because America's seven thousand charter schools primarily serve disadvantaged urban populations, and because the charter sector contains far more elementary and middle schools than high schools, Advanced Placement has not loomed large there. Yet a handful of prominent charter networks (and independently operated or "mom and pop" charter schools) beg to differ, for they have placed AP near the curricular center of their high schools and, sometimes, their middle schools. Unsurprisingly, the tightest embrace has come from networks that obsess about getting their graduates into colleges, especially competitive four-year colleges. For the most part, however, they also focus on poor and minority youngsters and thus can fairly be said to partake of the widening view that AP is no longer just for privileged kids; it's also a way to accustom disadvantaged students to challenging academic work, give them confidence that they can handle such work, incorporate college aspirations and possibilities into their own sense of reality, and, when successful, propel those young people forward with a nationally recognized credential attesting to their capacity to engage in heavy-duty academics and perhaps speeding their progress toward a valuable, marketable degree and the upward mobility that often follows.

Although schools of every sort have been working to boost pupils with weak basic skills and sketchy backgrounds to higher levels of achievement, often including success in AP classes and exams, parts of the charter sector have racked up extraordinary accomplishments. In the 2018 *U.S. News* rankings of the country's top high schools, for instance, almost a quarter of the five hundred gold award winners were charters.[1] On Jay Mathews's Challenge Index in 2018—based primarily on AP exam participation— almost 18 percent of the top five hundred were charters (more than private schools), including eight each from KIPP and IDEA, six from YES Prep, five from Uplift, four from Summit, and three from BASIS.[2] (We say more about several of these networks below.) One reason for charters' awesome record in such rankings may be that so many of their students are underserved minorities, which (combined with AP results) is a key component of the *U.S. News* algorithm. But as we shall see, charter schools also possess some institutional features that amplify their capacity to boost AP success.[3]

We see many examples of earnest effort toward that end. The Noble charter network, which enrolls about 12 percent of all Chicago schoolchildren, accounts for a quarter of that city's AP exam volume. Achievement First (AF)—which operated thirty-four schools in 2018, five of them high schools, in Connecticut, New York, and Rhode Island—has created model AP curricula to be used across its network, and proudly declares that "the average AF high school student will take five Advanced Placement classes before they graduate, including a math AP and a science AP."[4]

In New York City, the high-flying Success Academy charter network, led by the redoubtable Eva Moskowitz, requires all eleventh graders to sit for AP exams in World History and English Literature—and offers AP math and science, too.[5]

The Uncommon Schools network includes nine college-prep high schools (and more than forty elementary and middle schools) in Massachusetts, New Jersey, and New York. Although its curriculum varies somewhat by campus, several schools have succeeded with the "AP for All" approach, insisting that every student take as many as four Advanced Placement courses and exams, and their pass rates have generally been strong. But passing isn't everything, for Uncommon's leaders are convinced that such courses—in the hands of capable teachers—yield value for almost all who take a sustained shot at them, including kids who end up with 2's and even 1's on the exams. The benefits they see include stronger study skills, better time management, the sense of accomplishment that comes from sticking with something hard for a full year—and greater success on mandatory state assessments.

Uncommon asked to participate in the College Board's 2018–19 pilot program for the four new ninth grade pre-AP courses in academic core subjects, and its nine high schools are among the hundred across the country that, as we write, are at work on this, along with schools in traditional districts such as Spokane, Washington.[6] They're developing lesson plans and availing themselves of the College Board's online benchmark exams. The Uncommon network's goal is to make high-quality pre-AP available to all of its freshmen, then give them the opportunity to transition into full-fledged AP classes in subsequent years.

Also in the works is a possible partnership between Uncommon and another high-performing charter network to develop detailed curricular materials aligned with AP frameworks and make these broadly available via open-sourcing as well as to their own teachers, many of whom are new to the classroom and grateful for access to proven lesson plans and materials already developed by successful veteran instructors.[7]

At the sprawling KIPP network—some 209 schools in twenty states and the District of Columbia, including twenty-seven high schools—Advanced Placement is also rising in importance, in large part because of the sobering discovery (from a self-study in 2011) that KIPP schools were doing well at getting kids into college but not nearly enough of them were completing degrees. One major reason was that KIPP's curriculum had emphasized basic skills and sophisticated preparation for state assessments, not the "deeper learning," analytic thinking, argumentation, and extended writing that many college courses demand. The upshot—at KIPP and several other high-performing charter networks that had employed the "no excuses" formula—was adjustments in curriculum and pedagogy so as to prepare their pupils better for postgraduation academic success. Advanced Placement was there to be deployed. One might term its expanded use part of an intentional shift from "test prep" to true "college prep."[8]

KIPP's new goal is to have a version of "AP for All" in every high school, along with sufficient pre-AP efforts to equip many more "KIPPsters" with the skills and background to do well in those classrooms. Half a dozen schools are piloting this, in most cases starting with AP English Language and Composition, and the network is working with the National Math and Science Initiative on curriculum, student supports, and—especially—teacher preparation. Experience has shown—KIPP's been around since 1995—that recruiting and retaining enough first-rate teachers is the greatest challenge in growing a high-performing, high-intensity, multi-state network of charter schools that successfully prepare disadvantaged youngsters for college and beyond. That challenge intensifies when what those kids are being asked to learn is as intensive as a well-taught AP course, for even the smart, committed young university graduates who are typically drawn to teaching positions like these cannot be counted on to bring with them all that content knowledge, much less the sophisticated pedagogical skills that they will also need.[9]

IDEA Public Schools

Perhaps the most AP-centric of the major charter outfits—as well as the fastest-growing network in the land—is Texas-based IDEA Public Schools. Founded in the deeply impoverished and heavily Hispanic Rio Grande Valley in 1998 as an after-school program by Teach For America participants JoAnn Gama and Tom Torkelson, IDEA received its first charter for a full-fledged school in 2000 and slowly expanded in "the Valley," town by neighboring town, until 2012, by which time its impressive track record with minority youngsters had caught the eye of Bill Gates as well as the charter-minded Walton Family Foundation and the multi-foundation Charter School Growth Fund, all of which urged Torkelson and Gama to reach further. With generous infusions of philanthropic dollars, IDEA looked to expand into Austin and San Antonio. Austin's then superintendent invited them to open schools in the state capital, but she was soon forced out and multiple political dustups and pushbacks followed (not unlike some of the issues NMSI faced there around the same time, see chapter 4). Meanwhile, NBA basketball star David Robinson asked them to come to San Antonio, where IDEA began by converting a private Christian school that Robinson had founded into one of its trademark charters.

Although those two cities differ culturally and politically from IDEA's home base, this initial expansion stayed within the Lone Star State and thus within the rules, academic standards, accountability framework, and demographics of Texas. But that, too, was to change. Emboldened by more invitations, donor dollars, and an ever-stronger student performance record, IDEA has been growing like a zucchini in August. By 2018–19, it ran seventy-nine schools with more than 45,000 kids, was planning to open another nine campuses the following year, and had ratified an audacious expansion plan that aims to operate 173 schools for 100,000 pupils by 2022.[10] Besides adding schools in Fort Worth, El Paso, and Houston (while enlarging its footprint in its first three Texas regions), IDEA launched its first out-of-state schools in southern Louisiana in 2018—Baton Rouge, then heading toward New Orleans—and expects to open in Florida by 2021, while seeking additional expansion sites in other jurisdictions.

IDEA schools are fairly standardized in structure and, at most sites, in size and operations. They divide each campus into an "academy" that goes through fifth grade and a college-prep program from sixth grade through high school. They're open admission and, when space is available, will take students off waiting lists through at least eighth grade. Consistent with IDEA's origins, their target population in Texas has been disadvantaged girls and boys from immigrant/Latino backgrounds, and that target is being hit. In spring 2018, 89 percent of IDEA's Lone Star pupils were economically disadvantaged (according to state data) and 34 percent were English language learners.[11]

IDEA's significance in this book is not just its bumptious growth plan and stunning track record in educating poor and minority youngsters—they can boast 100 percent college acceptance and nearly 100 percent matriculation for their graduating seniors over eleven consecutive years—but also the fact that Advanced Placement is central to the network's high school curriculum. In 2014, they proclaimed "AP for all IDEA students," and their high schools now insist that every pupil take a full suite of Advanced Placement courses and the exams that follow.

The impetus came from returning alums who reported that they were not truly prepared for the rigors of college academics, particularly at the competitive campuses where IDEA aims to send its graduates. Network leaders view degrees from such institutions as the most likely to "break the poverty cycle," and those are also the colleges best able to supply students with decent counseling, workable financial aid packages, and other supports. But Torkelson and colleagues, mindful that "kids need college preparatory coursework before they get to college," pooh-pooh dual-credit offerings from community colleges in favor of the AP approach, which is also likelier to yield transcripts and exam scores that the admissions and placement teams at Tier I and Tier II institutions can parse and will take seriously.

A few IDEA high schools have opted instead for the International Baccalaureate program, which is okay with network leaders so long as the school has an exceptional principal, a tight-knit culture, and a stable, dedicated teaching team that understands and values the IB approach.[12] Mostly, though, IDEA high schools are bastions of Advanced Placement.

The plan is for every pupil in those schools to take eleven Advanced Placement courses, and IDEA's core curriculum is vertically aligned, featuring pre-AP and AP courses in English, math, social studies, science, and Spanish. The entire social studies program, for example, consists of four consecutive AP courses. Also mandatory in most IDEA schools are the two AP English courses, twelfth grade Calculus AB or Statistics, and at least two AP science courses, although—mindful of the challenge of staffing every AP class every year with a capable instructor—campuses have some discretion as to which courses are offered and which are required of all pupils. Individual schools may also add AP electives such as foreign languages and studio arts, and students can access a selection of online AP offerings developed by Brigham Young University.[13]

The network's goal is for 30 percent of graduates at each IDEA high school to earn the designation of "AP Scholars," which the College Board confers on students who achieve at least three scores of 3 or better. Some 24 percent of 2018 graduates across the IDEA network hit that target, the same proportion as the previous year. It's tough going, though. Network leaders expected an upward bump in 2018 that they didn't get, and they acknowledge that some of their schools are doing far better at this than others.

Why the AP emphasis? As in other charter networks that make heavy use of it, school leaders see multiple advantages. William Corbit, who directs college counseling at an IDEA school in Brownsville, explains it this way:

> AP classes are rigorous, college-level classes that can afford a student the opportunity to earn college credit if they receive a passing score (3, 4, or 5) on an AP course exam. These credits can potentially save students and their families thousands of dollars in college tuition . . . and help more students and families afford a college education. AP courses also offer college admissions officers a consistent measure of course rigor across high schools, districts, states, and countries. . . . When admissions officers see "AP" on students' transcripts, they have a good understanding of what a student experienced in a particular class and how well the course prepared the student for the rigor of college. . . . At IDEA, we believe that if every student is going to succeed in college, then every student should engage with college preparatory coursework. . . . As we have expanded AP access to more students, AP passing rates have increased. Not only do IDEA's high-quality teachers find innovative ways to teach students challenging content, but they also differentiate the lessons for students at different learning levels.[14]

Intensively dosing every student with multiple AP classes in open-enrollment schools full of poor kids is audacious in the extreme, and many IDEA schools are seeing lots of 1's on the end-of-year AP exams. In 2018, those minimal scores came back on 63 percent of the 12,539 exams taken by IDEA students. Scores of 3 and higher were attained on just 19 percent of that year's exams, with another 18 percent scoring 2. Those rates were almost the same as the previous year, although it's no small feat to hold them steady when 2,557 more AP exams were taken in 2018 than in 2017, which translates to some 449 more qualifying scores earned across the network. The young people who accomplished that have much to celebrate, as do their teachers, even when IDEA as a whole clearly has far to go before its results match its aspirations, especially because it's pursuing both rapid expansion and high-level performance.[15]

Not surprisingly, the data look worse at the network's newer schools and better where the AP program is well established and those teaching it have at least a few years of experience under their belts. A handful of IDEA schools have become exceptionally strong on the AP front. (Hence the four that made it onto *U.S. News*'s "gold" list in 2018, and the eight among Jay Mathews's top five hundred.) Still, across the network there are way too many disappointing scores on far too many exams.

As we heard from teachers and leaders at many other schools, IDEA educators insist that getting a 2 has value for students even if it doesn't count as a qualifying score. It signals that a young person grappled with college-level work and took something away from the experience. A score of 1 is harder to justify, however, for it could mean that a student "almost got a 2" or it could signal that she merely sat in class and learned next to nothing.

The IDEA team isn't complacent. They view all those 1's (and, for that matter, the large number of 2's) as a problem in need of a solution, particularly because a qualifying score is what signals to universities—and the world—that one has indeed succeeded in a college-level course. They know it's exceptionally hard to grow as rapidly as IDEA is doing *and* to boost the effectiveness of curriculum and instruction at the same time. (For example, the network is currently hiring some 1,400 additional or replacement teachers every year.) The current solution strategy has multiple elements:

- IDEA has teamed up with NMSI to boost teachers' mastery of AP content (in STEM subjects and English) and to supply students with extra instructional sessions on Fridays and Saturdays, plus other sources of tutoring and encouragement. Kids get gift cards for attending those sessions—and teachers get bonuses when their students earn qualifying scores.
- An ambitious curriculum overhaul is focused on the middle grades and designed to strengthen IDEA's pre-AP offerings to better align with what lies ahead.
- With NMSI's help, IDEA schools administer a series of interim assessments to their AP pupils during the school year, yielding data that helps teachers see who is learning what and whether corrective steps are indicated. Administrators, too, can view progress (or not) and gauge whether AP participation is benefiting pupils who may still not perform well on the exams. Such evidence of within-year

gains is also good for the morale of hardworking instructors whose pupils may get low scores in May. Noted an assistant principal in one IDEA high school that we visited: "Although they don't meet AP standards, we see progress."

- By commencing full-on AP courses in ninth grade and following up in successive years, particularly when there's also been solid pre-AP grounding, IDEA helps students gradually up their games, with the hope that a score of 1 or 2 the first time around becomes a 2 or 3 in tenth grade and so forth. It's assumed that the more experience one gains with study skills, analytic thinking, lots of homework, much writing, and other AP-level challenges, the better one will handle them.

- Student attitudes get attention, too. IDEA accompanies AP (and the rest of its curriculum) with participation in the national initiative called AVID, which seeks from the early grades to get prospective first-generation college goers on track both academically and attitudinally for what college can do for them, while assisting teachers and administrators to "provide the key academic and social supports students need to thrive."[16] Getting kids into a "college mind-set" also entails pep-rally type treatment. At the start of a tenth grade AP World History class at one IDEA school we visited, everyone rose and recited a sort of pledge that included the words "We want 3 or higher. . . . We will be college ready."

- Starting in kindergarten, IDEA's school design—like that of most high-performing charter networks that target disadvantaged kids—incorporates longer-than-usual days and years as well as much homework. Everybody understands that when there's limited academic support at home, a college-bound youngster needs more from school. A Stanford analysis concluded that IDEA students learn the equivalent of eighty extra days of math and seventy-four of reading instruction during a school year compared with ordinary public schools.[17]

- When hiring new high school teachers, IDEA gauges whether candidates possess the content knowledge, instructional prowess, and willingness to handle AP classes. They need not bring all that with them, as the job includes mentoring and extensive staff development (in part via NMSI), but they must arrive with the requisite mastery of their field plus a strong desire to share that knowledge with young people. Hence the hiring process may even include asking prospective instructors in AP subjects to take a sample AP exam themselves.

What sets IDEA and other charter networks apart from traditional school systems seeking to infuse AP into more high schools is that charters are relatively nimble, they're expanding rather than static or shrinking, and they have the freedom to hire people (teachers, principals, central office personnel, and such) who share a commitment to AP. Because most high-performing networks now run from kindergarten (or earlier) through twelfth grade, they're far better able to align curricula and expectations across grades and avoid the paralyzing problem faced by high schools that have no sway over their feeder schools and must take in—and try to remediate—ninth graders whose elementary and middle school education was sorely lacking.

Free in most places from state certification, tenure laws, and teacher unions, charter schools are also able to replace anyone who can't or won't pitch in. And they can construct compensation systems that reward teachers with bonuses when their pupils succeed at AP. So instead of imposing "yet another reform" on a relatively inert bureaucratic system, they can tug on all the levers that must move for this to work. And if they have a solid track record, such as IDEA and the other networks named here, they can often bring in grant dollars and philanthropic subsidies to help cover ancillary costs and fill staffing gaps.

That doesn't make it easy to turn disadvantaged kids into AP Scholars (or successful college matriculants), particularly when a fast-growing, open-access network serving thousands of kids from what were once called "deprived" backgrounds is also bent on achieving AP success for every pupil. But IDEA has a fighting chance, a coherent plan, stable leadership, and a very solid start.

BASIS and Beyond

An even more robust start can be observed in the BASIS network, which contained twenty-five charter schools by 2018 (plus some tuition-charging private schools in the United States and China) and which has also brought Advanced Placement into the core of its curriculum.

Although BASIS demographics vary, many of its schools enroll more middle-class youngsters, including the progeny of educated professionals (more than a few of them immigrants) who take for granted that their kids will go to college and who see these high-powered schools as heat-generating missiles aimed at the admissions office. In the BASIS charter school in Washington, DC, for example, just 16 percent of pupils come from low-income families—and the school (though generously financed with public dollars) "request[s] an annual contribution of at least $1,500 per student" to supplement its budget.[18]

BASIS offers a traditional, liberal-arts-oriented curriculum but accelerates it faster than typical schools in the district, charter, and private sectors. Thus algebra may commence as early as sixth grade and AP math may be taken as soon as ninth. AP science may also start that year, AP English arrives for sophomores, and juniors and seniors take the new Capstone courses.

Network leaders offer an unconventional rationale for this reliance on AP. Because they wanted to confer *autonomy* on classroom teachers, BASIS needed an external gauge of how well students were learning. So instead of prescribing a detailed system-wide curriculum and pedagogy, they chose to rely on a set of respected national tests as a third-party validation of the schools' (and instructors' and pupils') success. The IB and Cambridge systems (discussed in the next chapter) were not good fits for various reasons, so they "backdoored into AP." But now it's huge. The average BASIS student sits for a dozen AP exams during his/her high school (and sometimes middle school) years, and the network has racked up an enviable 87 percent pass rate on those exams. Nobody can graduate without taking at least seven AP courses and six exams—and passing at least one of the latter. That's a slam dunk for many BASIS pupils but remains a steep climb for some who must be coaxed, guided, and tutored to ensure that they eventually—perhaps as late as May of senior year—squeak by with a 3 on a single exam. Although BASIS attracts more than its share of able, hardworking students (and demanding parents), its charter schools, like others in the sector, are open enrollment and have lottery-based admissions. So the BASIS schools serving inner-city pupils in Tucson and Phoenix enroll many kids from disadvantaged backgrounds who—particularly if they don't board the BASIS express in the early grades—may struggle with its curricular demands.[19]

AP is not, however, everyone's choice in the charter sector. Just as several IDEA high schools have opted for the International Baccalaureate, the well-regarded Uplift network of twenty charter schools in the Dallas–Fort Worth area—half of them with high school grades—has embraced IB and worked it into the core curriculum. School leaders earnestly explain why they find IB superior, and their website boasts that "we develop well-rounded International Baccalaureate scholars who think critically, are confident in themselves, and appreciate diverse ideas and people."[20] They contend that "an International Baccalaureate education combines academic rigor with social and emotional growth, creativity, and global thinking" and "helps scholars become not only problem-solvers, but also people who understand community, connection, and how they are a part of it all."[21]

Like some of the private schools described in chapter 10, a handful of high-performing charter networks want nothing to do with either AP or IB. At Great Hearts Academies, twenty-eight schools that now educate about 15,000 youngsters from kindergarten through high school in Arizona and Texas, they prefer to construct their own classical, great-books curriculum, an approach that has proven hugely popular with families, many of them with college-educated, middle-class parents who take as given that their daughters and sons will go to college and want them to have a traditional liberal arts preparation, complete with Socratic dialogues in class. Great Hearts old-fashionedly states that it "cultivates the hearts and minds of students in the pursuit of Truth, Goodness and Beauty."[22]

Observing a Great Hearts high school literature classroom is akin to watching a "Harkness table" discussion at Exeter, albeit with twice as many kids in the room.[23] Much of the dialogue takes place among students, with the teacher functioning more as provocateur, referee, and occasional helmsman. This is very nearly the opposite of a structured, cover-the-content, teacher-centric curriculum aimed to prepare pupils for an end-of-the-year exam that comes from somewhere else. While Great Hearts schools must abide by the accountability regimes of the states in which they're located—and they've fared well on those metrics as well as on college admissions—they don't seek (or think they need) other external assessments such as AP, nor are they willing to submit their courses for College Board approval.

Like the prep schools, however, they're not completely immune. Some Great Hearts academies administer Advanced Placement exams to interested students via outside-of-class "AP clubs," and school leaders say they welcome the use of AP exams to help students obtain college credit. Toward that end, however, they find a better fit between their curriculum and a separate College Board offering called the College Level Examination Program (CLEP, discussed in the next chapter), the results of which are also accepted on many campuses for potential degree credit. CLEP is simply a set of exams, however, and while they reflect implicit curricular assumptions, they're more flexible than the frameworks-and-syllabus-based AP approach.[24]

Diverse approaches to education are the essence of charter schooling (and other modes of school choice), so there's no reason to think that all schools in that sector should embrace the same curriculum or judge their students' academic progress on the same external exams. Vive la différence. Yet we also see solid reasons for college-oriented middle and high schools—not just charters—to embrace AP (or International Baccalaureate). Internally, AP offers a rigorous curriculum that spans all the core academic subjects, a curriculum that's the same in Tampa and Baton Rouge—and Boston and Palo Alto—as in Brownsville. Properly taught by knowledgeable instructors, it gives kids more than a taste—a brimming plateful—of college-level academic work that assists them to glimpse what lies ahead and to test themselves against a rigorous course of study. Unlike state assessments, which link to idiosyncratic academic standards, typically deploy low-level, machine-readable "bubble tests," and in most places are spotty in their coverage of high school content, AP exams can be studied for—and are worth studying for. The exam is aligned with the course framework and taps into the skills and knowledge that the course seeks to impart. Even better, external exams like AP and IB place student and teacher on the same team: "United, we can triumph over that tough test." It's not teacher judging student and it's not (usually) an exam that teachers scorn or fear.

Externally, AP brings benefits, too, and doubly so for charters. Unlike long-established private and public schools with reputations familiar to college leaders, curricula that haven't changed much in ages, and grading scales that can easily be interpreted by admissions staffers and professors, charter schools are mostly new, their internal norms and standards are not widely understood beyond their own walls, and (though the good schools are striving to change this) they don't benefit from long-lived and mutually trusting relationships with institutions of higher education. AP supplies a universal metric or common currency by which their students and student work (and the school itself) can be judged.

In the quest for college credit during high school, however, the AP program is facing more competition than ever, and schools are considering more alternatives. To that quickening academic marketplace—and other challenges that Advanced Placement faces today—we turn next.

Notes

1. *U.S. News and World Report*, "U.S. News Best High Schools Rankings," accessed November 7, 2018. https://www.usnews.com/education/best-high-schools/rankings-overview.

2. Jay Mathews, "Jay Mathews Challenge Index High School Rankings 2018," accessed February 1, 2019. https://jaymathewschallengeindex.com.

3. Nina Rees, "Charter Schools Stack Up Well," *U.S. News and World Report*, April 27, 2016. https://www.usnews.com/opinion/articles/2016-04-27/charter-schools-boost-the-education-odds-for-disadvantaged-students.

4. Achievement First, "How We Work: In the Classroom," accessed November 7, 2018. https://www.achievementfirst.org/how-we-work/teaching-and-learning/.

5. Success Academy Charter Schools, "Our Approach: High School," accessed November 7, 2018. https://www.successacademies.org/our-approach-high-school/.

6. Jim Allen, "Spokane Public Schools' Pre-AP Offerings Unique in Nation," *Seattle Times*, October 28, 2018. https://www.seattletimes.com/nation-world/spokane-public-schools-pre-ap-offerings-unique-in-nation/.

7. Uncommon Schools, Uncommon Collegiate Charter High School, "Student Life: Academics," accessed November 7, 2018. http://uncommoncollegiate.uncommonschools.org/ucc/student-life/academics?_ga=2.170855776.1786429271.1523301320–806293731.1523301320.

8. Robert Pondiscio, " 'No Excuses' Kids Go to College," *Education Next* 13, no. 2 (2013).

9. KIPP, "Results: How We Measure Success," accessed November 7, 2018. https://www.kipp.org/results/national/#question-3:-are-our-students-progressing-and-achieving-academically.

10. IDEA Public Schools, "Our Story: History," accessed February 1, 2019. https://www.ideapublicschools.org/our-story/history; IDEA Public Schools, "Our Story: Expansion and Growth," accessed February 1, 2019. https://www.ideapublicschools.org/our-story/expansion-growth.

11. Daniela Doyle and Juli Kim, *Built to Grow: How IDEA Public Schools is Expanding to Serve a Million Students* (Chapel Hill, NC: Public Impact, 2019), 5. https://publicimpact.com/wp-content/uploads/2019/02/Built_to_Grow_How_IDEA_Public_Schools_is_Expanding_to_Serve_a_Million_Students.pdf. The demographics will change in Louisiana, which has a small Latino population but many disadvantaged African American youngsters.

12. Torkelson favors AP himself, but cofounder JoAnn Gama noted that IDEA's first high school was an IB school, so it's not an alien concept.

13. Brigham Young University, Continuing Education, "BYU Independent Study: About," accessed November 7, 2018. https://is.byu.edu/about/.

14. William Corbit, "With AP for All, IDEA Lays a Foundation for College-Readiness for Students," *Academics* (blog), *IDEA Public Schools*, December 5, 2018. https://www.ideapublicschools.org/news-events/with-advanced-placement-for-all-idea-lays-a-foundation-for-college-readiness-for-students.

15. Data supplied by IDEA Public Schools.

16. Advancement Via Individual Determination, "Get the Inside Scoop: What AVID Is," accessed November 7, 2018. https://www.avid.org/what-avid-is.

17. Kisella Cardenas, "IDEA Students Receive 80 Extra Days of Math Instruction and 74 Extra Days of Reading Instruction, Stanford University Finds," *Academics* (blog), *IDEA Public Schools*, July 7, 2018. https://www.ideapublicschools.org/news-events/idea-students-receive-80-extra-days-of-math-instruction-and-74-extra-days-of-reading-instruction-stanford-university-finds.

18. Jay Mathews, "A Little School Demands a Lot—More Than Any Other in D.C. Is That Good?" *Washington Post*, May 20, 2018. https://www.washingtonpost.com/.

19. June Kronholz, "High Scores at BASIS Charter Schools," *Education Next* 14, no. 1 (2014).

20. Uplift Education, "The Uplift Model," accessed November 7, 2018. https://www.uplifteducation.org/Page/14520.

21. Uplift Education, "International Baccalaureate," accessed November 7, 2018. https://www.uplifteducation.org/domain/3147.

22. Great Hearts, "Pillars of a Great Hearts Academy," accessed November 7, 2018. http://www.greatheartsamerica.org/great-hearts-life/great-hearts-curriculum/pillars/.

23. Phillips Exeter Academy, "Harkness," accessed November 12, 2018. https://www.exeter.edu/exeter-difference/how-youll-learn.

24. College Board, "CLEP: Home," accessed November 7, 2018. https://clep.collegeboard.org/.

PART III

Challenges and Opportunities

8

Competition Stiffens

For three decades, Advanced Placement was the principal—indeed, almost the exclusive—mechanism for systematically bringing college-level courses into US secondary schools and for giving high school students the opportunity to demonstrate their mastery of such material.

Alternatives were few and episodic, though some had been around for ages. Long before AP began, exceptionally strong students could occasionally accelerate, skip grades, and enter college earlier than their age-mates. Some high schools arranged for youngsters who had exhausted their own offerings to leave for part of the day to travel to nearby campuses to take more advanced courses alongside regular college students. More recently, some schools teamed up with nearby community colleges to offer continuous programs—often career-oriented—that commence in the latter years of high school and continue more or less seamlessly toward a certificate or associate's degree, thereby blurring the distinction between "secondary" and "postsecondary."

Historically, however, such arrangements were localized and ad hoc, the work of particular schools, districts, and colleges, or responses to specialized situations and the pleas of individual students and families. Before the mid-1980s, the only real programmatic alternative to AP was the small International Baccalaureate (IB), which slipped in from Europe in 1971.

The early-access-to-college-courses scene began to change in 1985 when Minnesota lawmakers created a statewide "postsecondary options" program "to promote vigorous academic pursuits and to provide a wider variety of options to high school students by encouraging and enabling secondary pupils to enroll full-time or part-time in nonsectarian courses or programs in eligible post-secondary institutions."[1] This recalled one of the Ford Foundation's experiments three decades earlier—placing high achievers into college when younger than typical freshmen—though, as we saw in chapter 1, that approach was sidelined in the 1950s (due to "social adjustment" problems) in favor of bringing college courses into high schools AP style.

Four years later, Ohio launched a similar program for high school juniors and seniors, and several other jurisdictions soon followed.[2] Then, starting around 2000, many states ramped up their use of "concurrent" or "dual" enrollment options whereby young people could take—and get credit for—college courses while still in high school.[3]

Today, sundry forms of dual credit, dual enrollment, and concurrent enrollment are the principal alternatives to AP as sources of a college-level academic experience for high school students. In this chapter, we look closely at dual credit (DC) in its near-stupefying complexity, with a particular focus on how it has unfolded in Texas, and we touch on several other alternatives to AP. First, however, let's review what's worth looking for.

Key Criteria

If a course, cluster of courses, or program taken by high school students is meant to yield college credit, placement in advanced undergraduate courses, acceleration toward a degree, even an entire associate's degree stapled to one's diploma, several questions should be asked of it:

- Is its content truly college level and is it graded or scored such that it's equivalent to college in rigor?
- How much and in what ways does it actually benefit students who succeed at it?
- How robust is the return on investment for those who put time and money into it?

One should also ask what it displaces in the high school that might possibly yield greater net benefit. Does it consume resources—money, administrator energy, instructional time, classroom use—that could be deployed to tutor students who lag behind, to provide opportunities in the arts or health or civic engagement, or to augment and diversify the school's extracurricular offerings? That question is so situation specific, however, that here we can only flag it. But as we examine DC and other AP alternatives, we seek to shed some light on the first three; in appendix I, we delve deeper into the extant literature that bears on the second and third of them.

Other Pathways

Advanced Placement and dual credit are by far the widest paths to college-level work and possible credit during high school, but they're not alone. The Europe-based International Baccalaureate (IB) program, originally conceived as a way to provide a consistent education for the high school children of international diplomats who frequently moved around the planet, has sought since 1968 to "encourage students across the world to become active, compassionate and lifelong learners who understand that other people, with their differences, can also be right." IB today offers four curriculum programs spanning the elementary, middle, and high school grades.

Most akin to AP is IB's "Diploma Program," which takes place in approved high schools and consists of a suite of IB-designed courses and student projects that are externally reviewed.[4] The IB organization describes it as "a rigorous, academically challenging and balanced program of education designed to prepare students aged sixteen to nineteen for success at university and in life." It spans two years—eleventh and twelfth grades in US schools—and students typically choose six courses from an array of subjects and must fulfill several additional requirements.[5] Participating schools must offer the full package, although students not pursuing the IB Diploma may—as in AP—opt for individual courses. Unlike AP, most IB subjects are available at either a "standard" or a "higher" level, the latter going deeper and consuming more classroom hours. To earn an IB Diploma, students must complete at least three higher-level courses.

IB is truly international, with a presence in at least 150 countries, but its US footprint is small when compared with Advanced Placement. Some 960 American schools offer the IB Diploma and over 153,000 public school students were enrolled in that program in 2015–16, versus the 2.8 million who took at least one AP class that same year (see table A.5 in appendix II). In other words, AP in the United States is about eighteen times the size of IB.[6]

Like AP, the IB program is unevenly distributed across the land. Twenty-three states enroll fewer than a thousand students each in it, while California, Florida, Virginia, and Texas each contain between nine and twenty-two thousand. Participation is often concentrated in a few districts within a state. In 2015–16, for example, 90 percent of Illinois's public school IB Diploma students (about 3,200) were enrolled in the Chicago Public Schools (CPS), which was more than the statewide totals in thirty-six states. Chicago began in 1997 to introduce IB into thirteen ailing high schools (one or two classrooms at a time, not whole-school interventions) and by 2018 it boasted the nation's largest IB operation, with twenty-two high schools offering the Diploma Program and thirty-four elementary schools participating in IB programs aimed at younger pupils.[7] While the Diploma Program proper commences in eleventh grade, Chicago students started pre-IB coursework as freshmen.[8]

Analysts have reported positive results for IB in Chicago. One study showed that those who stuck with the program for four years were 40 percent more likely to attend a four-year college than similar peers, 50 percent more likely to attend a selective college, and significantly likelier to persist through college. But because students self-select into IB, able and motivated youngsters are mostly who's opting for these courses—an issue we take up in appendix I—and 38 percent of those who began Chicago's Diploma Program in ninth grade dropped out before eleventh. Still, recalling that the schools studied were largely made up of minority youngsters, these effects remain striking. Although just 20 percent of Chicago IB students earned the full Diploma by the end of their fourth year (compared with 70 percent nationally and 80 percent internationally), it's probably true that sustained exposure to the program's rigor, content, and strong pedagogy—with or without a Diploma at the end—is associated with greater success thereafter, and a growing body of research supports that claim.

Nor is IB the only alternative to AP and dual credit. Over four hundred schools in thirty-one states (and the District of Columbia) work with UK-based Cambridge Assessment International Education, which boasts a global network of ten thousand schools in 160 countries. Cambridge offers four stages during the K–12 years (closely mirroring the English secondary school sequence), with the "advanced" stage (Advanced International Certificate of Education, or AICE) offered to sixteen- to nineteen-year-olds. Unlike AP or IB, this program is connected to an actual university—Cambridge, with the prestige that entails—and unlike IB (but akin to AP and often DC) it affords schools a menu of courses: 125 of them! Proponents note that it's cheaper than IB, with no candidacy or student registration fees and lower annual school fees. Cambridge is even smaller than IB, however; just 111,000 AICE exams were taken in 407 US schools in 2016–17.[9]

Students (and former students) may also establish credit on entry to college by passing exams developed by the College Level Examination Program (CLEP), which, like AP, is run by the College Board. Unlike AP, however, CLEP exams are not linked to any pre-set course framework or curriculum, making them popular with homeschoolers, some charter schools, and adults seeking a college credential later in life. The exams probe skills and knowledge that may come from any source—independent reading, life experience, internships, online study—and they can be taken anytime. This option is also expanding among younger students who glimpse the possibility of establishing college credit based on experience gained outside the classroom, and it's well-suited to philanthropic ventures such as the Modern States Education Alliance, which orchestrates and subsidizes access to an array of online college courses with the goal of compressing the time and cost of obtaining a degree.[10]

Although the CLEP program is growing in high schools in some locales (such as Louisiana and Florida's Orange County), the College Board positions it chiefly as an option for students in specialized circumstances: when AP is not available; if they are home schooled; or as a chance to take another stab at an exam similar to AP after having already taken an AP exam. For example, a student may want a higher score without waiting another year to retake the exam.[11] They also promote CLEP as a way for dual-credit students to convert that coursework into more nationally transferable credits based on external examinations.[12] Again, though, we're looking at small numbers. Just 17 percent of the roughly 177,000 CLEP examinees in 2015–16 were high schoolers, and just 13 percent were under eighteen, while almost a third were in the military.

The Dual-Credit Surge

In 2010–11, according to the federal National Center for Education Statistics (NCES), two million American public high school students participated in some form of dual credit. Within that number, some 600,000 took part in courses with a "career and technical" orientation while the other 1.4 million opted for courses with an academic focus. The latter number is properly compared with the 1.7 million US public high school pupils who, according to the College Board, sat for at least one Advanced Placement exam in the same year.[13]

As we were completing this book, NCES reported additional dual-credit data, this time the percentage of youngsters completing high school in 2013 who at some point in their education had taken at least one dual-credit course: a very impressive 34 percent.[14]

If we assume that figure can roughly be split into the same two portions as NCES did for dual-credit participation in 2011—smack in the middle of the high school careers of the graduating class of 2013—we can estimate that 24 percent of the class of 2013 had at some point taken at least one dual-credit course of the academic sort, which may be compared with 33 percent of that class that, according to the College Board, took at least one AP exam during their high school years, and the 20 percent of graduates who had earned at least one score of 3 or higher on an AP exam.[15]

Direct comparisons of this kind grow more difficult after 2013. The College Board reliably produces exam-taking data every year, up through (as we write) the high school class of 2018. However, there are absolutely no national dual-credit data after 2015–16, and those come from a different federal source—the Office for Civil Rights (OCR)—which obtains them in a very different (and we think less reliable) fashion than NCES. But analysts have precious few other places to turn for national data or for most state-level dual-credit data, though some jurisdictions—including Texas and Ohio—track this on their own.

Irksome as they are, such data lacunae and discrepancies are more understandable when one considers how blurry is the definition of dual credit, how many forms it takes, and the many different ways—and locations—that it's delivered. Because OCR phrases its dual-enrollment survey question in very general terms, and depends on schools and districts to respond, there's much scope for variation, misunderstanding, and error.

Apologetic that we don't have more reliable data, we can still use OCR to compare participation in—and access to—AP, dual credit, and the International Baccalaureate during 2015–16, depending what state one lives in (see table A.5 in appendix II). We see, for example, that in prosperous coastal states such as Massachusetts, Maryland, and California, AP course enrollment dwarfs dual credit, while in Indiana, Iowa, and Kansas, more students can be found in dual credit.

Growth rates also appear to differ. In Texas, where we benefit from the state's own administrative data over multiple years, we see phenomenal DC expansion: from nearly 18,000 students in 2000 to over 133,000 in 2016. The Lone Star State now contains 11.3 percent of the country's dual-enrolled students compared with 9.6 percent of its eleventh and twelfth graders.[16] Public school AP examinees in Texas, however, numbered over 270,000 (across all grades) in 2016, more than twice the number of dual-credit students— though it was thrice in 2000, indicating that dual credit is gaining on AP even as both programs grow.[17] In Ohio, some 50,000 students took part in dual enrollment in 2015–16, closing in on 57,000 (public) AP exam-takers in the Buckeye State that year.[18]

In some jurisdictions—Indiana and Florida, for example—public school systems are *required* to offer some dual credit. Texas law states that "each school district shall implement a program under which students may earn the equivalent of at least twelve semester credit hours of college credit in high school," though this requirement may be met via online offerings, AP, or IB as well as dual enrollment.[19] In Ohio, young people are advised that "if you are an Ohio student in grades 7–12, you can apply for College Credit Plus admission to any Ohio public or participating private college."[20]

Depending on the state, the high school, and the college, these arrangements take several forms. "Concurrent" enrollment generally means a student takes a college course, typically on a college campus, while still enrolled in high school, but that course ordinarily counts only for college credit and doesn't show up on one's high school transcript. The class may meet during the school day—in which case the high school normally releases the student to attend it—or at another time. But it isn't really part of the K–12 system and is usually paid for by whatever combination of state subsidy and tuition a regular college student would employ, though concurrent-enrollment students don't presently qualify for federal financial aid.[21]

"Dual" enrollment (or credit) courses are different, in that they ordinarily count for both high school *and* college, require some joint programming that involves both institutions, may take place either in the high school or at the college, and are paid for from a combination of K–12 and higher-ed funds (which often means that taxpayers are hit twice).[22]

Dual credit has emerged as a sizable alternative and potential threat to AP, primarily because, from the standpoint of students and their parents, these courses hold great appeal. They look easier and friendlier—and sometimes cheaper—and they also offer a near-certain route to credit at a nearby college. All that's needed is for one's instructor to give one a passing grade in the class, and in these days of grade inflation that's not hard to get.[23] By contrast, the intimidating end-of-year AP exam may or may not yield a score that may or may not be accepted for credit of some kind at the college where one ends up.

DC courses are typically developed by individual colleges and taught either by college faculty—often part-time or "adjunct" instructors—or by the high school's own teachers, provided they satisfy qualifications set by the college and its accrediting body, which generally means holding at least a master's degree in the subject being taught.[24] Although most often conducted within a high school building—NCES puts that portion at 86 percent[25]—these classes usually follow a college schedule. They have a semester- or year-long syllabus (contrasting with the nightly or weekly assignments typical of high school), classes meet twice or thrice a week, and students seeking more contact with the instructor must report for office hours.

For those who take and pass these classes, dual credit holds out the promise of college credit in advance of matriculation. That's the easy part and an obvious and legitimate source of DC's attraction. Policies and practices vary widely, however, regarding how and where that credit may transfer beyond the college that first confers it. Even more convoluted—but akin to AP in this regard—is the matter of exactly how that credit works. Does it count toward one's major, for example? Does it actually replace specific entry-level classes that one must otherwise take, either for "distribution" purposes or in pursuit of a particular major or program? Or is it generic "credit hours" that may apply to a degree or certificate but don't replace anything in particular?[26]

Early College High School

An increasingly popular form of dual credit is the "early college high school" (ECHS) model, which offers a structured program that may comprise a student's entire schedule during all four years of high school and that, if successfully navigated, can result in an associate's degree as well as a high school diploma at the end of those years. That AA (or the credits earned toward it) may also be transferable to a four-year institution en route to a bachelor's degree. In practice, about one-third of ECHS students manage to earn the AA before graduating, but the average graduate exits high school with some thirty-eight college credits in his or her backpack, which is a solid start and a welcome form of acceleration and economizing, particularly considering that most ECHS students come from low-income and/or minority backgrounds.[27]

The ECHS version has been strongly encouraged—and subsidized—by the Gates Foundation and other major funders, and skillfully advanced by the Boston-based Jobs for the Future organization. By 2014, some 280 ECHS programs were operating across the country (up from forty-six just ten years before), with eighty thousand students enrolled.[28] By 2018, Texas alone—a state with about 2,500 high schools—had designated almost two hundred ECHSs, with some districts going for them in a big way. Dallas, for example, operates ECHS programs on twenty-three of its high school campuses in partnership with the Dallas County Community College District.[29]

A variation of the early-college model, this one supported and encouraged by IBM, is usually called P-TECH (Pathways in Technology). It has a

STEM and/or career orientation, and, while it may also yield an associate's degree, it aims more at industry certifications than at transferability to four-year academic programs.[30]

The specific design of a P-TECH or ECHS program can take various forms and come with varying rules, depending on state policies and funding arrangements as well as the terms worked out between high schools and participating colleges. Locations vary, too. The ECHS program may have a dedicated facility where everything happens, or students may spend part of their time—often the first two years—inside a high school building and the remainder on a college campus.[31]

Unlike the structured academic menu of an ECHS, however, by far the most common form of dual credit remains à la carte.[32]

What's the Rush?

Why all the enthusiasm to expand dual credit? Motives are multiple, not entirely harmonious, and not wholly selfless, although in most respects they parallel efforts by educators, policy makers, and philanthropists to widen access to AP (and, in some places, to IB or Cambridge). The push to give students access to college and college-level courses and opportunities to earn credit before leaving high school is intended by its many boosters to address a host of problems that plague American education at the macro-level and individual pupils at the micro-level. These include:

- The boredom and wheel-spinning of many young people, most often seniors, who have completed their high school graduation requirements and are coasting as they wait for their diplomas.
- The desire of advanced students to pursue subjects that interest them in greater depth than their high school offerings allow, combined with the inability of many school systems to supply a rich-enough array of advanced courses, often because the systems (and individual schools within them) lack money, suitable teachers, or sufficient enrollment.
- The benefit to high school pupils, especially those from disadvantaged and "first-generation" families, of previewing what college is like so they're better prepared to surmount the challenges that await within the ivy gates and—it is hoped—to persevere, do well, and complete degrees once they reach those gates.
- The desire of many high school students to get a head start on college, whether to save time and money in an era of soaring costs,

to be spared from dull introductory courses taught in large lecture halls, and/or to deepen and widen their options for course-taking once they matriculate.

- The push by policy makers to elevate academic performance in high schools (and their feeder schools), give a rocket boost to able disadvantaged youngsters, get more of them into and through college—and save some tax dollars by minimizing course duplication and, perhaps, student remediation.
- The appetite of colleges themselves to maximize enrollments and revenues by teaching some students who haven't yet matriculated and—via familiarity and course credit—recruiting more of those students to enroll in their institutions.

The last of those rationales smacks of institutional self-interest on the part of colleges—and it's not the only time in these pages that such motives appear. It's important to note that, after growing rapidly for decades until about 2010, postsecondary enrollments then began to flatten—the post-recession economy was brightening and making more jobs available—and a number of non-elite colleges are "really scraping for students," which makes high school pupils an inviting target, above all for nearby community colleges.[33] (The Community College of Baltimore County, for example, shrank from 72,000 to 62,000 students between 2009 and 2018.) For them, enrolling precollegiate students is a win-win, as they get both an immediate bump in state subsidies (which are usually tied to enrollments and credit hours) and also better odds that these young people will later enter their institutions as regular students. By fall 2010, 15 percent of new takers of community college courses were high school pupils on the "dual" path, and for many such institutions the dual-credit population now accounts for a quarter or more of their enrollment.[34] Recall, however, from chapter 3 that the national high school population has essentially leveled off and will soon shrink a bit.

Setting aside collegiate self-interest, the other explanations for expanding DC offerings and participants appear legitimate from the perspective of students, parents, educators, and policy makers, for many of whom dual credit seems to have near-term advantages over AP or IB. It's almost always easier to get a passing grade from a friendly teacher who shares the classroom with you—and thereby nail college credit—than to pass a tough external exam marked by people who never even see your name. The chance to save time and money in college is an obvious plus, as is early exposure to collegiate expectations and routines. The material studied may also be more interesting and stimulating than what's on offer in standard high school classes.

Advanced Placement brings different advantages. It has built-in quality control, highly regarded national standards, courses attached to transparent and uniform frameworks, scores that are understood throughout higher education, and—though this gets complicated—the credit that it potentially yields may be deployed in any university, including those far across the country, not just at a single nearby institution or within one's home state.

College credit is not, however, all that matters to students navigating the twisted channels of DC, AP, and IB. In most places, such courses carry additional "weighting" on one's grade point average. (So may a school's own "honors" classes.) This typically means that an "A" grade goes into one's GPA calculation as worth five points rather than four, a "B" is worth four rather than three, and so on. In the many situations where GPA and/or class rank matters to students—and admissions offices—those extra points are highly valued. Which also means that, if a DC class and an AP class carry the same weight, but the DC course is thought easier, then alongside the angst-inducing prospect of the AP exam a strategic student may weigh the odds of getting a higher grade from the dual-credit instructor and thus more of those coveted GPA points.

Competition in Texas

The admissions office of any selective college is apt to pay at least some attention to GPA and class rank, but Texas is the paradigmatic example of a place where these things matter hugely. As a way of diversifying entry into its public universities and enhancing opportunity across a vast state with fast-changing demographics, all without running afoul of political and judicial bans on race-based affirmative action, Lone Star lawmakers moved in 1997 to guarantee admission to state universities—including the flagship University of Texas at Austin and the almost-as-exclusive Texas A&M at College Station—to any student who graduates in the top 10 percent of his or her (public) high school class.[35] (Texas has some 300,000 graduates every year.[36])

The pros and cons of such a policy are debatable on many dimensions. What's not arguable is that it has catalyzed an arms race among high school pupils to work their way toward the top of their classes based on GPA calculations. And in today's Texas, it's common knowledge that, to have a chance of nearing that destination within many high schools, one *must* take—and do well in—multiple classes with weighted grades that yield extra heft in the GPA algorithm. That certainly includes AP—but if it's easier to find a dual-credit course and obtain an honors grade from its instructor, why not take the path of less hassle, less homework, and greater immediate payoff?

Which of course gives rise—in Texas as everywhere that dual credit has taken off—to issues of quality control, rigor, and true college equivalency. Controversy surrounds the question of whether dual credit is anything akin to a gold standard—even bronze—when it comes to vouchsafing actual learning and giving young people a lasting boost up the mobility ladder.

The problem is that it's so uneven, with rigor and quality almost entirely in the hands of individual instructors deployed by individual colleges. Some DC purveyors—such as UT/Austin's OnRamps program—adhere to bona fide university standards.[37] (Almost every campus within the sprawling UT system offers its own forms of dual credit—evidence that DC isn't confined to community colleges.[38]) The early-college model is also somewhat more amenable to quality control; at least its architects and operators think comprehensively about what students need, including a coherent curricular sequence, guidance counseling, and other supports. À la carte dual credit, however, in most cases lacks any uniform norms or external review of learning.

That hasn't stopped eager Lone Star lawmakers, many of whom seem to think that, if dual credit can save their constituents money and time in college, everyone should have it. This has led to a "Wild West" atmosphere in which it's pretty easy for young Texans to establish "college readiness" and thus qualify for DC classes that can begin as early as ninth grade. Economist David Troutman, in a major recent study of dual credit (and AP) within the UT system, noted the "tsunami of incoming college credit produced by dual credit programs within Texas." He reports several dimensions—grades, perseverance, and such—on which students entering UT with dual credit fare better than those without (although those with AP credit fare better still), and his study has already been seized on and applied to justify every sort of dual credit across the state, though its data were drawn exclusively from students matriculating at UT campuses.[39]

There's no longer a limit to how many credits young Texans can accumulate in this way, and both two- and four-year institutions may legally deliver DC anywhere in the state, not just in their own territory (though community colleges generally keep it within commuting distance). For Texas's many rural high schools, it may also be cheaper and easier to team up with a reasonably nearby community college and offer DC courses than to pursue AP or IB.[40]

Dual credit has become a sizable part of what many Texas colleges now do—and for many it's now a vital part of their revenue stream. Based on the state's own data, the number of young Texans participating in some form of DC now makes up 10 percent of all higher education enrollments (compared with about 1 percent in 1999). In community colleges, dual-credit students comprise a fifth of overall enrollment (up from 3 percent), and on some campuses it's reached half. Community colleges remain the primary source (93 percent) of DC offerings in Texas, though several student-hungry four-year institutions have also become major players, and other campuses—such as those in the UT system—despite a surfeit of traditional students, engage in dual credit both to do right by qualified high school pupils in their communities and to assist more of their own entrants to save time and money.[41] Texas, it may be recalled, is a place where holding down the cost of college has become something of a political obsession.[42]

As a result, Texas today has more DC students than any other state, and the number is rising fast. Yet it's struggling to balance that expansion with concerns about consistency and quality across its many providers and instructors. Commissioner of Higher Education Raymund Paredes estimated in January 2018 that some 40,000 of the high school students then enrolled in dual credit—more than a quarter of the 150,000 participating statewide—had not met Texas's college-readiness standards. Testifying before a legislative committee two years earlier, he cautioned:

> Dual credit is not going to be the magic bullet in helping us achieve our education goals. We have a very limited pool of college-ready students in our high schools. If we don't make sure these courses are sufficiently rigorous what will inevitably happen is universities will not accept these dual credit courses.[43]

The National Alliance of Concurrent Enrollment Partnerships is doing its best to establish quality standards for DC programs and is keen to accredit programs that comply with those standards. As of 2018, 107 programs in twenty-two states were on that list—but none was yet to be found in the Lone Star State.[44]

Nothing is simple in the vast and varied Republic of Texas—and how it handles dual credit in the years ahead will, at minimum, be instructive for forty-nine other states. We can only hope that it doesn't lead to disappointment along the way for a number of young Texans even as it brightens the future for others.

Back to the Big Questions

IS IT REALLY COLLEGE LEVEL?

Although some Advanced Placement courses are undeniably harder than others, the AP program has striven with fair success over the years to establish and adhere to uniform standards for judging student learning via end-of-year exams that are uniform everywhere, and also to ensure—via elaborate standard-setting sessions, scoring procedures, and psychometric equating from year to year—that those who score 3 or better on the exams have in fact demonstrated mastery of a college-equivalent course. (We revisit this in the next chapter.)

Dual credit, however, has no fixed standard. It's up to the college that sponsors the course to determine its content and say what criteria will be employed in evaluating student mastery of that content and—as with college courses generally—that's all pretty much in the instructor's hands. The assertion that college-level content has been satisfactorily mastered rests on that person's word—and on a course grade that signifies less and less in an era of rampant grade inflation and easy "credit recovery."[45] Although state rules usually stipulate that young people must demonstrate "college readiness" before enrolling in dual-credit classes, that threshold also turns out to be uneven, often low, and loosely enforced. On the whole, it seems that the push—by colleges, politicians, philanthropists, advocates, parents, and often by high schools themselves—to get more kids into dual-credit courses is more forceful than the push to gauge bona fide college readiness and monitor classroom rigor.

DOES IT TRULY BENEFIT STUDENTS?

Benefit may take many forms, including the experience of successfully wrestling with advanced content before reaching college; the enhancement of one's admissions prospects; the establishment of credit upon arrival on campus; and stronger odds that one will successfully complete college and go on to further achievements, ideally including a trajectory of upward mobility for one's self and one's children.

Many of these benefits are nebulous and long term. Those that are easiest to measure in the here and now are the kind that occur during college—and there we find any number of studies that—regrettably—yield no clear bottom line. Generally, the research on dual credit, as on AP, has been positive, showing that participants notch higher levels of high school graduation, college enrollment and persistence, stronger college GPAs, and enhanced completion rates. But did dual credit (or AP) *cause* that to happen or was it a correlate of something that likely would have happened anyway, considering who the participants are? This is what analysts fretfully term a "selection effect" and, in the absence of well-designed experiments with proper control groups, it's not possible to be sure whether there's a causal connection between an "intervention" and an "outcome" associated with that intervention. Experiments in this realm are scarce, however, mostly confined so far to the limited domain of early college high schools (and there, as we see in appendix I, the effects of participating are generally positive).

Also bedeviling definitive conclusions regarding the impact and outcomes of dual credit are its sheer variety of options and formats, the variation in access and participation rates, and the diversity of policies, practices, and funding arrangements. Equitable access is a particularly sensitive issue, as the recent NCES data compilation makes clear that black and Hispanic high school students are significantly less likely to participate in dual credit than white and Asian students. In similar fashion, just 26 percent of the daughters and sons of parents with less than a high school education themselves took part in dual credit, compared with 42 percent of the progeny of those with college degrees.[46] Do such discrepancies arise because schools attended by disadvantaged youngsters are less likely to make this opportunity available? Because the youngsters themselves are ill-prepared to take advantage of it, or are deterred from even trying it? Probably all of the above.

The benefit to students may also depend in part on their own traits. A youngster who isn't intellectually ready for college-level work during eleventh or twelfth grade—assuming he or she can access dual-credit classes in the first place—surely gains less from the experience than one who is well prepared to exploit this opportunity for advanced learning. Yet one tantalizing College Board study, comparing the collegiate boosts associated with AP versus dual credit, divided students into quartiles based on their SAT scores. Analysts found that, for those in the lowest quartile, having taken AP in high school was associated with significantly stronger performance in college than having taken dual credit, whereas the differences in college bounce were much smaller among higher-ability students.[47]

HOW ROBUST IS THE "RETURN ON INVESTMENT"?

AP and DC both cost money, as does IB, though how much and who pays are quite different. With AP, the district incurs costs in getting teachers properly trained and kept up to speed on course content and pedagogy, and in providing students with suitable textbooks, labs, and IT. The College Board says start-up costs for a new AP course in a high school range from $3,200 for English to twice that for science courses.[48] A 2009 study of three school districts, however, by Marguerite Roza (now at Georgetown), found that spending on AP courses in two districts significantly outpaced outlays on regular and remedial courses, leading to the estimate that a district's average per-pupil spending in its high schools could be as much as $1,700 annually for an AP course, compared with about $700 for a regular course. That could mean that adding a thousand kids to the district's AP rolls may add a million dollars to its budget—or draw similar resources from elsewhere. Roza also found that AP teachers—teacher salaries being a major driver of class expenditures—are generally more senior and earn almost $17,000 more than teachers of remedial courses. And they taught far fewer students.[49]

A school also faces opportunity costs if deploying teachers, labs, and other resources for AP means that other instructional needs go unmet. And someone—state, school, parents, or some combination—must pay exam fees that are nearing $100 a pop, plus ancillary fees associated with getting scores reported. AP does not, however, cost colleges anything, except lost revenue when the credit they confer on successful exam-takers results in reduced tuition payments or state subsidies.[50]

The International Baccalaureate is relatively expensive, as participating schools must pay various fees to the IB program and students (or their schools) also face substantial charges for having materials reviewed and exams scored.[51] IB schools must also pay nearly $10,000 annually for two to three years before they are even authorized to offer the Diploma Program.[52] And schools offering IB incur other operating expenses akin to those of AP.

Dual credit poses different kinds of cost considerations. In many states, including Texas, the taxpayer may pay twice—in part or in full—because public funds usually flow both to the K–12 district enrolling the student (generally based on pupil head count) and also to the public college that's responsible for the DC class, since students in that class qualify for the credit-hour tally that's normally a key part of the formula by which the college is funded. There are multiple examples in active DC states where such students generate a quarter of the college's revenue.[53]

A careful study of the taxpayer-borne costs of dual credit in three states (Georgia, Florida, Ohio), this one also undertaken by Marguerite Roza (with Caitlin Brooks), found that dual enrollment "triggered some double funding" in all three jurisdictions and that, in two of them, the net cost to the public purse of having these credits acquired during high school was greater than if students deferred such courses until they actually matriculated.[54] That finding doesn't cancel the possible benefit of accelerated study for the students themselves; it simply says that taxpayers are making a greater investment in the education of those students.

While some colleges waive for DC pupils the tuition and fees that they charge their regular students, in many cases either the district or the family must cover those costs as well.[55] Another cost associated with DC (but not AP or IB) is job loss by high school instructors when growing numbers of their pupils receive more of their education from people employed by colleges. As dual credit expands, the major US teacher unions are growing restive over this.[56]

How all this works out in terms of return on investment depends, of course, on how that return is calculated, over what period of time, and for whom. Optimally, an ECHS student completes high school with an associate's degree as well as a diploma, and either goes into the world prepared for gainful employment or saves as much as two years in time and tuition (and "banked" financial aid) while pursuing a bachelor's degree and perhaps beyond. In other cases, however, students emerge with a few credits that turn out to have limited applicability to their intended course of study—and may not even be able to circumvent remedial courses after matriculating.

Moreover, because the credit that a student gets may initially be usable only at the institution that confers it, this can constrain the student's postsecondary opportunities even as it enhances them, and can lead to "undermatching" of strong young scholars who find themselves channeled into the nearby community college instead of even applying to institutions that might do them more good. This problem diminishes if the dual credit is widely transferable, including to four-year institutions, but its transferability is typically limited to public colleges within the same state—and credit transfer remains a challenge throughout higher education.[57]

Dual credit is the only source of college-level work during high school that comes close to rivaling—and may in fact already equal—AP in scale and penetration, and it's inevitably a source of concern for AP proponents. They're not panicked, as AP also keeps extending its reach and raising its participation levels. The larger point, however, from a public-interest perspective, is that absent better mechanisms for ensuring student readiness and quality control, and without some check on self-interest among enrollment-hungry colleges, dual credit could turn out to disappoint more than a few of those who think they'll get ahead by engaging in it. But enrolling in AP or IB can ultimately yield disappointment, too, if no useful credit follows, if the class proves unmanageably difficult (or the instruction inadequate), or if the hard work that it demands squeezes out other opportunities.

Capacity Gaps

Just as the mandated, top-down expansion of AP has raised capacity issues at the high school level, so too has the push to spread DC across entire districts and states. A 2016 episode in Indiana illustrates the challenge of finding enough qualified instructors.[58] Because the Hoosier State requires its public high schools to offer dual-credit classes, some three thousand individuals teach them. In an effort to ensure that those instructors have adequate command of the subjects that they're teaching, Indiana's main college-accrediting body—the Higher Learning Commission, formerly known as the North Central Association of Colleges and Schools—ruled in 2015 that they must possess master's degrees or the equivalent in those subjects.

A master's degree seems a low bar for someone teaching a college course, but this requirement caused palpitations in Indiana high schools and the colleges whose courses they were handling. How, the schools wondered, could they possibly make these opportunities available to their students— and comply with the law that said they must—if their teachers couldn't (or didn't want to) obtain a master's degree? Quoth the head of the Indiana Association of School Principals: "Every—literally every—principal I've talked to, and in some cases superintendent, has said we'll have a very, very limited amount of teachers able to teach dual credit."[59]

By December 2016, Indiana had persuaded its accreditor to grant a reprieve. Hoosier teachers now have until 2022 to comply with the master's-degree requirement. One wonders how many of them will retire by then— and how many more reprieves and extensions may follow. Meanwhile, a nontrivial number of young Hoosiers will be earning college credit based on course grades from high school teachers who don't possess advanced degrees in the subjects that they teach.

Comparing the Options

Both AP and DC are employed (by students, parents, educators, policy makers, schools, colleges) for so many different purposes that there's no single metric on which to compare them. Those who value academic rigor and depth, as we do, will tend to favor Advanced Placement, as will those—again includ-ing ourselves—who see the country (and particularly its neediest students) benefiting from a high-quality national high school curriculum and from uniform standards by which to gauge student learning in relation to that cur-riculum. But we also acknowledge the obvious allure of dual credit as a policy-amenable way to give more young people—again, especially, those from disadvantaged backgrounds—a preview of college, a chance to enter the culture and mind-set of the college-bound, and the opportunity to test themselves as possible college students. Nor is there any doubt that credit earned in this way can accelerate and reduce the cost of college degrees while fending off ennui and wheel-spinning in the final years of high school. We also observe that with a flat (or shrinking) national high school population in coming years, it's likely that competition between proponents of both DC and AP will only intensify and probably get nastier, especially as enrollment-strapped colleges advance further into the domain of high schools (with inevitable pushback from the teachers' unions).

But the interaction between AP and DC is not a zero-sum game. Society benefits from kids having options by which to enrich, enliven, and advance their learning. We're cheered and encouraged by the young people we met in high schools in several states who now avail themselves of two or three or more of these options. They and their counselors and parents assemble courses like a jigsaw puzzle, with different ones serving different purposes in their school, on their transcript, in their daily schedules, in their pursuit of college admissions, and beyond. We also met some who chose courses more because of favorite teachers or classmates and paid scant attention to the auspices under which the courses were offered. At the same time, we encountered principals, superintendents, and state officials who viewed—and sometimes favored—AP and DC as alternate paths for different student populations, typically with Advanced Placement (and IB) associated with better-resourced youngsters headed to competitive, four-year colleges, often distant from home, while seeing dual credit as suited to first-generation stu-dents who don't have a lot of sophisticated support at home, need encour-agement and help to get to (and succeed in) college, and are apt to make their way toward open-access campuses within driving distance of where they live.

Although that kind of distinction runs the risk of segmenting—indeed, tracking—the student population, it's not crazy to view the programs in that way, so long as one also bears in mind the challenges of equitable access associated with both programs. There will—and should—be ample options, exceptions, and overlaps, as AP is employed to lift the horizon and widen the opportunities for more young people from every kind of background, and as dual credit offers a varied and flexible supply of curricular additions and accelerants for kids from more privileged circumstances as well as sizable numbers of poor and minority youngsters. We would hate to see these two approaches turn into mutually exclusive paths for different kinds of students. But it's also folly to see them as wholly interchangeable.

Notes

1. Joe Nathan, Laura Accomando, and Debra Hare Fitzpatrick, *Stretching Minds and Resources: 20 Years of Post-Secondary Enrollment Options in Minnesota* (Minneapolis: Hubert H. Humphrey Institute of Public Affairs, University of Minnesota, 2005), 11. http://centerforschoolchange.org /wp-content/uploads/2012/09/stretching.pdf.

2. Jeffrey M. Jordan and Wendy Cantrell, *Post-Secondary Enrollment Options Program for Ohio High School Students* (Columbus: Ohio Department of Education, 2009). http://www.wcsoh.org /docs/PS_EOpts%5B1%5D.pdf.

3. Nancy Hoffman and Amy Robins, *Head Start on College: Dual Enrollment Strategies in New England 2004–2005* (Washington, DC: Jobs for the Future, 2005). https://jfforg-prod-prime.s3 .amazonaws.com/media/documents/HeadStartOnCollege.pdf.

4. *International Baccalaureate Diploma Programme: Standard Level and Higher Courses* (Geneva: International Baccalaureate Organization, 2015). https://www.ibo.org/globalassets/publications /recognition/slhl-brief-en.pdf.

5. *General Regulations: Diploma Programme* (Geneva: International Baccalaureate Organization, 2014). https://www.ibo.org/globalassets/publications/become-an-ib-school/dp-general -regulations-en.pdf.

6. IB and AP course enrollment data here come from the OCR dataset from 2015–16, derived from reports by districts in fifty states (and the District of Columbia). US Department of Education, Office for Civil Rights, "Civil Rights Data Collection," accessed November 7, 2018. https:// ocrdata.ed.gov/. Data in the text are numbers of students reported to be enrolled in at least one AP course. For phrasing of the questions that yielded these totals, see *2015–16 Civil Rights Data Collection: School Form* (Washington, DC: US Department of Education, Office for Civil Rights, 2016). https://www2.ed.gov/.

7. Chicago Public Schools, "CPS Stats and Facts," accessed November 7, 2018. https://cps.edu /About_CPS/At-a-glance/Pages/Stats_and_facts.aspx; Vanessa Coca and others, *Working to My Potential: Experiences of CPS Students in the International Baccalaureate Diploma Programme* (Chicago: University of Chicago, Consortium on Chicago School Research, 2012), 3. https://files.eric .ed.gov/fulltext/ED532512.pdf; David Steiner and Ashley Berner, *Chicago's Use of the International Baccalaureate: An Education Success Story That Didn't Travel* (Baltimore: Johns Hopkins School of Education, Institute for Education Policy, 2015). http://edpolicy.education.jhu.edu/wp-content /uploads/2015/10/ChicagobaccalaureatemastheadFINAL.pdf.

8. Coca et al., *Working to My Potential*, 8.

9. Stephen Sawchuk, "In Age of High Tech, Old-School Cambridge Curriculum Makes Unlikely Gains," *Education Week*, February 21, 2018. https://www.edweek.org/ew/articles/2018/02/21/in -age-of-high-tech-old-school-cambridge.html.

10. Modern States Education Alliance, "About: Who We Are," Accessed February 5, 2019. https://modernstates.org/about-us/who-we-are/.

11. Kitty Porterfield, "Online Program Offers Easy, Cheap Way to 'Earn College Credit for What You Already Know,'" *College Fix*, July 2, 2018. https://www.thecollegefix.com/online-program -offers-easy-cheap-way-to-earn-college-credit-for-what-you-already-know/; Carol McCall, "Loui-siana Should Celebrate Our Progress in Education," *Nola.com*, November 8, 2017. https://www.nola .com/opinions/index.ssf/2017/11/louisiana_education_progress.html; *Save Time and Money with CLEP Exams* (New York: College Board, 2018). https://clep.collegeboard.org/pdf/clep-military -brochure.pdf. College Board, "CLEP: Student Advising," accessed November 7, 2018. https://clep .collegeboard.org/develop-your-clep-program/inform-students/student-advising.

12. Authors' correspondence with Trevor Packer of the College Board.

13. Nina Thomas, Stephanie Marken, Lucinda Gray, and Laurie Lewis, *Dual Credit and Exam-Based Courses in U.S. Public High Schools: 2010–11 (NCES 2013–001)* (Washington, DC: US Department of Education, National Center for Education Statistics, 2013). https://nces.ed .gov/pubs2013/2013001.pdf; College Board, "AP-Archived Data 2011," accessed February 8, 2019. https://research.collegeboard.org/programs/ap/data/archived/2011.

14. *Dual Enrollment: Participation and Characteristics (NCES 2019–176)* (Washington, DC: US Department of Education, National Center for Education Statistics, 2019). This report is based on data from the High School Longitudinal Study of 2009 (HSLS:09), a nationally representative study of more than 23,000 young people who entered as ninth graders in 2009. https://nces.ed .gov/pubs2019/2019176.pdf.

15. Because the NCES survey's question on dual credit (for the Class of 2013) was broad and did not distinguish between academic or CTE focused dual credit courses, we assume the ratio of dual credit participation in 2013 was similar to that reported in the NCES 2010–11 survey (70:30 in favor of courses with an academic focus). The AP comparison comes from *The 10th Annual AP Report to the Nation* (New York: College Board, 2014), 40–41. http://media.collegeboard.com /digitalServices/pdf/ap/rtn/10th-annual/10th-annual-ap-report-to-the-nation-single-page.pdf.

16. US Department of Education, Office for Civil Rights, "Civil Rights Data Collection"; Trey Miller and others, *Dual Credit Education in Texas: Interim Report* (Santa Monica, CA: RAND, 2017). https://www.rand.org/content/dam/rand/pubs/research_reports/RR2000/RR2043/RAND _RR2043.pdf. The share of overall eleventh and twelfth graders comes from College Board, "AP-Archived Data 2016," accessed February 8, 2019. https://research.collegeboard.org/programs/ap /data/archived/ap-2016.

17. Note that the AP figure for Texas shown in table A.5 represents class enrollment as reported by OCR. The number in the text is the number of public school students to take at least one AP exam that year as reported by the College Board.

18. The Ohio Department of Higher Education estimated 54,000 dual-enrollment students in 2015–16. *College Credit Plus: Overview of Year One 2015–16* (Columbus: Ohio Department of Higher Education, 2016). https://www.ohiohighered.org/sites/ohiohighered.org/files/uploads/CCP/CCP _overview_2016_11032016.pdf.

19. *Dual Credit: Frequently Asked Questions* (Austin: Texas Education Agency, 2011). https:// www.gpisd.org/cms/lib01/TX01001872/Centricity/Domain/5469/TEA_Dual_Credit_FAQ.pdf.

20. Ohio Department of Higher Education, "College Credit Plus: Frequently Asked Questions," accessed November 7, 2018. https://www.ohiohighered.org/ccp/faqs.

21. Such aid—Pell grants, subsidized loans, and such—may not be used for college courses taken by students who are still enrolled in K–12 schools, although the US Department of Education is running an experiment for up to 10,000 dual-credit students, meant to determine whether earlier access to federal aid boosts their college-going and college-completion rates. See *Higher Education: Policy Platform* (Iowa City, IA: ACT, 2018), 11. https://www.act.org/content/dam/act/unsecured /documents/pdfs/Policy-Platform-Higher-Ed-2018.pdf; "Fact Sheet: Department of Education Launches Experiment to Provide Federal Pell Grant Funds to High School Students Taking College

Courses for Credit," press release, US Department of Education, October 30, 2015. https://www
.ed.gov/news/press-releases/fact-sheet-department-education-launches-experiment-provide
-federal-pell-grant-funds-high-school-students-taking-college-courses-credit.

22. Education Commission of the States, "50-State Comparison: Dual/Concurrent Enrollment
Policies," March 25, 2016. http://ecs.force.com/mbdata/MBQuestRTL?Rep=DE1404.

23. As we discuss further on, some colleges employ more systematic and seemingly rigorous grading practices, occasionally even using AP exam results to demonstrate satisfactory
coursework.

24. Although many high school teachers hold master's degrees, those are often in education
rather than the academic discipline being taught. Such credentials rarely satisfy the accreditation
rules.

25. *Dual Enrollment: Participation and Characteristics*. Among the roughly one-third of 2013
graduates who had taken any dual credit while in high school, 80 percent reported doing so within
their own school, 8 percent in another high school, 17 percent on a college campus, and 6 percent
online. (Respondents could designate more than one venue.)

26. Catherine Gewertz, "Are Dual-Enrollment Programs Overpromising?" *Education Week*,
September 6, 2016. https://www.edweek.org/ew/articles/2016/09/07/are-dual-enrollment
-programs-overpromising.html.

27. Nancy Hoffman, "Early College Models Morph, but Keep Their Edge," *Point of View* (blog),
Jobs for the Future, March 16, 2015. https://www.jff.org/points-of-view/early-college-models-morph
-keep-their-edge/.

28. *The Early College High School Initiative at a Glance* (Boston: Jobs for the Future, 2001).
https://www2.ed.gov/about/offices/list/ovae/pi/hs/04summit/b_cenhancing_jv.pdf; Jobs for
the Future, "Early College," accessed November 7, 2018. https://www.jff.org/what-we-do/impact
-stories/early-college/.

29. Gene Davis, "TEA Announces Early College High School Designations for 23 Dallas ISD
Campuses," *The Hub* (blog), *Dallas ISD*, April 24, 2017. https://thehub.dallasisd.org/2017/04/24
/tea-announces-early-college-high-school-designations-for-23-dallas-isd-campuses/.

30. Abby Ellin, "A High School Education All in One," *New York Times*, November 1, 2018.
https://www.nytimes.com/2018/11/01/education/learning/a-high-school-education-and-college
-degree-all-in-one.html; Maryland State Department of Education, "Pathways in Technology
Early College High School (P-TECH) Program," accessed November 7, 2018. http://www
.marylandpublicschools.org/programs/Pages/ptech/index.aspx.

31. For more on the distinction between ECHS and generic dual credit in the Ohio context,
see Geoff Zimmerman, "Why Early College High Schools Provide an Important Pathway," *Ohio
Gadfly Daily* (blog), *Thomas B. Fordham Institute*, September 24, 2018. https://edexcellence.net
/articles/why-early-college-high-schools-provide-an-important-pathway.

32. ECHS may also offer some choice among courses, depending on a school's size and its
arrangement with the partner college. See, for example, *Application for ECHS Designation Benchmark 4: Curriculum and Support 2017–2018; South Grand Prairie Early College High School* (Austin:
Texas Education Agency, 2018). https://www.gpisd.org/; and Bard High School Early College
Cleveland, "Overview," accessed November 7, 2018. http://bhsec.bard.edu/cleveland/academics/.

33. Jon Marcus, "Panicked Universities in Search of Students Are Adding Thousands of New
Majors," *Washington Post*, August 9, 2018. https://www.washingtonpost.com/news/grade-point
/wp/2018/08/09/lots-of-new-college-majors/?utm_term=.31d7c312661b.

34. John Fink, Davis Jenkins, and Takeshi Yanagiura, *What Happens to Students Who Take
Community College "Dual Enrollment" Courses in High School?* (New York: Community College
Research Center, Teachers College, Columbia University, 2017), 1. https://ccrc.tc.columbia.edu
/media/k2/attachments/what-happens-community-college-dual-enrollment-students.pdf.

35. After many disputes and some modifications, UT Austin is required to admit no more than 75 percent of its entering class via high school class rank—and the crush of numbers now means that one must be in the top 6 percent to traverse that entry path onto the flagship campus.

36. Data on public high school graduates in Texas are available at Texas Education Agency, "Accountability Research: Completion, Graduation, and Dropouts," accessed November 7, 2018. https://tea.texas.gov/acctres/dropcomp_index.html.

37. University of Texas at Austin, OnRamps, "Experience College before College," accessed November 7, 2018. https://onramps.utexas.edu/.

38. David R. Troutman and others, *The University of Texas System Dual Credit Study: Dual Credit and Success in College* (Austin: University of Texas System, 2018). https://www.utsystem.edu/sites/default/files/documents/ut-system-reports/2018/dual-credit-and-success-college/utsystem-dualcreditstudy.pdf.

39. Steve Taylor, "UT System Study Vindicates STC's Pioneering Work with Dual Credit," *Rio Grande Guardian*, August 12, 2018. https://riograndeguardian.com/ut-system-study-vindicates-stcs-pioneering-work-with-dual-credit/; "UT System Study Delves into Impact of Dual Credit Courses on Student Success in College," press release, University of Texas System, August 1, 2018. https://www.utsystem.edu/news/2018/08/01/ut-system-study-delves-impact-dual-credit-courses-student-success-college. We discuss the important findings from this study in appendix I.

40. Miller et al., *Dual Credit Education in Texas*, 39, 40.

41. Angelo State University, "Angelo State Dual Credit Programs," accessed November 8, 2018. https://www.angelo.edu/dept/dual_credit/; and the University of Texas of the Permian Basin, "UTPB Dual Credit/Early College High School Program," accessed November 8, 2018. https://www.utpb.edu/academics/dual-credit/index.

42. Lauren McGaughy, "Key Senator Pitches Four-Year Tuition Freeze at Texas Public Colleges," *Dallas News*, January 19, 2017. https://www.dallasnews.com/news/higher-education/2017/01/19/key-senator-pitches-four-year-freeze-texas-college-tuition; "Perry Pushing Tuition Freeze, $10,000 Degrees," *Rio Grande Guardian*, October 2, 2012. https://www.statesman.com/news/20121002/perry-pushing-tuition-freeze-10000-degrees.

43. Ralph K. M. Haurwitz, "Texas Higher Education Chief Raises Concern about Dual-Credit Courses," *Austin-American Statesman*, January 11, 2018. https://www.statesman.com/NEWS/20180111/Texas-higher-education-chief-raises-concern-about-dual-credit-courses; Steve Taylor, "Paredes: Dual Credit Is Not a Magic Bullet for Education in Texas," *Rio Grande Guardian*, May 16, 2017. https://riograndeguardian.com/paredes-dual-credit-is-not-a-magic-bullet-for-education-in-texas/.

44. National Alliance of Concurrent Enrollment Partnerships, "About NACEP," accessed November 8, 2018. http://www.nacep.org/.

45. Michael Hurwitz and Jason Lee, "Grade Inflation and the Role of Standardized Testing," in *Measuring Success: Testing, Grades, and the Future of College Admissions*, ed. Jack Buckley, Lynn Letukas, and Ben Wildavsky (Baltimore: Johns Hopkins University Press, 2018).

46. *Dual Enrollment: Participation and Characteristics*.

47. Jeffrey N. Wyatt, Brian F. Patterson, and Tony F. Di Giacomo, *A Comparison of the College Outcomes of AP and Dual Enrollment Students* (New York: College Board, 2015).

48. College Board, "AP Central: Consider the Costs," accessed November 8, 2018. https://apcentral.collegeboard.org/about-ap/start-grow-ap/start-ap/how-your-school-can-offer-ap/consider-costs.

49. Marguerite Roza, "Breaking Down School Budgets," *Education Next* 9, no. 3 (2009).

50. Students and families may incur other costs if schools make them purchase textbooks, if they obtain supplemental materials on their own, and if they sign up for private exam coaching. They may also face opportunity costs if the AP homework burden keeps them from doing other things.

51. International Baccalaureate Organization, "Assessment Fees and Services," accessed November 8, 2018. https://www.ibo.org/become-an-ib-school/fees-and-services/assessment-fees-and -services/.

52. International Baccalaureate Organization, "Fees for Candidate Schools," accessed November 8, 2018. https://www.ibo.org/become-an-ib-school/fees-and-services/fees-for-candidate -schools/.

53. Ashley A. Smith, "College Courses in High School," *Inside Higher Ed*, November 29, 2016. https://www.insidehighered.com/news/2016/11/29/dual-enrollment-rise-texas-community -colleges.

54. Marguerite Roza and Caitlin Brooks, *College Credit in High School: Doing the Math on Costs* (Washington, DC: Georgetown University, Edunomics Lab, 2017), 1. http://edunomicslab.org/wp -content/uploads/2017/11/Dual-Enrollment-V2.pdf.

55. "Fact Sheet: Expanding College Access through the Dual Enrollment Pell Experiment," press release, US Department of Education, May 16, 2016. https://www.ed.gov/news/press-releases /fact-sheet-expanding-college-access-through-dual-enrollment-pell-experiment.

56. Many colleges also have unionized faculties—which are presumably delighted with the additional work, particularly in light of dwindling numbers of traditional students.

57. Alexandra W. Logue, *Pathways to Reform: Credits and Conflict at the City University of New York* (Princeton, NJ: Princeton University Press, 2017). Logue's fine book details vividly her personal experience with the City University of New York's Pathways program, which was plagued with challenges of credit transferability among its nineteen constituent colleges.

58. Shaina Cavazos, "Dual Credit Classes Are Safe for Now: Teachers Have Five Years to Get New Training," *Chalkbeat Indiana*, December 21, 2016. https://www.chalkbeat.org/posts/in/2016 /12/21/dual-credit-classes-are-safe-for-now-teachers-have-5-years-to-get-new-training/.

59. Shaina Cavazos, "Educators Warn Dual Credit Courses Could Dry Up after Rule Change for Teachers," *Chalkbeat Indiana*, October 1, 2015. https://www.chalkbeat.org/posts/in/2015/10 /01/educators-warn-dual-credit-courses-could-dry-up-after-rule-change-for-teachers/.

9

Does Platinum Bend?
Standards under Stress

Perhaps the greatest asset of the Advanced Placement program over nearly seven decades has been its capacity to set and maintain lofty academic standards for high school students and to sustain those standards during times when many forces push to relax them. That's an extraordinary accomplishment, considering all that's happened in American education during this period.

Academic standards of various kinds have become a big deal, a growth industry, and an endless source of controversy, especially when accompanied—as they usually are—by student tests. Many thoughtful educators and policy makers, ourselves included, believe that higher expectations are essential for higher achievement, although not sufficient unto themselves.[1] That belief is what motivated Henry Gradillas and Jaime Escalante to embrace AP for their low-income Latino students in the 1980s and led to the much-noted Garfield High School success story (see chapter 2). Because it's meant to equal college-level curricula and instruction, AP sets higher expectations than do conventional high school courses. It's widely recognized, deeply rooted, broadly understood, and not particularly controversial, despite the fact that it's a form of national curriculum.[2] It's entirely private, done by educators and nonprofits, hence not a government thing, even when encouraged and subsidized by localities, states, and sometimes even Uncle Sam.

AP's nongovernmental character is rare in the world of education standards, at least since 1989. That was the year—half a decade after the nation was declared "at risk"—that state governors and President George H. W. Bush convened in Charlottesville, Virginia, and emerged from their "summit" with an ambitious set of national education goals for the year 2000.[3] This gave rise to an important if obvious question: If (as Goal 3 stated), "by the year 2000, all students will leave grades four, eight, and twelve having demonstrated competency over challenging subject matter including English, mathematics, science, foreign languages, civics and government, economics, arts, history, and geography," who was to specify what is "challenging subject matter" and who would define and gauge students' progress toward "competency?"[4]

In response, Congress created the National Council on Education Standards and Testing to "explore the desirability and feasibility of establishing national education standards and a method to assess their attainment" and a National Education Goals Panel to monitor and report on how the country was doing in pursuit of the summit targets.[5] In 1994, the Clinton administration and Congress joined to pass both the "Goals 2000: Educate America Act" and the "Improving America's Schools Act," which required states to set their own K–12 academic standards in reading and math and devise suitable assessments of student performance against those standards, giving teeth to these requirements by making dollars from the big federal Title I program contingent on states' compliance.[6] Washington's pincers tightened further in 2002 when, at the behest of President George W. Bush, Congress passed the "No Child Left Behind Act," which refined the mandates for standards and assessments and added a heavy dose of accountability whereby schools and districts that did not meet their state's standards were subject to various interventions.

Many complications, modifications, and pushbacks followed, and the situation grew even more fraught as political divisions deepened during the Obama era, the more so after 2010 when the governors and state education chiefs promulgated the "Common Core" academic standards for English and math, and Washington added strong incentives for states to adopt those standards and participate in multistate tests. Although the pincers loosened with 2015's "Every Student Succeeds Act," the entire quarter-century sequence left many—teachers, parents, state and local officials, conservatives, and more than a few liberals—hostile both to governmental micromanagement of schooling and, especially, to anything that smacked of government-prescribed standards, curricula, and tests. The only thing worse, in the view of such critics, were standards, curricula, and tests that bore the adjective "national."

With just a few exceptions and caveats, the Advanced Placement program has been immune to this suspicion, rancor, and resistance—truly remarkable, considering that it's national and that it consists of standards, curriculum frameworks, and exams.

The Woes—and Lows—of Testing

Academic standards can be a maze and a distraction, the more so when they—and the tests associated with them—rain down from all directions. What with state assessments, district-wide tests, formative and summative tests, teacher-created tests, college-entrance tests, placement tests, the National Assessment, the multi-nation Programme for International Student Assessment (PISA) and Trends in International Mathematics and Science Study (TIMSS) programs and more, all of them incorporating some sort of explicit or implicit standards, grading scales, and reporting systems; confusion and suspicion—if not outright fear—afflict many educators, and it's no surprise that anti-testing and "opt out" movements have spread among parents.

Although many of these assessments are intended to ensure educational rigor and to hold schools—and sometimes students and teachers—accountable for achievement gains, there are ample ways to feign rigor while ensuring that test results don't cause undue stress or lead to politically troublesome levels of failure. Mostly, this means setting respectable standards yet making it relatively easy to pass the tests based on them.

The psychometrics are too complex to unpack here, but we can supply a few hints. Test questions can be made easy—concentrating on the simpler intellectual expectations within the standards and giving short shrift to the complicated stuff; the questions can be solid but passing scores can be set low; or the cut scores may be robust but other, less punishing, bits of the accountability system outweigh them.[7] On balance, it's not easy for politicians to make hard decisions affecting every school and student in their state or community and end up denying promotion or graduation to many youngsters or to declare that lots of schools are failing. Budgetary and capacity challenges also arise when large numbers of kids or schools are deemed lacking, as citizens, parents, taxpayers, and educators naturally demand that extra resources and help be furnished to rectify the situation.

Lowering expectations for students can take other forms besides diluting academic standards and easing passing scores. Inflating teacher-conferred grades also lowers them, not so much "defining deviancy down" as "raising mediocrity up." When student work that formerly earned a C now gets a

B, and when yesterday's B work is rewarded today with an A-minus, the teacher or school or education system has relaxed its standards.[8] When course credit can be "recovered" by tens of thousands of high school pupils through means—often online courses from commercial vendors—that are far easier to pass than the original teacher-taught-and-graded courses for which those students did not get credit, standards have again fallen.

Teachers, schools, districts, and states all have powerful short-term incentives to make it easy to pass someone who might previously have failed and to confer "honors" on young people who in an earlier era might have just scraped by. It's so much friendlier and more gratifying to give students a pleasant outcome—a passing grade, a course credit, a diploma, an honors designation—than to convey (and have to explain and defend) unwelcome news. The appearance of success brings praise, promotions, bonuses—and fends off potentially harsh interventions for student, teacher, school, or district. It reduces the chance of being accused of discrimination. It boosts graduation rates—a key coin of the education policy realm in recent years—and discourages dropping out. It may save the system money by cutting the incidence of grade repetitions, makeup classes, and summer schools. It gets politicians re-elected. It helps kids move on to the next level by elevating their GPAs and enhancing their transcripts. It avoids embarrassment for one's bosses. It encourages voters to support the next school levy or bond issue. And so much more.

Yet there are downstream costs for students and society alike. The most obvious example is rampant remediation (and its equivalent with other labels) for college students, often leading to disappointment, frustration, expense, and finally quitting college. Those who persevere rack up additional costs of their own—both what they must pay the college over a longer period of time (often with the help of loans that carry their own burden) and the opportunity costs of not working while in student status.

Also visible (and audible) are employers who must expensively train newcomers to their workforce in things they should have learned in school—or pay extra for people who possess additional credentials. Some must look overseas for the expertise they need, which isn't easy given the endless fracas over immigration.

How AP Is Different

While all this has been roiling the policy sphere, the College Board has been giving hundreds of thousands of high school students direct experience with the kinds of academic expectations, coursework, and assignments that are typical of colleges—four-year colleges that are the hoped-for destination of most of these young people (and their parents). It's also been giving them experience with multi-hour end-of-course exams that resemble college "finals." Kids who survive in these classes and do well on the exams can fairly be said to have tested themselves against college-like academics.

Nobody would claim that every AP class in every subject is equally rigorous or equally well taught in every classroom of every school. Some of the newer additions to the course roster, particularly in social studies (for example, Psychology, Human Geography), may be rigorous on their own terms but are essentially self-contained, that is, without prerequisites or the expectation that students have already completed a sequence of courses in the same field. Still, AP has always included an external exam that's anonymously scored; the College Board and ETS put much effort into both the psychometrics of that exam and the training of those who appraise students' work; and a score of 3 or higher is widely accepted for college credit and placement out of the corresponding freshman course. These features, taken together, have enabled AP to sustain its reputation for high standards that are identical whether a student lives in rural Montana or suburban Boston and that is hailed by policy makers across most of the land. Indeed, the most oft-heard response of politicians is, "We want more of it in more schools and we want more kids to participate in it." That's very nearly the opposite of the storms that blew up around No Child Left Behind and the Common Core State Standards.

On balance, one might fairly say that, at a time when schools and students are being evaluated mainly on the basis of their results but when the standards by which those results are judged are difficult for educators and states to sustain at a lofty level, Advanced Placement is (along with the National Assessment and perhaps the PISA and TIMSS exams) one of just a few durable sources of intellectual rigor. Even scarcer—AP and the International Baccalaureate are all but alone here—is sustained rigor on measures that affect the lives and prospects of individual students rather than statistical samplings that touch nobody in particular.

This isn't easy to maintain, particularly with mounting evidence that many of the disadvantaged high schoolers being drawn into AP are finding it hard to pass the exams—and it's far from foolproof. Stiffer competition from dual-credit offerings by colleges adds to the pressure to make AP more appealing to students by dumbing it down, mindful that the alternatives are generally less daunting to embark on, easier to pass, and a surer source of college credit. The colleges don't help, either, when they soften their course prerequisites, inflate their own students' grades, and blur the distinction between "remedial" and "credit bearing" courses. In the face of all this, AP minders at the College Board deserve credit for diligently working at quality control and the maintenance of rigor, going about this via several different strategies and mechanisms.

Framework Development

Every AP course has a "framework" or "course description" supplied by the College Board and intended to communicate to teachers what their students need to learn in order to have a reasonable chance of succeeding on the exam in that subject. Also available to teachers and pupils are sample questions from previous exams and rubrics from the scoring of those exams, all intended to help them understand how the tests are structured, what sorts of things they can expect to be asked, and the characteristics that distinguish a high-scoring exam paper from one that gets a 1 or 2.

In the past, many course descriptions were almost perfunctory—a few pages—while others were quite detailed, closer to an actual course outline.[9] The College Board has been gradually revamping the older ones, along with a regular cycle of reviewing and renewing all of them, intending—by the 2019–20 school year—to have the fuller version and supporting materials available for all thirty-eight subjects.

That's a big and extremely elaborate undertaking, but a much-needed one, for as the program expands, as thousands more "nontraditional" AP students enter its classrooms and sit for its exams, and as swarms of new teachers take on the challenge of teaching them to a college-level standard, it's important that participating schools and instructors have easy access to clear, comprehensive materials, and that the program itself be transparent in its expectations so prospective students and their parents can see what lies ahead and so college admissions offices, placement offices, and professors can see what young people showing up with AP exam scores actually studied in those high school classes.

Course frameworks also need periodic updating—even replacing—as academe shifts its disciplinary approaches. Although introductory college courses in some subjects change at a glacial pace, others evolve more rapidly. In recent years, for example, the humanities have become notably more multicultural and "postmodern" on many campuses, and both the sciences and social sciences have given greater attention to deep understanding and student engagement with the material rather than passive ingestion of lecture-style surveys.

Since AP courses are meant to be equivalent to introductory college classes, changes in the content or emphasis of the latter must eventually find their way into AP frameworks and exams. What makes this doubly complicated is that the AP course is meant to be accepted across the broad and variegated landscape of collegiate education in the United States *and* to serve as a high school class that often must align with state academic standards, be acceptable to parents, taxpayers, schoolteachers, and local officials, and satisfy local diploma requirements.

Doing this right takes time. In fact, it takes about seven years to add a new AP subject or direct a soup-to-nuts revamp of an existing course framework, along with all the paraphernalia associated with a new, framework-aligned exam that is psychometrically sound and intellectually equivalent to its predecessors and counterparts. All that involves multiple committees of teachers and professors as well as intensive work by College Board and ETS staffers. It must satisfy multiple constituencies, including those who will teach it and those on university campuses who are being asked to acknowledge its value. And when one is dealing with a sixty-year-old program whose reputation—and the legitimacy of its role in American education—rests on general confidence in those single-digit exam scores from 1 to 5, the stakes are very high indeed.

Course Audit

Since 2007, the College Board has required prospective teachers of classes labeled "Advanced Placement" to obtain prior approval of their course syllabi. This process is intended to respect the instructors' pedagogical freedom while ensuring that what they teach aligns with the core content of a given AP course, corresponds to that course's national framework, and provides reasonable confidence that students in a given teacher's class will learn the essential content and skills that the May exam will probe. A further purpose is to provide colleges the assurance that any course labeled AP—wherever and whatever the high school may be—has common elements.

The audit process arose from several sources:

- When AP changed the content of its Comparative Government course in 2005, it replaced France with Iran on the list of six countries studied. Yet the first round of the revamped exam showed that a quarter of the students sitting for it had not known of the change, that is, it had not filtered from the College Board through teachers to pupils. This obviously disadvantaged those students and denied them at least some of the benefit of the course. It also showed Board officials that, while their program was in touch with schools, it had few links to actual teachers. The course-audit process was a way of creating that direct contact and a communications channel whereby teachers could learn about changes in course content and approach and be encouraged to seek additional professional development to equip themselves to refract such changes into their own classrooms.

- Around the same time, Florida started rewarding schools with added funds when pupils scored 3 or higher on AP exams, which led a number of schools to channel more students into AP classes, whether or not the kids were prepared to succeed there. Inevitably, many weren't. Some instructors put in charge of those additional AP sections were similarly ill-equipped to handle them, hadn't had the relevant preparation, lacked proper textbooks, and more. The course-audit process discouraged schools from this sort of shoddy program expansion by requiring both teachers and principals to sign off on submissions to the College Board that indicated a decent level of preparedness. (Trevor Packer notes that a collateral benefit was to cause schools to bestir themselves to equip teachers with essential instructional requisites, such as freeing up lab space for bona fide AP science classes.)

- With AP participation growing rapidly and extending into high schools with which they had scant familiarity, some college admissions people asked the College Board to vouch that courses labeled "Advanced Placement" on an applicant's transcript were legitimate. It seems that some schools had been cutting corners, such as transcript entries for things like "AP Ceramics." Today, course audit means any course that a high school dubs "Advanced Placement" has at least been reviewed and okayed by the College Board.

The audits themselves are generally done by college faculty engaged to review the syllabi submitted by high schools (and organizations offering online versions). But the process is not foolproof. Some teachers have been known simply to xerox the syllabi that others have previously gotten approved. There are crib sheets and tip sheets for teachers (and homeschoolers)—as well as extensive College Board guidance—on how to prepare a syllabus to gain approval.[10] And while the audit process tends to reinforce the "national curriculum" aspect of AP, that very sense of uniformity is off-putting to some schools and teachers who crave the freedom to design their own courses or simply don't want to submit to external scrutiny. For a handful of schools— mostly the elite independent sort—initiation of the course audit was the last straw, the College Board move that led them thereafter to decline to dub their courses AP.

Teacher Readiness

The College Board's Trevor Packer characterizes AP teachers as the "beating heart" of the program. Thousands of them are passionate about it. They love their subjects, much as college professors do. They love teaching eager pupils and high achievers and welcome the sense that they and their students are a team that struggles together to triumph over that tough exam in May. (Of course, they love it even more when their kids do well on the exam.) They welcome the sense of professional distinction and personal accomplishment that comes with AP engagement, and they enjoy the help and camaraderie of other AP teachers, both in their schools and districts and with the far-flung cadres that get together virtually (often via "AP Central"[11]) and face-to-face at summer workshops, national conferences, and cast-of-thousands exam-scoring sessions in June.

It isn't easy, though, to teach AP courses well. Besides mastering the content—and keeping up as frameworks and exams get revised—the pedagogy is challenging, the more so as the "new AP" seeks deeper understanding on the part of students, not just acquisition of a body of knowledge. Helping kids learn to reason, to analyze, to argue, to write, to work successfully with fellow pupils, to extract essential information from sometimes-obscure primary sources, to explain why something happened the way it did or how to solve a complex problem—none of this is simple, little of it is instinctive, and much of it goes well beyond typical teacher preparation in the United States. It becomes still harder as nontraditional students are encouraged to enter AP classrooms in substantial numbers. Because some (or many) are less prepared than yesterday's AP pupils—weaker study skills, scant acquaintance with challenging content, limited writing experience, minimal practice with long-term assignments and heavy homework loads, and probably also meager support at home—the instructor must engage in more classroom differentiation and "scaffolding" than he or she was accustomed to doing. The teacher must also find ways to do that without skimping on the appetites and challenges of the traditional AP population, all the while navigating touchy political and inter-personal situations within the school and perhaps with parents.

Although the term "professional development for teachers" is routinely thrown about in discussions of education reforms and their implementation, and although many hopes are vested in it (and frequently dashed), in the AP realm it's taken seriously and often done well. A principal with whom we spoke said his high school sends all its AP teachers back to the summer insti-tutes on a five-year cycle, and they return "renewed and on fire." The College Board takes considerable pains to develop workshop materials and train presenters and, in order to display the AP imprimatur, the two-hundred-odd outfits that host such workshops—mostly universities, but also groups like NMSI and MassInsight—are required to use those resources. Other oppor-tunities for teachers arise at College Board gatherings of various kinds, and many teachers who sign on as exam graders declare that those laborious weeklong work sessions in cavernous convention centers yield the most valu-able PD they've ever had.[12] The AP team also makes available ample material online and in print to assist practitioners in successfully teaching AP courses and preparing students for the exams. Much of this is teacher generated and available via the AP Central website, which also hosts discussion groups and other networking possibilities. Accessible there as well is a College Board–coordinated "teacher mentoring" program—increasingly valuable as veteran AP instructors retire and are replaced by neophytes, and as the program's growth draws in thousands more instructors who suddenly find themselves responsible for AP classes. Although the quality of instruction in such classes varies from school to school, the PD opportunities available for motivated teachers are impressive, and some participants term it the most substantive in their experience, not to mention the best taught and most relevant to actual classroom work as well as their own intellectual growth.

An inherent weakness of this kind of professional development, however, is that it's usually voluntary—and some teachers must pay out of pocket to obtain it. That can mean those who need it most never get it, or must settle for some dilute version. And special challenges arise in situations—as in Fort Worth and New York—where school or district leaders decide to inaugurate or beef up AP in schools that haven't had much of it and where veteran teach-ers aren't accustomed to it and don't necessarily want to change their ways even when organizations like NMSI are standing by to assist. Kids who are persuaded to set foot in those teachers' AP classes may not get what they expect—or what they need.

The Exam

Because the AP exam score is widely recognized by universities as a basis on which to make course-placement decisions and confer credit, and because the exam in most disciplines contains content drawn from a hypothetical universal version of an introductory course in that subject, preparing students to succeed on the exam serves as a kind of curricular standardization that shifts classrooms away from instructor digressions and teachers' favorite topics toward a broad-gauged (but often deep) approach to the subject. Because the AP exam is neither written nor scored by the student's own teacher, it also creates a positive incentive for instructors and students to raise their game, working together in pursuit of a high standard, and focusing on important content and skills. That, at least, is the College Board view. On the other hand, what some see as "instructor digressions," others view as "teacher professionalism," that is, we encounter the fear that AP turns teachers into deliverers of someone else's syllabus rather than creators of their own. (Similar objections are raised to statewide academic standards and certainly to state- or district-dictated curricula and constraints on the choice of instructional materials.)

Several elements of the exam cycle serve to maintain rigor and keep it consistent from year to year, even as course frameworks evolve and specific test questions change. This is easiest, of course, when changes are slight. "Common item equating" enables the College Board and ETS to deploy re-used multiple-choice items to calibrate new essay questions that still relate to the familiar framework. When a wholly new framework or exam format arrives, the calibration challenge mounts, but the exam makers employ procedures intended to ensure (and then verify) that it's "just as hard as before." Standard-setting is multifaceted, with some of it coming in advance of exam creation and some occurring after the test itself has been constructed, administered, and scored on a rubric, but "cut scores" have not been established. The test makers engage a panel to set "aspirational" standards for how successful college students should be expected to do on the new test items, then they apply those standards to actual exam papers to see how the score distribution looks. (Often they administer the new questions to a sample of actual college students.) Since kids don't change much from year to year, if the distribution is wildly discrepant from prior years, they go back for further rounds until Packer and his team are satisfied that it hasn't become easier. Indeed, introduction of a new framework or exam generally means that scores decline for at least a couple of years until teachers adjust their curricula and pedagogy to what's changed and students get accustomed to—in some cases—different sorts of exam questions.[13] So far, Packer says, despite an inherent risk of standards slipping when a new exam launches, the calibration procedure has always worked. Teachers of the course are also surveyed and asked to take the exam, score it, and set standards for it, and Packer reports that they're usually tougher than the expert panels comprised mainly of professors.

Because scores do typically dip when the framework or exam is replaced, and because this tends to alarm teachers and may discourage parents and school leaders, Packer writes to AP teachers of the subject—a note they can share with the principal—explaining why the change was made. In his experience, teachers are generally okay with this, though there is a risk—more from political leaders—that when major efforts are made to widen AP participation (as in New York's "AP for All" initiative, see chapter 5), there should also be a commensurate rise in qualifying scores. The College Board, too, seeks to grow participation in the program, because it's convinced it can benefit more kids and because it adds to the Board's revenues. This leads to pressure—and temptation—to make it easier, which Packer acknowledges could pose problems going forward.

Scoring

With more than five million AP exams now completed by students worldwide during the first two weeks of May, with every single one of them containing portions—often sizable portions—that must be evaluated by expert human eyes rather than tallied by scanners, and with teachers, schools, colleges, and students all clamoring to get the results ASAP, it follows that the exam-grading process is an enormous operation. Well over ten thousand high school teachers and college professors are brought together in the first half of June, filling immense convention centers in four or five cities, there to be confronted with towering piles of exam papers or their online equivalents, even as hundreds more readers tackle identical scoring duties from home or office.

ETS organizes all this on a nearly unimaginable scale and with as many logistical challenges, security concerns, and issues of standardization and consistency as a major military undertaking. Even more impressive than all the housing, feeding, plane ticketing, and networking that's involved is the extensive training and retraining of that multitude of exam readers and the pains taken to ensure that scores are equivalent no matter which reader makes the judgment on which student's response to a question, and regardless of whether that student's paper is reviewed during the first morning or the final afternoon of the weeklong process. Elaborate scoring rubrics are constructed, then refined and refined again, for each part of each exam question, and supervisory structures and quality control procedures are implemented, all in a secure facility and with student and school identities masked. At the pinnacle of the human hierarchy that's responsible for doing this right is a "chief reader" for each of the thirty-eight AP subjects, generally a senior professor with decades of experience not only with their discipline but also with the AP courses and exams in that field.

Although the scale is now vast, something like this has been going on throughout the sixty-odd years of AP's existence, and while it's a bit old-fashioned—other large-scale assessments generally make greater use of technology and "remote" scoring—it's a cherished and respected part of the AP process, and teachers and professors vie to be part of it. Yes, they're paid, but not very much. It seems that the camaraderie is at least as important, and participants report that they seldom otherwise get a chance to team up with peers in their field whose day jobs are on both sides of the high school diploma divide.

So far, research by Nat Malkus of the American Enterprise Institute shows that the College Board has a strong track record when it comes to maintaining quality and rigor even as the program has grown.[14] It's easier for more students to access AP classes but apparently no easier to earn qualifying scores on the exams. Although we see some evidence that nontraditional students are apt to sign up for classes such as Psychology and Human Geography rather than Calculus and Physics, it's nonetheless true that, for the AP program writ large, the passing rate has declined as participation has risen, which attests to successful maintenance of standards.

The College Board is also proud that as the program has ballooned and become more diverse in recent years, the "mean AP score" for all students has barely budged: 2.84 in 2017, down slightly from 2.88 in 2007, indicating that the exam-taking population can grow while maintaining a high bar for rigor.

Look a decade further back, however, and the picture changes somewhat, for the mean score in 1997 was 3.02. The difference between that number and the 2.84 of 2017, while numerically small, is essentially the difference between a score qualifying, or not. How to explain what happened?

Between 1997 and 2007, we saw uneven growth of the program, and racial differences that had a greater impact as minority numbers rose. Black and Hispanic students earned 1's and 2's more often than their white and Asian classmates, and their participation rose faster.

This changed after 2007 as scores began to be distributed a bit more evenly. For example, the number of exams taken by black students more than doubled since 2007, but so did their numbers of 1's, 2's, 3's, 4's, and 5's, at very similar rates—a big change from the preceding decade. Hispanic students followed a similar trajectory. All this helped maintain a relatively stable mean score and suggests that there's merit in the optimism of the College Board and many booster organizations and policy makers that more—and more equitable—AP participation can proceed apace with sustained performance levels. The bigger challenge is that relatively evenhanded growth in exam scores has not closed preexisting achievement gaps. So it remains the case that disproportionately large numbers of black and Hispanic youngsters are earning 1's and 2's on their exams.[15]

One major contributor to AP's impressive record of quality control is that Packer's own hand has been on the AP tiller since 2003. His commitment to educational rigor is unchallenged, and he's proud of the program's gold-standard reputation.[16] But he also cites teachers as a reliable force for quality. In his experience, any move to inflate qualifying scores will collide with AP instructors' own instincts about the quality of desirable student work. In other words, he sees teachers' expectations for their students—and perhaps for their field—as a source of rigor maintenance in the face of political pressures that push in the opposite direction. Also helpful in fending off such pressures is widening access to new sources of help for AP students and teachers, including a vast virtual library of resources related to each of the thirty-eight subjects that's supposed to be operational by summer 2019.[17]

Yet it's no time for complacency. Any transition from elite to mass invites dilution of quality and any move to promote greater equity of outcomes invites easing of standards. The Advanced Placement program has skillfully sailed through these treacherous shoals for decades, but it would be a big mistake to let go of that tiller.

Notes

1. On the matter of high standards, we're honored to be in the company of such eminent thinkers as the late Kenneth Clark and Ronald R. Edmonds.

2. Sheila Byrd, *Advanced Placement and International Baccalaureate: Do They Deserve Gold Star Status?* (Washington, DC: Thomas B. Fordham Institute, 2007). A few AP subjects have proven controversial in recent years (see more in chapter 11).

3. Alyson Klein, "Historic Summit Fueled Push for K–12 Standards," *Education Week*, September 23, 2014. https://www.edweek.org/ew/articles/2014/09/24/05summit.h34.html; *The National Education Goals Report: Building a Nation of Learners* (Washington, DC: The National Education Goals Panel, 1999). https://govinfo.library.unt.edu/negp/reports/99rpt.pdf; Maris Vinovskis,

From a Nation at Risk to No Child Left Behind: National Education Goals and the Creation of Federal Education Policy (New York: Teachers College Press, 2009).

4. *National Education Goals Report*, vi.

5. The National Education Goals Panel, "History, 1989 to Present," accessed November 8, 2018. https://govinfo.library.unt.edu/negp/page1–7.htm. Strictly speaking, the Goals Panel was initially created within the Executive Branch in 1990, then reconstituted by statute two years later.

6. "Summary of Improving America's Schools Act," *Education Week*, November 9, 2018. https://www.edweek.org/ew/articles/1994/11/09/10asacht.h14.html.

7. There are myriad additional pathways around rigor, such as exempting many children from the tests, promoting them based on teacher grades rather than test scores, and conferring diplomas on the basis of cumulative "Carnegie units" rather than passing exit exams.

8. Michael Hurwitz and Jason Lee, "Grade Inflation and the Role of Standardized Testing," in *Measuring Success: Testing, Grades, and the Future of College Admissions*, ed. Jack Buckley, Lynn Letukas, and Ben Wildavsky (Baltimore: Johns Hopkins University Press, 2018).

9. Compare, for example, the course descriptions of Macroeconomics and Music Theory with German Language and Culture and Chemistry. College Board, AP Central, "Courses," accessed November 8, 2018. https://apcentral.collegeboard.org/courses.

10. Halle Edwards, "How to Pass Your AP Course Audit," *PrepScholar* (blog), December 18, 2015. https://blog.prepscholar.com/ap-course-audit; Shelly Olson, "How I Passed the AP Audit," *Practical Homeschooling* 83 (2008). http://www.home-school.com/Articles/ap-audit.php; College Board, AP Central, "AP Course Audit," accessed November 8, 2018. https://apcentral.collegeboard .org/courses/ap-course-audit/about.

11. College Board, AP Teacher Community, "Welcome to the AP Teacher Community," accessed November 8, 2018. https://apcommunity.collegeboard.org/.

12. National Math and Science Initiative, "Laying the Foundation Program," accessed November 8, 2018. http://www.nms.org/Our-Approach/Laying-the-Foundation.aspx; Mass Insight Education and Research, "2018 Summer Institute," accessed November 8, 2018. http://www.massinsight .org/2018summer/; College Board, "AP Annual Conference: 2018 Program," accessed November 8, 2018. https://apac.collegeboard.org/program.

13. In testing generally, scores decline when the test changes, only to rebound as teachers and students adjust. In the case of AP, foreign language results were the exception, as the College Board intentionally eased its expectations to correspond to the current level of college courses.

14. Nat Malkus, *AP at Scale: Public School Students in Advanced Placement, 1990–2013* (Washington, DC: American Enterprise Institute, 2016). https://www.aei.org/wp-content/uploads /2016/01/AP-at-Scale.pdf.

15. Alina Tugend, "Who Benefits from the Expansion of A.P. Classes?" *New York Times Magazine*, September 7, 2017. https://www.nytimes.com/2017/09/07/magazine/who-benefits-from -the-expansion-of-ap-classes.html; Steve Farkas and Ann Duffett, *Growing Pains in the Advanced Placement Program: Do Tough Trade-Offs Lie Ahead?* (Washington, DC: Thomas B. Fordham Institute, 2009). http://edex.s3-us-west-2.amazonaws.com/publication/pdfs/AP_Report_7.pdf.

16. Jay Mathews, "The Triumph of Advanced Placement," *Washington Post Magazine*, October 23, 2018. https://www.washingtonpost.com/news/magazine/wp/2018/10/23/feature/meet -the-man-who-made-advanced-placement-the-most-influential-tool-in-american-education/ ?utm_term=.5459f80eb407.

17. College Board, AP Central, "Launching in 2019: New AP Resources and Processes," accessed November 8, 2018. https://apcentral.collegeboard.org/about-ap/news-changes/ap-2019.

10

Elite Dropouts

Does the expansion and democratization of Advanced Placement erode its value for the big-name schools and universities that helped create it back in the mid-twentieth century? Education historian Jack Schneider certainly thinks so: "One unintended but foreseeable consequence of the expansion of AP," he wrote in 2009, "has been a declining level of prestige and achievement associated with the program. . . . The popularity of AP has brought about a great demand for it, and, in meeting that demand, educators and reformers have weakened the status of AP in high-status high schools. . . . [I]s AP a mark of a 'top' school or the mark of an average one?"[1]

Recall that Advanced Placement emerged in large part from the labors of a small cadre of representatives from privileged private schools and colleges, including Andover, Exeter, and Lawrenceville on the secondary level and Harvard, Princeton, and Yale at the university level. A one-line version of its original mission was to ease the transition of high achievers from prep schools into Ivy League institutions and colleges like Swarthmore and Williams, giving those kids a leg up—literally "advanced placement"—on their baccalaureate studies based on college-level work that they completed during high school.

This made perfect sense for the institutions that were involved and the student populations being served. It also carried an aura of status and a benchmark for others. ("If Albert's score on that exam is enough evidence for Yale to trust that he actually learned Yale-level history while at Choate, why can't the same exam give a boost to my Phyllis as she matriculates from New Trier to Northwestern?")

The standards built into that metric appear not to have slipped, but today AP can be found in many, many places and, while solid scores on its exams still denote serious academic accomplishment in high school, that's no longer exceptional. Almost a quarter of today's American high school graduates can boast a qualifying score on at least one AP exam. Plain old Middletown High School in Ohio offers five AP classes—and Middletown High School in Maryland offers a whopping twenty-two. One need not enroll in a posh prep school to participate in AP, nor must one's family move to Winnetka, Brookline, or Chappaqua.

What does this mean for elite private schools? In practice, it means that a handful of them have in various ways distanced themselves from AP—and their number is likely to grow, albeit in slightly hypocritical fashion. At the postsecondary level, it means that selective colleges, again mainly the private kind, are making it harder to earn credit via AP exams—and much harder to shorten one's time to degree.

In the Prep Schools

A high school might shun AP for any number of reasons. It may embrace a completely different sort of curriculum, perhaps specializing in theater, Arabic, agriculture, or careers in the hospitality industry. It may focus on a certain kind of young person, possibly individuals with a specific disability, addiction, emotional problem, or athletic specialty. It might feature a distinctive pedagogy, such as discovery learning, rather than a structured, teacher-delivered curriculum. It may favor the International Baccalaureate program or be affiliated with a singular college, employer, church, or other compelling linkage. It may seek to shield its students from competitive pressures so they can bloom in their own individual ways at their own speed. And so much more.

If it's an elite and pricey private school, it's legitimate to ask whether AP still adds the distinctive curricular cachet, exclusive aura of rigor, and college admissions boost that it once did, and, if not, then why continue to endure the hassles of participating in it—the calendar rigidities, the syllabus reviews, the increasingly prescriptive course frameworks, and more? After all, as the program has grown to encompass more subjects, as democratization makes it available to the masses, and as selective colleges grow stingier about conferring credit based on it, there may well come a crossover point where a school concludes that its benefits are dwarfed by its costs.

Author Finn described a family prep-school quest to AP chief Trevor Packer in autumn 2017: "Yesterday, my daughter and I visited two well-regarded independent schools in the New York City area with an eye toward possible high school choices for my granddaughter. Chatting with both admissions directors, they indicated that both schools have already withdrawn from AP history and English to give their teachers more flexibility, and they're studying the possibility of withdrawing from AP entirely for essentially the same reason. (One seemed pretty sure that students would still be able to take AP exams on campus; the other implied that they might have to take them elsewhere.) Question: Is it possible that, as the number of participating public high schools balloons, we're seeing significant defection by the private schools that, in effect, helped invent AP sixty years ago?"

Packer replied that "the number of private schools offering AP courses continues to grow steadily and rapidly" but also acknowledged some distancing by high-status schools. He noted, for example, a recent decision by Choate Rosemary Hall—one of the earliest schools to institute Advanced Placement—to cease offering AP-labeled courses (although it continues to administer the exams and its teachers decide whether to continue aligning their classes with AP frameworks).[2] On the other hand, he added, the program's new "Capstone" courses (see chapters 3 and 12) have begun to re-engage some private schools that had previously foresworn AP.

The fact that millions of young people across the land are joining—and often succeeding—at Advanced Placement courses at little or no cost to themselves in 2019 has definitely eroded the program's exclusiveness, and—as we discuss further on—AP's ubiquity and the ballooning number of entering students with scores of 3 or better has led many colleges to reconsider awarding credit based on those scores. For expensive independent schools, the program's inclusion of thousands more schools and pupils also means that offering it on one's campus is no longer a plausible justification for charging lofty tuitions, not when it's "being given away free down the street" and when the colleges that one's graduates go on to are making it harder to enter with degree credits already harvested via Advanced Placement exam scores.

That doesn't mean prep school students (and their parents) have stopped wanting AP for themselves, simply that offering it no longer marks a school as high-leverage and distinctive. What's more, some instructors at some prestigious schools fret that AP course syllabi and exams foster a wide but ultimately shallow curriculum and that they can do a better job—and perhaps justify their own status, salaries, and professional worth—by developing their own advanced courses rather than being bound by frameworks set by outsiders.

As we saw in the previous chapter, that binding tightened—and College Board supervision grew stricter—as AP leaders sought to assure integrity and quality control for their fast-growing program via measures such as course syllabus review, even as they also responded to the "wide but not deep enough" criticism by revamping course frameworks and exams. With the revamps, however, came greater specificity and detail as to what might (and would not) be included in the exams, and this, plus the syllabus review, was too much for some prep school teachers, particularly in the humanities, as they saw their pedagogical freedom as well as their school's curricular distinctiveness being bridled by those people in New York. "Why should an independent school like ours," rhetorically asked one school head whom we interviewed, "teach a curriculum created by someone else?"

The College Board acknowledges much grumping among private school teachers after AP commenced reviewing course syllabi in 2007 but also says it encountered little actual rejection of the program by schools. Indeed, Packer noted, the total number of AP-participating private schools (those offering AP-branded courses) continued to rise—from some 3,085 in 2006 to 5,179 in 2018. Yet some of the country's best-known prep schools have stopped designating their courses "AP," and at least one well-regarded public high school (Scarsdale) has followed suit.

Often, though, such rejections turn out to be more cosmetic than binding. At Scarsdale High School, the teacher-designed alternatives are called "Advanced Topics," but the course catalog acknowledges that "students in these college-level courses may choose to take Advanced Placement (AP) examinations linked to the subject area."[3] The school also covers exam fees for students who find them burdensome—and excuses kids from class on AP exam days in May.

New York City's private Fieldston School made rather a big deal of abolishing AP courses back in 2001, well before syllabus reviews started, declaring at the time that teaching such courses resulted in too narrow and confining a curriculum, yet even now several of Fieldston's math and science courses follow or approximate the AP syllabus—and this, too, is acknowledged in the school catalog.[4]

Seventeen years later, the heads of eight prominent private schools in the DC area boasted in the *Washington Post* that "we have jointly come to recognize the diminished utility of Advanced Placement courses. Consequently, collectively we agree that we will better equip our students for further study and for life beyond the classroom by eliminating AP courses from our curriculums entirely by 2022."[5] They will, however, also continue to administer the AP exams.

A few months earlier, Phillips Academy's (Andover) stance made it into *Business Insider* via an article titled "The best high school in America helped create the fast-growing AP program—but now it does things differently." School head John Palfrey told the journalist that "we were one of the founding AP schools in the 1950s [but] we have decided over the time that teaching to the AP is not the best way of teaching," though he was apparently referring specifically to US history and his school continues to offer College Board–sanctioned AP classes in five subjects, mostly math. Ambivalence is evident, too, in an information sheet distributed to Andover students that tells them how to register for AP exams while cautioning that "these exams are very expensive and take up extensive time for preparation and missed classes. AP exams are not required for college applications."[6]

Up the road at Phillips Exeter, instructors in some subjects were gradually parting company from AP before 2007, but the College Board's insistence on auditing course syllabi pushed them over the edge. After a debate, the faculty voted to cease submitting their instructional plans to any external review. Their view had long been that "we teach the AP content and go beyond it," and school leaders say that, for the most part, that's still the view of those who teach math, science, and language courses, where students are advised that, if they do well in class, they'll be well prepared for the AP exam in that subject. That's what the Academy's course catalog implies:

> Exeter does not subscribe to the AP program but many courses at Exeter are taught at or beyond the AP level and are sufficient preparation for AP exams; Exeter administers the AP exams on campus each May. AP exams are scored from 1–5 and there are several advantages to scoring a 4 or 5 including earning college credit or receiving an exemption from college distribution requirements or lower-level requirements in specific disciplines.

Not every part of the school agrees, however. The History Department declares in near-belligerent terms that

> the department does not confine itself to teaching in order to prepare students for standardized tests. We believe that such an approach would compromise our commitment to student-centered discussion, close

reading of primary and secondary sources, and independent research and writing. *Those students wishing to take AP exams in history are strongly advised to undertake sustained review on their own.*[7] (Emphasis added)

Advisors who assist Exeter seniors with college applications also note that the selective universities to which most apply don't weigh AP scores very heavily as part of their admissions decisions and aren't overly impressed by students taking AP courses, if only because so many of their applicants do just that. It's worth noting, however, that most such institutions have long experience with kids applying from Exeter and other well-established prep schools (such as the octet in Washington), so their admissions teams already possess what an Academy staffer characterized as "a whole database of how various Exeter graduates have performed at their college." In other words, the admissions team can parse course grades, teacher recommendations, and SAT scores and determine fairly well how a given candidate from Exeter is likely to fare on their campus.[8] This is harder for youngsters applying from more obscure high schools, and in those situations—Exeter administrators recognize this—a student's AP track record may make more difference.

Historian Schneider suggests much the same thing, writing that "while AP may no longer carry much distinction on transcripts from private, high-status high schools, it does carry weight on transcripts of students at poorly funded public high schools. When course quality is questionable, AP provides a baseline of substance and rigor."[9] He notes that teachers in such schools "also have reasons to hang on to AP" as a good source for their own professional development and colleagueship with peers around the land and goes on to suggest that the potential reward of doing well on AP exams also helps them motivate students to study harder!

Even the most exclusive schools have trouble spurning AP altogether, much as some of their instructors might wish it. Other teachers, particularly in STEM fields and perhaps foreign language, don't feel overly constrained by AP frameworks—their courses wouldn't be very different without that external structure—and many instructors find both personal validation and potential benefit for their students from successes on those end-of-year exams. As seems to have happened at both Scarsdale and Exeter, as well as Fieldston and Choate Rosemary Hall, parents insist on access to AP for their daughters and sons—"They leave no stone unturned in their quest to advantage their kids in the college admissions sweepstakes" acknowledges an Exeter administrator—and many students are keen to bypass introductory courses when they reach college, such as future engineering majors hoping to skip calculus. For them, as we found in some upscale suburban public schools, course placement with the help of AP seems to matter more than starting with actual degree credit.

As a result, Exeter administers AP exams on the prescribed timetable—kids pay their own fees—and the results are reported back to the Academy, which tabulates and tracks them, shares them with teachers, and often discusses them with department chairs. Moreover, even as the Academy's two-page "profile" of itself—a document given to colleges that may not know the school—boasts that "all academic departments offer courses well beyond the normal secondary school level, which is why we are not part of the College Board's Advanced Placement Program," the same profile reports that "the distribution of scores is: 5 or 4–90 percent; 3–7 percent; 2 or 1–3 percent."[10] In sum, Exeter is not oblivious to AP—and probably couldn't be even if it were more determined. The Advanced Placement mind-set and potential benefit that AP course-taking and exam scores may confer on its students are too deeply ingrained for even this proud, wealthy, two-century-old independent school to disregard.

That seems broadly to be true for most of the 160-odd, mostly private schools that have joined the Independent Curriculum Group (ICG), dedicated to the proposition that good schools create their own curricula and aren't dictated to or homogenized by externally shaped courses and academic standards, much less by those ghastly "standardized tests."[11] Many of the same schools also belong to the Mastery Transcript Consortium, which is trying to devise entirely new ways of demonstrating their students' academic accomplishments without traditional letter grades or test scores.[12] We salute both ventures and wish them well. A virtue of private schools is the freedom to pilot different ways of doing things. Yet important as autonomy and teacher-built curricula are to such schools' philosophies of education, and vital as it is for their reputations and revenue streams to be distinctive, inner-directed, and relentlessly independent, it's next to impossible for them to resist the gravitational pull of AP, at least to the extent of administering (or enabling pupil access to) the exams and—often—also assuring their students that completing certain of their courses will prepare them for those exams. ICG director Peter Gow estimates that only about thirty of his member schools (at the secondary level) offer *no* AP—or International Baccalaureate—classes.[13]

Gravitational pull—and student and parent insistence—does not entirely explain the persistent (or revived) involvement of most private schools with AP, even when it no longer makes them distinctive or justifies their tuition. Some school heads confide to Packer that the rigorous marking of AP exams actually helps them and their teachers push back against grade inflation and withstand pressure from aggressive parents to elevate their children's report-card grades. After all, a student who cannot attain a 4 or 5 on the AP exam surely does not deserve an A in that subject! As public schools have also learned (sometimes to their chagrin and discomfort) from student results on state assessments, a chasm between teacher-conferred grades and external exam scores is hard to explain. For independent school instructors rattled by prosperous and pushy parents (and sometimes kids) fretting about college admissions and demanding higher grades—even insisting that otherwise they're not getting their money's worth!—AP exams can provide a helpful dose of reality. Moreover, the new AP Capstone courses appeal to some private schools because they don't specify particular content, instead allowing students and teachers to select their own topics while being held to a high standard for critical thinking and research.

For the overwhelming majority of US independent schools, Advanced Placement (and sometimes the International Baccalaureate) remains a necessary and popular part of their curriculum, expected by parents, sought by students, welcomed by teachers, and sometimes valued by administrators because of its role in influential high school ratings and rankings that families consult when winnowing their school options. Whatever their motivations, those who lead the more than half of America's ten thousand private high schools that participate in the AP program don't seem to be losing much sleep over it, save perhaps for the challenge of keeping up with the program's expansive list of course options.[14] Far more common are boasts on their websites and recruitment literature about how many AP classes they offer and—not quite as common—how well their students do on the exams. Indeed, by not offering AP, they would actually dim their luster and likely erode their market share in a particular community. Insofar as some schools have issues, it's mainly the most exclusive (and often most expensive) of them—and those that focus on something other than conventional preparation for traditional colleges. Vermont's Putney School, for example, prides itself on its "progressive" curriculum and explicitly disavows Advanced Placement, even in calculus.[15] Should the Mastery Transcript group make serious headway, college admissions offices would no longer see A's and B's (and the odd C) in old-fashioned courses labeled US History, Geometry, and Spanish 3. Nor would they see applicants' GPAs and class ranks. Instead, they would see teachers' opinions of whether a candidate can "understand non-western history, politics, religion, and culture" and has developed "flexibility, agility, and adaptability."[16] That's a far cry from the AP approach.

The AP program itself throws one more curve ball at independent (and many public) schools, which is its rigid calendar whereby every exam is given on a fixed date and time during the first half of May. This creates all manner of challenges for schools whose own calendars range widely, with some starting in mid-August and ending in May while others commence well after Labor Day and continue deep into June. Still others operate year-round and some have semesters in Washington or work-study projects in developing countries. Some build their curricula on a semester basis, others on a trimester, and some favor short intensive courses while others stretch them over the full academic year, even into multiyear sequences. The upshot is myriad opportunities for mismatch between how a school—especially one struggling to be distinctive—organizes itself and how the College Board forces conformity, not only in course content but also very forcefully in calendar.[17]

Packer and his team are well aware of the issue but so far cannot picture any reasonable alternative to uniform scheduling of exams. Altering it would be hugely expensive, would raise tough issues of test security, complicate exam scoring, and generate new allegations of unfairness and advantage. Someday, perhaps, that will get worked out, most likely with the aid of technology, but probably not soon.[18]

Meanwhile, the defection from Advanced Placement by private schools, though visible and newsworthy thanks to the exalted profiles of some defectors—and the irony that they include some of the same schools that once rushed to enlist in the program, indeed to create it—is a mouse alongside the fattening hippo of schools that continue to sign up for it and offer it in more subjects to more students. Moreover, few defectors have totally rejected AP. They may not submit their syllabi for review but they almost all make it possible for their students to sit for the exams, they track the results, and in many cases their instructors, whether out of commitment or obligation, acknowledge that what they're teaching is well-aligned with what the exam writers look for.

In the Universities

Dartmouth College made a media splash in 2012 with the announcement that it would no longer accept AP exam results for credit toward the bachelor's degree. The dean of the faculty later clarified that AP scores—as well as IB results and kindred indicators of successful prior college-level work—would continue to be used to waive students past entry level courses in particular subjects and for other placement decisions.[19] Indeed,

Dartmouth—confusingly—will confer something it calls "credit upon entrance" to students with high scores on certain exams, yet that kind of credit does not count against the thirty-five units that must be earned *while at Dartmouth* in order to obtain a degree. Nor, therefore, do AP results shorten anyone's time to degree or lighten the cost burden. In sum, every entering student must take a full load of courses from Dartmouth faculty— and pay a full four years of tuition. It's acknowledged that they may have done college-level work in high school, but that doesn't free them to do any less of it while in college.

A handful of other selective-admission institutions now employ similar practices. Following in the Dartmouth mode, the Harvard faculty voted in early 2018 not to give students any credit in the future "for work completed prior to their matriculation" unless that work was done at Harvard itself, such as via summer or extension courses. Individual departments may still use AP and IB results for course placement, but the dean of undergraduate education haughtily declared that few faculty members regard those high school classes as truly equivalent to what they teach, so—reported the alumni magazine— "it makes no sense to allow students to count them toward earning an A.B. short of Harvard's 'curated eight-semester experience.'" Several professors objected that this decision eliminated the option for students with compelling personal, health, or financial reasons to compress their undergraduate experience, but the dean quashed such protests by terming it inequitable to grant advanced standing to a minority of students who have accumulated AP or IB credits while denying it to others.[20]

Brown University says much the same thing, explaining to students that "Advanced Placement exam scores are not eligible for course credit at Brown, but students may use certain AP scores to enroll in higher-level courses and/ or to satisfy concentration requirements. In other words, AP credit will not increase your course credit total."[21]

At Amherst, too, the policy says, "We do not accept such courses for credit or advanced standing, although some Amherst academic departments will allow you to forego introductory-level courses in areas in which you have already completed rigorous work."[22]

This denial of credit toward degree contrasts vividly with the personal experience of author Finn, who entered Harvard at a time (1962) when that institution cheerfully offered the option of full sophomore status—an entire year of credit—to any matriculant who presented at least three AP scores of 3 or higher, and nobody suggested that this was unfair or inequitable to those who arrived without that option.

Half a century later, especially at upscale private institutions, such acceleration is practically unheard of, and any credit that gets conferred typically hinges
on higher AP scores. MIT gives it only for 5's. Stanford recognizes a few 4's but
otherwise also demands 5's. Duke and Oberlin insist on at least a 4 and in many
subjects a 5, with such decisions made by individual departments. At Wellesley,
only calculus allows a 4; in all other fields, one must score 5's.

Nor is this form of "grade inflation" confined to Ivy-type institutions.
Examining the credits awarded to incoming students by the University of Kansas on the basis of AP scores, we also see 4's and 5's creeping in (the latter
especially in foreign languages).[23]

The College Board's Trevor Packer estimates that about 7 percent of US
colleges now give credit only for scores of 5. But among the top ten universities ranked by *U.S. News* in 2018, only the University of Chicago granted
any credit for 3's (mostly in the same languages that Kansas has raised the
ante on!) along with a bevy of 4's and 5's.

Why this score inflation and credit denial? Is it that passing the test has
grown easier? As discussed in the previous chapter, that appears not to be the
case. Is it—as the Harvard dean insisted—that colleges like his have concluded
that it's not truly equivalent to what they teach? That professors can't bear to
acknowledge that someone else might teach it as well as they do? That their
academic freedom and intellectual integrity are compromised by accepting
courses taught by lowly high school teachers? That the professoriate's mounting distaste for "survey courses" in general has biased them against the kinds
of content that formerly typified the "101" level in their own departments? Or
simply that they're hungry for tuition dollars—and butts-in-seats in their own
entry-level courses—and are therefore loath to confer credit on entry, creating
an ever-larger dilemma—and potential revenue loss—as ever-more students
arrive on their doorsteps with ever-more AP qualifying scores.

So far as we can determine, some of all of that is happening. It's no secret
that colleges and universities, proud of their independence, are costly places
to operate, and getting more so, and that they're also notoriously inefficient.[24]
Neither is it a secret that moves to make them more efficient—which would
surely include granting credit for things learned elsewhere, expediting students' progress to degrees, saving parents and taxpayers money, and perhaps
clearing classroom space to serve more students—are typically resisted by
those whose own livelihoods are affected as well as those whose comfortable, customary modus operandi may be disrupted.

In pursuit of better understanding of the factors at work as colleges consider how to respond to swelling numbers of applicants with AP qualifying

scores, we visited with a veteran admissions officer who has decades of experience in selective universities. Although asking to remain anonymous, he acknowledged that AP course taking and course grades—and sometimes exam scores—are one way that institutions like his assemble evidence that applicants have tested themselves against the most challenging curriculum available in their high schools, which attests to both their enterprise and their achievement. In the end, however, his prestigious university is loath to grant much credit on the basis of courses taken in high school.

He's not alone in viewing Advanced Placement as a valuable transcript marker. When the eight Washington-area private schools declared in 2018 that they were ceasing to teach AP classes, one of their explanations was that "AP courses on high school transcripts are of diminished significance to college admissions officers." Yet a couple of weeks later, the admissions chiefs of more than a dozen eminent campuses—Duke, Stanford, MIT, Columbia, and so on—replied that "the expansion of AP across the country, from the Rio Grande Valley to Chicago, has increased, rather than diminished, our ability to find and enroll students from a wide range of backgrounds who have challenged themselves with college-level coursework in high school."[25]

Transcripts, said the experienced admissions person with whom we spoke, remain the most important documentary evidence, but they're easiest for an admissions committee to parse when the university has a database for a particular high school based on long experience with its graduates. That's apt to include places like Exeter and the DC-area prep schools that now eschew AP, but parsing transcripts is far harder when the school is unfamiliar. (His own institution sees transcripts from more than five thousand high schools!) Also important is the school context, which is—again—hard to evaluate at a little-known school. Some places offer many more advanced opportunities than others, and, because much AP gate-keeping persists, not all kids are equally welcome in such opportunities as are available.

There's also such a thing, he noted, as taking too much AP. He and his colleagues try to be sensitive to the balance in a kid's life; is she taking five or six AP classes at once and neglecting other activities and interests? (Some applicants display AP courses on their transcripts "in the teens.") Alternatively, has she so many other responsibilities and obligations (for example, siblings, jobs) that she can't realistically manage—and do well with—a heavy load of hard classes? A secondary school may actually be wise, he said, to encourage limits on how many advanced classes a student takes.

In his experience, AP and IB seem to enjoy equal footing, but sometimes the admissions office sees only the course grades, not the exam scores, as students themselves control which colleges get their scores, and those decisions may be affected by the College Board's fee structure. (Everyone can direct one free score report to the college of their choice, but sending more costs $15 apiece.) On the other hand, the "Common Application" that many colleges use has a place for optional self-reporting of exam scores, including AP, by students. Many colleges (including Yale and Princeton) expect applicants to supply their scores; if admitted, they may then need to furnish an official College Board report.

Occasionally, our veteran informant explained, AP exam scores can validate (or contradict) a student's performance in a course. For example, a very hard grader—a few remain, he said, mainly in Latin!—may give a B or C for the course while the student earns a 5 on the AP exam. And vice versa; the student may get a top grade in class but score 2 on the exam.

It's much harder, he noted, to interpret student performance in dual-credit courses as there's no fixed yardstick or external exam, only the instructor's grade. Occasionally, an admissions officer will dig deeper, perhaps examining the course description on a high school website to see what it really consisted of and whether it's legitimately "college level."

His own institution is extra fussy about dual credit, generally requiring that such a course actually have been taken on a college campus, not inside the high school; that it be open to regular college students and taught by a college faculty member; and that it not also be used for high school credit. As for AP, acceptable scores are sometimes 4's but more often 5's, but, like Dartmouth and others, his university seldom allows students to shorten its full eight-semester educational experience. (He declined to acknowledge that tuition dollars might be a factor in this reluctance.) Still, arriving with credit earned prior to matriculation creates many options for students during those eight semesters, such as double majoring, "triple minoring," internships, and community service. ("Kids spending this much money want some cachet with their degree, something special, something distinctive or extra, not just a sheepskin.") They may skip introductory and general-education courses and start with more advanced classes taught by the university's own faculty, although he pointed out that it's not always advantageous to do that. A future pre-med, for example, probably shouldn't skip the university's introductory biology course. Having studied the subject previously will help one do well in the course, which is important considering how closely medical schools scrutinize undergraduate grades. In cases like that, a strategic student may be smarter to apply any AP credit against a "distribution" requirement of some kind.

Scores

There's an obvious and legitimate rationale for variability in AP score acceptance from one campus to the next, inasmuch as "college-level work" is not uniform throughout the postsecondary universe. A 4 on an AP Chemistry exam won't mean the same thing to CalTech's Chemistry Department as to Pasadena City College's, just as a 5 in English Literature means one thing to Columbia and something else a few miles away at John Jay College.

Here's the College Board's definition of the scores:

5 = extremely well qualified
4 = well qualified
3 = qualified
2 = possibly qualified
1 = no recommendation

According to long-standing AP doctrine, "qualified" means one has satisfactorily completed the equivalent of an introductory-level college course in a particular subject and is therefore ready to handle the next course in that subject.[26] Yet it's hardly a surprise that CalTech and Pasadena City College view these scores differently. AP must of necessity postulate an all-purpose college-equivalent course and a universal definition of what "satisfactory" completion signifies. Yes, these definitions and decisions are carefully vetted with panels of professors, but colleges range widely in their curricula, admissions standards, and grading practices. A college department that lets a student waive an entry-level course toward its major in history, physics, or German is acknowledging that what was taught by a nameless high school teacher in Anywhere USA covered the content that the college expects to be lodged in the brains of students going into its own second-tier courses in that subject. It has, in effect, outsourced the shaping of that content to committees assembled by the College Board to create course frameworks. It has also acknowledged that the AP exam score it's being asked to accept as proof of student mastery has been judged by ETS-assembled readers in ways that are as rigorous and nuanced as that college faculty's own judgments of student work.[27]

All this becomes more momentous—and threatening to the professoriate and its fluid notions of curriculum—as the number of AP exam-takers and passers swells into the millions. (When author Finn graduated from high school, fewer than 22,000 AP exams were taken around the globe.)

Inevitably, we also come to money, which interacts in many different and often mischievous ways in college budgets with credits awarded via

Advanced Placement exams (and dual credit, IB, CLEP, and such). Most obviously, a college that lets someone graduate in three years rather than four may forfeit a quarter of the tuition revenue and/or state subsidy that that student would otherwise generate for its coffers. Institutions in high demand may easily be able to backfill with other students and tuition dollars, while open-enrollment colleges and those with declining student numbers don't have that option. But that's just the beginning of complexity. A research university that allows too many freshmen to enter Econ 202 won't have the hundreds of bodies in Econ 101 that make possible the teaching assistant stipends that enable dozens of economics graduate students to pursue their own PhD's. On the other hand, some departments on some campuses *save* money by not having to hire extra faculty, adjuncts, and teaching assistants, thanks to course enrollments that shrink because of AP credits.

Money also influences the growing popularity of dual credit. Simply put, the college offering a dual-enrollment course gets revenue—from somewhere, typically from the state if it's a public institution, perhaps from the high school, otherwise from the student's family, sometimes from more than one source— for doing so, whereas it gets no income by simply granting credit for high school–taught courses. If students who take a dual-credit class in high school then matriculate to the college that offered that course, the college benefits twice, as it gets the students, too, plus they bring revenue. (Recall that most dual-credit classes are offered by community colleges and other open-enrollment institutions, many of which now face enrollment shortfalls.)[28]

It doesn't work that way from the student's perspective. The more revenue the college gets from tuition, the more expensive college becomes for the student, and one of AP's advantages—acceleration as well as advancement—is lost.

In recent years, policy makers in some states—strongly encouraged by the College Board—have recognized that individual professors' preferences and biases can result in decisions to deny students credit for a traditional survey course simply because it does not reflect that instructor's vision. (Sometimes baser motives are in play, such as beefing up enrollment in professors' own classes.) In the case of public institutions, denying credit also burdens the state's budget if it means that undergraduates will linger on campus, taking taxpayer-subsidized classes from state-subsidized professors. Elected officials are also sensitive to parent and student concerns about the rising cost of college and therefore keen to devise ways to assist them to reduce the number of semester hours they must pay (or borrow) for.

In addition to pushing for more dual credit, such considerations have caused lawmakers in almost half the states to require their (public) universities to award credit for AP scores of 3 or better.[29] The College Board vigorously promotes such laws, doubtless mindful of its own revenues but also seeking to widen student access to AP and the associated benefits for young people. MIT and Harvard to the contrary notwithstanding, Board officials stoutly insist that because a score of 3 or higher has repeatedly been shown to predict success in subsequent college courses, colleges should confer credit on entry to students who bring such scores with them. It isn't something they talk about much, but Board lobbyists have had much to do with the statutes that mandate such credit as well as with state policies and programs that expand AP access in the high schools and subsidize exam fees.

Although the College Board is itself a membership organization consisting mainly of colleges and universities, when it comes to the economics of Advanced Placement its interests are not well aligned with those of its members. Colleges conferring AP credit may lose money—but the College Board loses money when students shun AP exams for whatever reason, including awareness that the colleges they're headed toward won't confer any benefit to them if they do well on those exams.

As we noted earlier, Advanced Placement has become quite a big deal for the College Board. Although the program nearly died in its cradle in the late 1950s due to the deficits it was running,[30] today the Board has a major financial interest in AP participation—the more so as ACT vies with the SAT for market share in admissions testing. So while its efforts to put a fence around dual credit—and mandate acceptance of AP scores—contain a substantial element of public-minded concern for educational rigor, quality, and opportunity, we also acknowledge its institutional self-interest.

Credit denial by universities is a much greater threat to AP than rejection by a handful of pricey prep schools. Although the latter retain a prestige aura, they contain just a handful of students, and almost all of them still give their students access to the exams. But if large numbers of postsecondary institutions decline to reward qualifying scores on those exams, then sizable numbers of youngsters in every sort of high school may decide that AP isn't worth the effort or the cost. More than a few will turn instead to the cheaper, easier, and more assured path of dual credit via classes that may be offered by the selfsame colleges that are cracking down on AP. What they may forfeit by making such a move is a lot more learning.

Notes

1. Jack Schneider, "Privilege, Equity, and the Advanced Placement Program: Tug of War," *Journal of Curriculum Studies* 41, no. 6 (2009): 10.

2. Grayce Gibbs, "Schools to Stop Offering AP Courses," *Choate News*, February 17, 2017. http://thechoatenews.choate.edu/2017/02/17/school-stop-offering-ap-courses/.

3. The Scarsdale High School math department actually designates two of its advanced courses "AB Calculus" and "BC Calculus," thus copying the AP terminology. Scarsdale High School, "2018–19 Course Catalog," 23, accessed November 8, 2018. https://www.scarsdaleschools.k12.ny.us/.

4. Yilu Zhao, "High School Drops Its A.P. Courses, and Colleges Don't Seem to Mind," *New York Times*, February 1, 2002. https://www.nytimes.com/2002/02/01/nyregion/high-school-drops-its-ap-courses-and-colleges-don-t-seem-to-mind.html; Ethical Culture Fieldston School, "Course of Studies 2017–18," accessed October 8, 2018. https://www.ecfs.org/.

5. Russell Shaw and others, "Our Schools Will Get Rid of AP Courses: Here's Why," *Washington Post*, June 18, 2018. https://www.washingtonpost.com.

6. Abby Jackson, "The Best High School in America Helped Create the Fast-Growing AP Program—But Now It Does Things Differently," *Business Insider*, November 2, 2017. https://www.businessinsider.com/phillips-academy-andover-doesnt-offer-advanced-placement-2017-11; College Board, AP Central, "AP Course Audit: Phillips Academy," accessed November 8, 2019. https://apcourseaudit.inflexion.org/ledger/school.php?a=MTU0Nzg=&b=MA; *Advanced Placement 2018 Registration Information* (Andover, MA: Phillips Academy Andover, 2018). https://www.andover.edu/files/APRegwebsite_2108.pdf.

7. *Course of Instruction, 2018–2019* (Exeter, NH: Phillips Exeter Academy, 2018), 27. https://exeter.edu/sites/default/files/documents/PEA-COI-10-12-2018.pdf.

8. The head of a Washington-area private school said much the same thing.

9. Schneider, "Privilege, Equity, and the Advanced Placement Program," 14.

10. *Phillips Exeter Academy, 2017–18 Profile for Colleges* (Exeter, NH: Phillips Exeter Academy, 2017). https://exeter.edu/sites/default/files/documents/Profile%20for%20Colleges.pdf.

11. Independent Curriculum Group, "The Principles of Independent Curriculum," accessed November 8, 2018. http://independentcurriculum.org/principles-of-independent-curriculum/; Independent Curriculum Group, "History," accessed November 8, 2018. http://independentcurriculum.org/about/#partner-list.

12. Mastery Transcript Consortium, "Home," accessed November 8, 2018. http://mastery.org/.

13. Personal conversation.

14. We approximated this number from NCES data. US Department of Education, National Center for Education Statistics, "Private School Universe Survey (PSS)," accessed November 8, 2018. https://nces.ed.gov/surveys/pss/tables1516.asp.

15. The Putney School, "Mathematics," accessed November 8, 2018. https://www.putneyschool.org/mathematics/.

16. Mastery Transcript Consortium, "About Us," accessed November 8, 2018. http://mastery.org/about/about-us.

17. Chester E. Finn, Jr., "Fancy Private Schools Swim in Lake Wobegon," *Flypaper* (blog), Thomas B. Fordham Institute, May 19, 2017. https://edexcellence.net/articles/fancy-private-schools-swim-in-lake-wobegon.

18. AP allows "late testing" under special circumstances, such as when a regularly scheduled exam conflicts with a religious holiday, when there's a natural disaster, bomb scare, epidemic, and such. College Board, AP Central, "Late-Testing Policies," accessed November 8, 2018. https://apcentral.collegeboard.org/ap-coordinators/exam-ordering-fees/late-testing.

19. "Dartmouth Issues Statement Clarifying Advanced Placement Decision," Dartmouth College, press release, February 8, 2013. https://news.dartmouth.edu/news/2013/02/dartmouth-issues-statement-clarifying-advanced-placement-decision.

20. The Harvard faculty did, however, open a path by which all students "will have the option of applying to the Graduate School of Arts and Sciences as an undergraduate in order to obtain a master's degree during their four years at the College." John S. Rosenberg, "Advanced Standing Reduced," *Harvard Magazine*, May 2018. https://harvardmagazine.com/2018/05/advanced-standing-harvard; Angela N. Fu and Lucy Wang, "Faculty Vote to Accept Changes to Advanced Standing," *Harvard Crimson*, February 7, 2018. https://www.thecrimson.com/article/2018/2/7/faculty-vote-advanced-standing-changes/.

21. Brown University, "The Brown Degree: Advanced Placement Examinations," accessed November 8, 2018. https://www.brown.edu/academics/college/degree/policies/advanced-placement.

22. Amherst College, "First-Year Applicants," accessed November 8, 2018. https://www.amherst.edu/admission/apply/firstyear.

23. University of Kansas, "Advanced Placement Credit," accessed November 8, 2018. https://admissions.ku.edu/freshman-requirements-deadlines/earning-credit-high-school-work/ap.

24. Preston Cooper, "The Exaggerated Role of 'Cost Disease' in Soaring College Tuition," *Forbes*, May 10, 2017. https://www.forbes.com/sites/prestoncooper2/2017/05/10/the-exaggerated-role-of-cost-disease-in-soaring-college-tuition/#6c2ce65d2b4e.

25. Shaw et al., "Our Schools Will Get Rid of AP"; Jay Mathews, "Attack on AP by Eight D.C.-Area Private Schools Flunks the Smell Test," *Washington Post*, July 15, 2018. https://www.washingtonpost.com/local/education/.

26. College Board, AP Central, "About AP Scores," accessed November 8, 2018. https://apscore.collegeboard.org/scores/about-ap-scores.

27. This also helps explain another expanding collegiate practice, which is to give entering students generic "credit toward degree" if their AP exam scores are satisfactory, but *not* allowing them to waive particular courses that it wants them to take on campus, sometimes including introductory courses taught by departments that refuse to outsource any academic decisions.

28. Jolanta Juszkiewicz, *Trends in Community College Enrollment and Completion Data* (Washington, DC: American Association of Community Colleges, 2016).

29. College Board, AP Program Results Class of 2017, "Expanding AP Access," accessed November 8, 2018. https://reports.collegeboard.org/ap-program-results/expanding-ap-access.

30. Eric Rothschild, "Four Decades of the Advanced Placement Program," *History Teacher* 32, no. 2 (1999): 183–84.

11

Advanced Placement
Fights the Culture Wars

Even before it launched, what would become the AP program was entangled with both partisans and critics of "liberal education" and caught in the curricular crosscurrents that flow—and lately seem to gush—through such topics.

As early as the 1930s and '40s, partly in reaction to the specialization, "life adjustment," and premature vocationalism that progressivism was injecting into American education, intellectual leaders such as Robert Maynard Hutchins, Mortimer Adler, and Jacques Barzun were pressing colleges to focus on "the great books" and the "life of the mind," and to ensure that their students got a well-rounded education.[1] The famous Harvard-authored "red book" of 1945, titled *General Education in a Free Society*, was a long, eloquent, and well-reasoned plea for a broad liberal education at the tertiary level.

That report, writes historian Tim Lacy, "quickened and nationalized the general education/liberal arts controversy, expanding the discussion broadly beyond higher education into the upper tiers of secondary schools. The report helped shape future discourse about advanced placement by limiting the program to survey courses that could form the core of a general education curriculum."[2]

Those working to strengthen "general education" in elite colleges—and to propagate that idea through the expanding universe of higher education—overlapped with the thinkers and doers who gave birth to AP, and who did so, at least initially, in many of the same colleges and their secondary-school counterparts, predominantly in the Northeast and Midwest.

Of the two Ford-supported initiatives that spurred AP's formation, one was clearly wedded to the ideals of liberal education. Led by prominent teachers of history and literature at high-status institutions, the 1952 report on "General Education in School and College" celebrated such cognitive and cultural traits as "thinks rationally, logically, objectively" and "sensitive to form and affected by beauty." It also linked that kind of education to the advancement of democracy itself: "Liberal education and the democratic ideal are related to each other in a thousand ways." Written as the Cold War chill was deepening, it hinted that a society full of technocrats and specialists would be more susceptible to totalitarianism, and that a fragmented curriculum of isolated individual subjects during high school and college contributed to "the failure to communicate . . . the full meaning and purpose of a liberal education."[3]

Yet the eternal tension between liberal learning, broadly conceived, and disciplinary specialization was evident in the second prominent Ford-funded initiative, the "Kenyon Plan." Gordon Chalmers, president of the eponymous Ohio college and spearhead of that project, "favored the study of particular subjects—specialties—over larger, interdisciplinary endeavors."[4]

AP emerged as a hybrid. Its courses and exams were decidedly subject specific: US History, Biology, Calculus, and such, not "great books" or "western civilization." Yet the first batch of AP exams were in subjects that, taken as a group, constituted a broad-gauged education. And the way that students were expected to demonstrate their mastery of those subjects was not through the kinds of machine-readable multiple-choice tests that characterized the SAT and kindred assessments—and that the Educational Testing Service reportedly tried without success to introduce into AP during the program's early days—but mostly via essays and other open-ended responses that would be reviewed by experienced college and high school educators. The exams were based on course outlines developed in similar fashion by veteran teachers and professors, as were the scoring rubrics by which those papers were graded.

Thus part of AP's enduring DNA was encouragement of liberal education as then practiced at top liberal-arts colleges, while another part was the push to escalate the curricular challenges available to able students in specific subjects at the high school level. Those dual motives were in reasonable balance at the outset, although ensuing decades have brought nonstop pressures from every direction to reshape AP as academic enthusiasms and educational priorities have shifted.

Pressure always builds where tectonic plates meet, and AP sits atop precarious geology. Not only is it buffeted by the asynchronous priorities and obligations of high schools and colleges, and tugged in different directions by devotees of liberal education on the one hand and disciplinary specialization on the other, it's also beset by the curricular and philosophical battles that emerge within each subject, usually beginning with the professors who teach it, some of whom also serve on the committees that decide what goes into those AP course outlines and exams.

Although AP's mandate is to bring college-level courses to high school students ready to tackle such challenges, that doesn't mean the educational obligations and instructional missions of colleges and high schools are identical. College attendance is obviously voluntary while high school is generally compulsory. One can choose one's college but is typically assigned to a high school. And while most colleges impose course requirements on their students, these generally involve options (for example, one humanities course, two science courses)—and even those can be sidestepped by going to a different university or choosing a different major. In high school, however, many courses are mandatory, not only at the generic level ("four years of English," "three years of math") but often also at the very specific level: "a year of US history," "a semester of civics." For many young people, high school is the final stage of their formal education, and for policy makers it's the last chance to ensure that everyone in the next generation has an adequate grounding in the fundamental knowledge, skills, and traits that they—and their society—will need to thrive.

Universal grounding of that kind is not the job of colleges, yet their faculties wield outsize influence over the content of AP courses delivered by high school teachers. They play large roles in the committees that shape the frameworks, devise the exams, and determine what sort of student performance should qualify for college credit.[5] But while the courses those professors offer to their own undergraduates are generally optional for those students—if you don't like the focus of one history or literature or government course, you can nearly always substitute another—that isn't how it works in high school. A few schools, mostly in the charter and "exam school" sectors, require pupils to take specified AP courses. More commonly, schools let students decide whether to sign up for the AP course in a given subject or stick with the standard curricular offerings in that subject, yet for the individual who selects the AP path, that's often his or her only exposure to that subject during high school. Few pupils take (for example) both regular US history and AP US History during their high school years, or both English 4 and AP English Literature, or both civics and AP US Government and Politics.

It's not quite the same in math, science, and foreign languages, where the AP course in a subject frequently follows a "regular" course sequence in that subject. Even in those fields, however, the AP course—in Biology or Chemistry, say—sometimes turns out to be one's only high school exposure to that particular scientific discipline.

The half-million young Americans who sat for the AP US History exam in 2017 will almost certainly enter college without having studied any other American history after middle school. That's a nontrivial fraction of the high school population—equivalent to about one-seventh of all diploma recipients—and that fraction includes lots of smart young people who are fated beyond their numbers to become college graduates and potential leaders in the fields they later enter.

Simply put, whatever content makes its way into a subject like Advanced Placement US History (henceforth APUSH) is very likely to be the only American history that these kids study in high school—and the same is true for some of their other AP courses. Which brings us back to the tectonic shifts that have rattled so many disciplines at the university level in recent years as tradition does battle with postmodernism, as old-style survey courses give way to specialized study of parts of a subject—often the parts favored by a particular professor—and as fierce arguments erupt about whether (for example) the past should be studied in terms of why people did what they did when they did it or should be critically examined through the lens of today's values and norms.

Often referred to as "culture wars," such conflicts extend far beyond academe, but they're especially intense among university faculty, particularly in the humanities and social sciences—and in the field of education itself. For AP to remain credible with both high schools and colleges, it must balance these contending forces. If an AP class strays too far into the esoteric, subjective, and sometimes doctrinaire realms of many college courses in these fields, it forfeits its ability to provide high school students with a broad and reasonably objective "universal grounding." But if it remains a simple survey course, particularly the kind that (in the case of history) concentrates on factual knowledge of things like elections, presidents, and wars, it will no longer convince professors in that field that doing well in it justifies college credit.

This needle isn't easy to thread—and threading it seemed to hold only middling importance for the College Board as the culture wars erupted on campuses and beyond. During the thirteen eventful years (1999–2012) that former West Virginia governor Gaston Caperton led the organization, the "New AP" initiative was launched but with more attention paid to pedagogical shifts and ensuring alignment with college priorities than to the role that the content of AP courses plays or fails to play in the "liberal education" of high school students.

The "New AP" ushered in some important rethinking of what an Advanced Placement course should teach and what sort of exam would best determine whether students learned it. The goal, says Trevor Packer, was to refocus these courses less on breadth of coverage of a subject—often criticized for being "a mile wide and an inch deep" and for putting too great a premium on simple recall of facts, dates, and formulas—and more on "what students need to be able to do with their knowledge."[6]

That meant more attention to reasoning, analysis, and understanding, not just "knowing," more emphasis on "thinking like a scientist (or historian)" and less on grasping the essentials of what earlier authors had put into textbooks (and into the exam guides that AP pupils often use to cram as May approaches). This shift in emphasis was itself a big deal and moved AP broadly in the curricular and pedagogical directions that much of higher education was heading. But it was also consistent with changes emerging in K–12 academic standards, notably the 2010 arrival of the "Common Core State Standards." Both the Common Core and the New AP pushed deeper and became more analytic, but that also meant reducing the breadth of content to be "covered," focusing more on essentials. In the AP case, that included giving teachers ampler guidance both as to what their courses needed (and by extension didn't need) to "cover," and what sorts of things students might be expected to understand and explain when exam time rolled around.

So far, so good. But campus-style trouble reached AP in a big way when the "New AP" framework for APUSH was published in mid-2012 to be put into practice in 2014, with its strong emphasis on deeper understanding of America's founding documents and key texts, for this also meant a corresponding reduction in coverage of events and people—some of them famous—and what turned out, in the eyes of dispassionate reviewers as well as critics, to be a bit of a leftward tilt.

The US History Fracas

How American history is taught on university campuses today, especially in elite institutions, is far distant from yesterday's standard survey course with its chronological, "main story" emphasis on wars from the Revolution to

Vietnam, presidents from Washington to Obama, epochal Supreme Court decisions, and a handful of seismic events like the Great Depression and the New Deal.

In the fall term of 2016, Amherst College offered *no* basic survey course in US history. Instead, it served up this menu: Science and Society in Modern America; US Carceral Culture; American Foreign Policy since the End of the Cold War; Sex and Law in Colonial America; the Long Civil Rights Movement; Intelligence and US National Security Policymaking; and An Introduction to US Latino/a History, 1848–Present.

The last of those was described in the catalog in these terms:

> Central themes include ethnic and national identity, migration, gender, and political mobilization. . . . The course pays particular attention to the 1960s through the 1980s when Latinos/as mobilized in defense of their rights and against economic exploitation and undertook the "decolonization" of their communities. We will address why their struggles took the form of the right to have rights, a rejection of stereotypes, and the right to define their own identities.[7]

At Yale, during the same (fall 2016) semester, here is the full list of lecture-style US history courses:[8]

HIST	107a	Introduction to American Indian History
HIST	119b	The Civil War and Reconstruction Era, 1845–1877
HIST	120a	American Environmental History
HIST	122b	The Origins of US Global Power
HIST	127a	US Lesbian and Gay History
HIST	135b	American Economic History
HIST	135b	The Long Civil Rights Movement
HIST	140b	Public Health in America, 1793 to the Present
HIST	147a	Media and Medicine in Modern America
HIST	171b	Women in Modern America
HIST	184a	The Rise and Fall of Atlantic Slavery
HIST	193a	Molecules, Life, and Disease: 20th Century

Not a bad list—indeed, much worth learning—but, once again, no standard survey was on offer.

That wasn't true everywhere, of course. That same semester, traditional-looking history surveys remained on the menu at—for example—the University of Wisconsin[9] and Georgetown.[10] The vast list of offerings at Ohio State included a solid few that focused on US history and some that might fairly be termed surveys.[11] Yet there's no obligation even for history majors at OSU to *take* those courses; they must simply select at least six credit hours "focusing primarily on North America and/or Europe."[12] For fellow Arts and Sciences students pursuing other majors, the "general education" requirements include three credit hours of "historical study," but myriad courses satisfy that requirement. Much the same obtains for undergraduates in Ohio State's College of Business. *Their* requirement says "three hours of history," but the smorgasbord of options in fall 2016 included such things as "Water: A Human History."

Broadly, we can say that, while students at nearly every college may take US history courses if they want to, it's rare that they must—and on some campuses the available offerings don't even include a basic survey. Which underscores the importance of whatever American history they encountered in high school—almost every state requires a year of it—because that is likely to be the last organized exposure they will ever have to any systematic study of the entirety of their country's past.

Which carries its own full measure of disputation. In fact, what gets taught across the entirety of K–12 social studies has long been fraught with controversy. How are major cultural conflicts handled? Does every immigrant and ethnic group get the curricular attention that its members are certain it deserves? Are various parts of the world given due deference and sufficient real estate in the textbooks?[13] And more.

Adding the AP wrinkle invites still greater controversy, for such a course must please college professors as well as the fractious primary-secondary crowd. The challenge for its creators and instructors is to provide a class that's broadly acceptable in the stormy world of K–12 social studies while also satisfying colleges as acceptable for credit when what their own faculty is teaching by way of US history is so specialized, even idiosyncratic. While individual universities (and, often, departments within them) determine what AP scores may yield what kinds of degree credit, the AP courses themselves are intended to be more or less universal, that is, potentially acceptable on every campus. How, then, to design a US history course framework that will satisfy both Amherst and Wisconsin even as it complies with state laws mandating a year of American history—and also work for public high schools that are ultimately answerable to the elected officials who write those laws, and whose states don't necessarily favor the same versions of that history?

The College Board's overhauled APUSH design still employed a chronological approach, spanning nine periods from 1491 to the present, but—befitting a "New AP" course—it emphasized depth, themes, concepts, and analysis more than just "knowing" and "explaining." That, however, was not the source of the ensuing uproar. The new framework was roundly denounced, primarily by conservatives, for misrepresenting the essence of the American story and ignoring key figures and events.

Among the critics were the Texas State Board of Education and the Republican National Committee, which passed a resolution stating that the framework embodied "a radically revisionist view of American history that emphasizes negative aspects of our nation's history while omitting or minimizing positive aspects."[14] Also heard from were such prominent right-leaning scholars as Harvey Mansfield, Victor Davis Hanson, and Leon Kass, who, with several dozen others, published an "open letter" declaring:

> There are notable political or ideological biases inherent in the 2014 framework, and certain structural innovations that will inevitably result in imbalance in the test, and bias in the course. Chief among these is the treatment of American national identity. The 2010 framework treated national identity, including "views of the American national character and ideas about American exceptionalism" as a central theme. But the 2014 framework makes a dramatic shift away from that emphasis, choosing instead to grant far more extensive attention to "how various identities, cultures, and values have been preserved or changed in different contexts of U.S. history with special attention given to the formation of gender, class, racial and ethnic identities." The new framework makes a shift from "identity" to "identities." Indeed, the new framework is so populated with examples of American history as the conflict between social groups, and so inattentive to the sources of national unity and cohesion, that it is hard to see how students will gain any coherent idea of what those sources might be. This does them, and us, an immense disservice.[15]

Enter David Coleman

About the same time the new APUSH framework was unveiled (2012), David Coleman took the helm of the College Board, bent on—among many goals—doing what he could to arrest the drift away from liberal arts that he had observed in both K–12 and higher education. Indeed, an admiring profile in *The Atlantic* that year described Coleman as "an utterly romantic believer in the power of the traditional liberal arts. A Rhodes Scholar whose conversation leaps gracefully from Plato to *Henry V*, he holds advanced degrees in English literature from Oxford and classical philosophy from Cambridge."[16] And he came to the College Board fresh from combat in the standards-and-curriculum battles at the K–12 level and as lead writer of the Common Core State Standards for English Language Arts, in which capacity he had emphasized the deep reading of primary texts and explicit attention to America's "founding documents."

What, he wondered, might the College Board do to strengthen liberal learning for more young Americans? And how, in particular, to do that with AP courses that also had to pass muster with university professors at a time when such learning was fading from many of their campuses?

As Coleman was formulating his own future plans and strategies, he was blindsided by the furor over the new APUSH framework, developed before he got there. But he swiftly took ownership of the problem, understood its significance both for the Board's general credibility and for his own agenda, and recognized the perilous prospect that the first high-profile controversy on his watch would be over a course that ought to embody and advance his own interest in broad-based liberal learning.

Accordingly, Coleman encouraged Packer and the AP team to take the criticism seriously and, at minimum, to seek some independent framework reviews. Which they did, consulting widely and asking independent historian Jeremy Stern to undertake a close examination. As it turned out, there were indeed substantive shortcomings in the document—"legitimate concerns," Stern termed them. As he wrote in the *History News Network* in 2015:

> While the concept and many parts of the content were sound, the framework too often took a tendentious and judgmental approach to history, appearing to urge condemnation of the past for its failure to live up to present-day moral standards. Such an approach—ignoring historical context in favor of current ideological and political priorities—is presentism, not history. . . . The 2014 version, for example, repeatedly singled out the British North American colonies as uniquely intolerant, violent and oppressive (unfavorably comparing them with the frequently brutal Spanish empire). . . . The Atlantic slave trade, discussed in 2014 almost uniquely in terms of British North America, in fact predated those colonies by a century, and the vast majority of slaves actually went to the Caribbean and Brazil; also, powerful African states captured and sold virtually all the slaves bought by European traders on the African coast. . . . In the 2014 version, western settlement was discussed almost entirely in terms of its dire impact on increasingly besieged native peoples, with no attention given to the settlers' aims and worldview (a crucial part of the story, whatever we think today of their actions in pursuit of those aims). . . . The

2014 framework seemed to invite students to condemn the use of the atomic bomb on Japan in 1945. . . . Coverage of the Reagan era—always difficult ground, given its contested place in today's political battles—came across as dismissive.[17]

Responding constructively rather than defensively to this analysis, Coleman and Packer reconvened (with some judicious changes) the panels that had forged the framework. They also invited advice from Stern and other external reviewers, and pushed for a revamp.[18] This yielded a revised framework in 2015 that drew praise from most of the earlier critics—and that deserves applause for threading such a sharp needle. It's neither progressivist nor conservative; it's balanced, covering essentials of the country's past and pressing teachers and students to dig deep in understanding why America's history unfolded as it did. Here's a pair of sample questions from the multiple choice portion of a practice exam:[19]

QUESTIONS 10 AND 11 REFER TO THE EXCERPT BELOW.

"Governments are instituted among Men, deriving their just powers from the consent of the governed. That whenever any Form of Government becomes destructive of these ends, it is the Right of the People to alter or to abolish it, and to institute new Government, laying its foundation on such principles and organizing its powers in such form, as to them shall seem most likely to effect their Safety and Happiness."
—THOMAS JEFFERSON, DECLARATION OF INDEPENDENCE, 1776

10. The excerpt was written in response to the:

   (A) British government's attempt to assert greater control over the North American colonies
   (B) British government's failure to protect colonists from attacks by American Indians
   (C) colonial governments' failures to implement mercantilist policies
   (D) colonial governments' attempts to extend political rights to new groups

11. The ideas about government expressed in the excerpt are most consistent with which of the following?

   (A) The concept of hereditary rights and privileges
   (B) The belief in Manifest Destiny

(C) The principle of religious freedom

(D) The ideas of the Enlightenment

Also revealing are the kinds of questions posed to students for the forty-minute essay portion of the APUSH exam. Here—from the same practice test—are their three options:

- Evaluate the extent to which trans-Atlantic interactions fostered change in labor systems in the British North American colonies from 1600 to 1763.
- Evaluate the extent to which new technology fostered change in United States industry from 1865 to 1900. [or]
- Evaluate the extent to which globalization fostered change in the United States economy from 1945 to 2000.[20]

This thought-provoking, analytic approach to US history is a far cry from the pre-2014 course, which was based on such an abbreviated framework that teachers had to scrutinize prior exams to get a sense of what their students might be expected to know—which could be just about anything. Such a mile-wide version naturally frustrated instructors and stressed students. Hence the "New AP" approach, which strives to distill pupil understanding of what's most important in a given subject.

Distillation, however, entails narrowing and choosing—and deepening means probing for the kinds of understanding and analysis that include judgment. In a field like history, that comes perilously close to "opinion" or "preference," which is what culture wars are all about. Because those conflicts are so intense in academe, and on the rise in some K–12 subjects as well, it's not hard to see why such a course can prove so contentious.

After a troubled start, however, the College Board recovered its balance in APUSH—and Coleman and company resolved to strive to get it right the first time when they revised the framework and exam structure for the next subjects that are especially vulnerable to this sort of contention, namely, civics and world history.

US Government and Politics

Almost every state requires its teens to take at least a semester of "civics," "government," or "American government."[21] As with US History, passing the AP course in US Government and Politics is one way of fulfilling that requirement—and, as in history, students who take that course are unlikely to take any other civics class before graduating. Here, once again, the AP course is also meant to satisfy colleges and universities that it's equivalent to what they teach in this realm.

Which is not to say that conventional introductory courses in civics and American government are ubiquitous on today's campuses, much less required of students. The closest Harvard came in 2016–17 was a one-semester course titled "American Government: A New Perspective," which the catalog described thusly:

> This course examines how American democracy and government work. Although the course serves as an introduction to American government, it also shows how well established institutions have been altered by modern politics, and it introduces students to key ideas in political science. We place particular emphasis on the increasingly significant role that electoral pressures and the permanent campaign play in the workings of American government.[22]

At Stanford, the Political Science Department came closest to undergraduate "civics" courses (fall 2016) with "The Federal System: Judicial Politics and Constitutional Law," "Introduction to American Law," and several offerings focused on that year's election.[23]

Political science majors at UCLA must take four of six lower-level courses in that department, one of which is "Introduction to American Politics"— but there's no requirement to take that one in particular.

Few US college students are required to take civics, and those who wish to may or may not find a survey-style course, meaning that, once again, what they learn in high school may be their final structured exposure to the principles, structures, procedures, and politics by which their country is (supposed to be) governed. But, once again, if it's an AP course, it must also satisfy college-level expectations.

Having learned from the APUSH rumpus and wanting both to avoid another ideological dustup and to promote thoughtful, well-informed citizenship—a priority for Coleman, now firmly at the Board's helm—when revamping its US Government and Politics course (which took effect in 2018), AP leaders joined forces with the National Constitution Center and other groups to identify key "founding documents" and Supreme Court cases for which there's broad—even bipartisan—agreement about the value of studying and understanding. Here's how the drafters describe their approach:

> A specified set of fifteen Supreme Court cases and nine foundational documents—including the Declaration of Independence and the Constitution—will now be required study. For each required Supreme

Court case, the National Constitution Center will publish articles for students showing both sides, where there was bipartisan agreement, and where there were differences.[24]

Coleman himself penned a powerful and lofty declaration of goals for the new course:

> AP U.S. Government and Politics offers students the opportunity to see how individuals and their ideas can shape the world in which they live; it invites them to explore central questions of liberty and justice in practice. The Supreme Court opinions explored in this course are not museum pieces but deeply felt expressions. They all represent real choices and decisions with enormous consequences. We aim for students to read them and discuss them with openness and insight.
>
> The ideas at the heart of the American Founding remain as vital and urgent as they were more than two-hundred years ago; it is our task as educators to make them vivid once more. . . .
>
> While this framework is new, its aims are timeless and its roots deeply embedded in the American experiment and the intellectual traditions that animated our founding. . . .
>
> For Aristotle, participation in civic life is necessary to live fully. President Eisenhower much more recently declared that "politics ought to be the part time profession of every person who would protect the rights and privileges of free people and who would preserve what is good and fruitful in our national heritage.[25]

So far, it appears, this revamped AP course is off to a smooth start.

World History

Fewer states require their students to study world history during high school than mandate US history and civics, but it—or something akin to it—is obligatory in Minnesota, California, Florida, and elsewhere.[26] Some 300,000 high school students take the AP World History exam each year, making it one of the most popular subjects on the list.

Its course description was revised as recently as 2017 to give teachers additional curricular guidance and bring the format into line with the New AP's emphasis on conceptual understanding, "thematic learning objectives," and core concepts.[27] But its content still spanned many millennia, stretching back to the Paleolithic era.

This, the College Board determined, was too much for a one-year course and—just as important—no longer mirrored courses taught on many college campuses. So in spring 2018, Packer's team announced that a new framework and exam would be promulgated in time for the 2019–20 school year.[28] The key change would be a sharp reduction in time periods. The new World History course would commence in 1450, that is, would consist of the latter half of the old framework's six historical "periods." Schools wishing to expose their students to earlier eras would be encouraged to adopt the new pre-AP course in "World History and Geography," intended for ninth graders.

Whereupon a new storm arose, this time—in contrast to APUSH—with protests coming mostly from the left side of the political-educational complex.[29] The main objection, voiced by some high school teachers (and a few entrepreneurs who "prep" students for the World History exam), was that commencing in the fifteenth century would make the course too "Eurocentric" by omitting the various Asian, Middle Eastern, and African civilizations that came before. (Of course, it would also omit the classical civilizations of Greece and Rome.) This, said some, would affront "students of color" who would no longer see much of their own heritage reflected in the course and therefore might not learn enough of it themselves, much less would their "majority" classmates.[30] Additionally, said some objectors, their schools might not be able to afford the Board's fees to mount the new pre-AP course, as those are financed by charges levied on the school or district rather than (via exam charges) on students and families.

After getting an earful of complaints at a conference, receiving a petition with some eight thousand online signatures, and innumerable tweets and other comments, AP chieftain Packer—by then closer to losing it than is normal for this seemingly unflappable man—signaled that the College Board would make further adjustments before rolling out its new World History course.

He and his colleagues moved swiftly to quell the uproar and by mid-July were ready with a revised plan. The revamped course would commence in 1200, which, said the Board's announcement, "Will ensure teachers and students can begin the course with a study of the civilizations in Africa, the Americas, and Asia that are foundational to the modern era."[31] Additionally, the Board promised—so long as it could identify sufficient support for this move among college faculty and high schools—to develop another addition to the catalog, to be dubbed "AP World History: Ancient." And the aforementioned pre-AP "World History and Geography" course would also remain available.

A reasonable accommodation, we would say, and one that the College Board insisted was based on input from "a range of stakeholders . . . who brought to light principled concerns and opportunities for improvement." But the early response from the field was mixed, as some insisted that the choice of 1200 was "arbitrary" and warned that the proposed ancient history course might never come to pass. We won't know for a while—but we can be pretty sure the fuss won't end for a while, either.

Vulnerabilities

Unlike the Common Core standards—which encountered much controversy for political reasons entangled with concerns about federal heavy-handedness and differing views of the Obama administration, and because states adopting these standards were, in effect, requiring every public school to adhere to them—Advanced Placement has the luxury of being private, voluntary, and generally immune to electoral politics.

But that doesn't immunize it against academic politics and contention or the intellectual contretemps that get fought over in journals and faculty meetings. This has proven not to be a huge issue in the natural and physical sciences, although controversies sometimes kick up there around hot topics such as evolution and climate change and, more broadly, in the long-running debate between those who believe that a traditional survey course is more important grounding than a "think like a scientist course" that goes deeper but covers less content. Still, science and math are relatively quiescent.

The main arenas for cultural warfare and curricular conflict in the AP program, as on the college campus, are in the social sciences and humanities. Which works of literature (if any) should a literature course require students to read—and which to omit? Are the authors sufficiently "diverse" and are their works analyzed in terms of what the author actually wrote or how we think those texts were influenced by factors in his or her life and circumstance?

In practice, the AP English Literature course framework ducks the "which author" problem by supplying a long and extremely diverse list of "representative authors," stating bluntly that "there is no recommended or required reading list" and inviting teachers to "select authors from the names below or may choose others of comparable quality and complexity."[32] No literary canon here, though the suggested readings do include the most prominent American authors across multiple genres—and there's a better-than-even chance that some of those authors will turn up in the passages that students are asked to analyze when exam time rolls around. Teachers are indeed free to assign other works, but there's subtle encouragement in the direction of enduring works and major writers.

No such subtlety is possible in social studies, however, and history has proven to be the main flashpoint so far, with recent efforts to overhaul both of AP's big history courses running into trouble, first from the right, then from the left. Both times, Packer and company—encouraged by Coleman—have gone back to the drawing board to try to set matters right without sacrificing the program's integrity or the commitment to do right by students and teachers— as well as parents, professors, and taxpayers—in a volatile academic domain.

It's impossible to know how long the AP program will maintain its rekindled attention to liberal learning, core documents, deep reading of primary sources and themes combined with due coverage of essential content, much less how successfully it can maintain a balanced handling of controversial topics. But Coleman is young, the attention appears serious, and the course frameworks themselves, once revised or replaced, have a long shelf life. In retrospect, the APUSH fracas may have been a necessary cold shower, a sober awakening to the care that must be taken when melding the expectations of a college-level course in the twenty-first century with the obligations of public high schools to prepare their pupils for citizenship, adulthood, further education, fulfilling careers, and a successful life in a land that remains heir to the best (and sometimes the worst) of Western civilization. More showers, however, probably both cold and hot, surely lie ahead.

Notes

1. Diane Ravitch, *Left Back: A Century of Failed School Reforms* (New York: Simon and Schuster, 2000).

2. Tim Lacy, "Examining AP: Access, Rigor, and Revenue in the History of the Advanced Placement Program," in *AP: A Critical Examination of the Advanced Placement Program*, ed. Phillip M. Sadler and others (Cambridge, MA: Harvard Education Press, 2010), 22. See more in chapter 1.

3. *General Education in School and College: A Committee Report by Members of the Faculties of Andover, Exeter, Lawrenceville, Harvard, Princeton, and Yale* (Cambridge, MA: Harvard University Press, 1952).

4. Lacy, "Examining AP," 26.

5. To see how the College Board describes the process, go to "How AP Develops Courses and Exams," accessed November 8, 2018. https://apcentral.collegeboard.org/about-ap/how-ap-develops-courses-and-exams. For a list of those who created and advised on the new AP Research course within the Capstone sequence, see *Course and Exam Description, AP Research, Part of the Capstone Program* (New York: College Board, 2017). https://apcentral.collegeboard.org/pdf/ap-research-course-and-exam-description.pdf. Note the combination of university faculty, high school instructors, and outside experts.

6. Christopher Drew, "Rethinking Advanced Placement," *New York Times*, January 7, 2011. https://www.nytimes.com/2011/01/09/education/edlife/09ap-t.html?pagewanted=all&mcubz=1.

7. Amherst College, "Course Catalog 2016–17," accessed November 9, 2018. https://www.amherst.edu/academiclife/college-catalog/1617?mmtid=489903.

8. *Yale College Programs of Study: Fall and Spring Terms, 2016–2017* (New Haven, CT: Yale University, 2016), 410–13. http://bulletin.printer.yale.edu/pdffiles/ycps.pdf.

9. University of Wisconsin–Madison, Department of History, "History Department Syllabi Library," accessed November 12, 2018. https://history.wisc.edu/undergraduate-program/syllabi-library/.

10. Georgetown University, "Class Schedule Listing for Fall 2016," accessed November 12, 2018. https://myaccess.georgetown.edu/.

11. *Course Offerings Bulletin, 2016–2017* (Columbus: Ohio State University, 2016), 232–46.

12. *Course Offerings Bulletin, 2016–2017*, "The History Major at Ohio State," accessed November 8, 2018. https://history.osu.edu/undergrad/major.

13. Courtland Milloy, "Students Gain an Appreciation for History after Learning There's More to the Story," *Washington Post*, November 21, 2017. https://www.washingtonpost.com/local/; "Texas School Board Approves Controversial Textbook Changes," *Need to Know* (blog), PBS, May 23, 2010. http://www.pbs.org/wnet/need-to-know/culture/texas-school-board-approves-controversial-textbook-changes/954/; Kathleen Porter-Magee, James Leming, and Lucien Ellington, *Where Did Social Studies Go Wrong?* (Washington, DC: Thomas B. Fordham Institute, 2003). https://edexcellence.net/publications/wheredidssgowrong.html.

14. Catherine Gewertz, "Republican National Committee Condemns New AP History Framework," *Education Week*, August 11, 2014. http://blogs.edweek.org/edweek/curriculum/2014/08/college_board_statement_on_ap.html.

15. An open letter from scholars concerned about Advanced Placement history, "Letter Opposing the 2014 APUSH Framework," *National Association of Scholars*, June 2, 2015, 2–3. https://www.nas.org/images/documents/Historians_Statement.pdf; Stanley Kurtz, "How the College Board Politicized U.S. History," *National Review*, August 25, 2014. https://www.nationalreview.com/corner/how-college-board-politicized-us-history-stanley-kurtz/.

16. Dana Goldstein, "The Schoolmaster," *The Atlantic*, October 2012. https://www.theatlantic.com/magazine/archive/2012/10/the-schoolmaster/309091/.

17. Jeremy Stern, "Left and Right May Not Be Happy with the New AP Standards: Here's Why You Should Be," *History News Network* (blog), *George Washington University, Columbian College of Arts and Sciences*, August 14, 2015. http://historynewsnetwork.org/article/160264.

18. Author Finn was among the critics. Frederick M. Hess and Chester E. Finn, Jr., "Getting Our History Right," *American Enterprise Institute* (blog), September 23, 2014. https://www.aei.org/publication/getting-our-history-right/.

19. *AP United States History Practice Exam: From the Course and Exam Description* (New York: College Board, 2017), 8. http://secure-media.collegeboard.org/digitalServices/pdf/ap/ap-united-states-history-ced-practice-exam.pdf.

20. *AP United States History Practice Exam*, 34.

21. Education Commission of the States, "50-State Comparison, Civic Education Policies: High School Graduation Requirements," December, 2016. http://ecs.force.com/mbdata/MBQuest2RTANW?Rep=CIP1601S.

22. *Course Syllabus, Government 30: American Government—A New Perspective, Fall 2016* (Cambridge, MA: Harvard University, 2016). http://wayback.archive-it.org/3671/20170601171514/https://canvas.harvard.edu/courses/18056/files/2701001/download?verifier=NE8sgA2rVDaYVColx9cAyWmaLdVFbGvfMnQIo5Gk.

23. Stanford University, "Bulletin: Explore Courses, Political Science," accessed November 13, 2018. https://explorecourses.stanford.edu/search?q=POLISCI&view=catalog&filter-catalognumber-POLISCI=on&academicYear=20162017&filter-term-Autumn=on&filter-departmentcode-POLISCI=on&page=0&filter-coursestatus-Active=on&collapse=.

24. College Board, AP Central, "AP U.S. Government and Politics: About the 2018–19 Redesign," accessed November 8, 2018. https://apcentral.collegeboard.org/courses/ap-united-states-government-and-politics/redesign-launching-fall-2018.

25. *AP U.S. Government and Politics: Course and Exam Description* (New York: College Board, 2018). https://apcentral.collegeboard.org/pdf/ap-us-government-and-politics-course-and-exam-description-effective-fall-2018.pdf.

26. Some state requirements are phrased as "world history or geography" or "world history, cultures, and geography." Education Commission of the States, "50-State Comparison, High School Graduation Requirements: Social Studies," March 22, 2007. http://ecs.force.com/mbdata/mbquest3NE?rep=HS07.

27. *AP World History: Course and Exam Description* (New York: College Board, 2017). https://apcentral.collegeboard.org/pdf/ap-world-history-course-and-exam-description.pdf?course=ap-world-history.

28. College Board, AP Central, "AP World History, 2019–20 AP World History Changes," Accessed November 8, 2018. https://apcentral.collegeboard.org/courses/.

29. Valerie Strauss, "AP World History Course Is Dropping Thousands of Years of Human Events—and Critics Are Furious," *Washington Post*, June 15, 2018. https://www.washingtonpost.com/news/answer-sheet/wp/2018/06/15/ap-world-history-course-is-dropping-thousands-of-years-of-human-events-and-critics-are-furious/?utm_term=.efa92dc779c4.

30. Alia Wong, "The Controversy over Just How Much History AP World History Should Cover," *The Atlantic*, June 13, 2018. https://www.theatlantic.com/education/archive/2018/06/ap-world-history-controversy/562778/.

31. Valerie Strauss, "College Board Restores 250 Years to AP World History Course after Outcry over Plan to Cut 9,000 Years," *Washington Post*, July 20, 2018. https://www.washingtonpost.com/news/answer-sheet/wp/2018/07/20/college-board-restores-250-years-to-ap-world-history-course-after-outcry-over-plan-to-cut-9000-years/?utm_term=.4df9f8c2407e.

32. *AP English Literature and Composition: Course Description* (New York: College Board, 2014). http://media.collegeboard.com/digitalServices/pdf/ap/ap-english-literature-and-composition-course-description.pdf.

PART IV

Looking Ahead

12

Making a Difference

Is Advanced Placement a vast and growing "scam," as political scientist John Tierney asserted in *The Atlantic* a few years back?[1] An overhyped educational extravagance with scant evidence that it does anyone much good?[2] A mere "cash cow for the College Board," as education critic Diane Ravitch declared in the *New York Times Magazine* in 2017?[3] Or is it, as veteran *Washington Post* columnist Jay Mathews insists, "the most powerful educational tool in the country," the closest thing American education has to a win-win initiative that raises academic standards, enhances the life prospects of millions of children, promotes some of the strongest teaching and deepest learning to be found in US high schools, acts as a powerful engine of school reform, and helps to preserve liberal learning at a time when that's under assault from many directions?[4]

Because we share the latter view, we can easily and enthusiastically contemplate a vibrant future for Advanced Placement, even as we recognize a number of ways in which the program's devotees aspire to more than it can presently deliver. In this chapter, we recap what we've learned—mostly positive—about AP, seeking to balance the good that it's doing against the challenges that it faces now and in the years ahead.

AP's Role(s) Today

ACADEMIC GOLD STANDARD

High achievement—and achievers—in American education can be identified and recognized in any number of ways from the National Merit Scholarship rolls to scores of 5 and 6 on PISA exams, 4 and 5 on PARCC exams, getting 800's on SATs or 35's on ACTs, reaching the "advanced" level on the National Assessment, gaining admission to highly competitive schools and colleges, and more, including winning less visible rewards such as Jack Kent Cooke and Carolyn Bradley scholarships. Meritocracy and merit-based recognition remain surprisingly robust in our K–12 and higher education systems, co-existing, however nervously, alongside our many efforts to remove barriers and advance equity, and managing to hold their own, however tenuously, in an era of grade inflation and academic standards that sometimes rise and sometimes sink.

Yet for all of that, there's something distinctive and peculiarly valuable about the Advanced Placement program and its standing in the realms of high school curricula, student aspiration, and academic accomplishment. The American Enterprise Institute's Nat Malkus says it "fills an important role in challenging high-achieving students, making it unique in an education system that has long focused on bringing up the performance of low-achieving public-school students."[5] Jay Mathews and *U.S. News* both use AP—participation rates and/or qualifying scores—as a key gauge of high school quality in their influential ranking systems. When Sheila Byrd and colleagues reviewed Advanced Placement (and IB) for the Thomas B. Fordham Institute in 2007, they found minor flaws yet termed it "mostly gold," because it sets

> high academic standards and goals for learning that are well delineated for teachers, students, and parents. Equally important, the exams . . . are well aligned to their standards, testing students on the content of their courses and considerably more. Students are also expected to make sense of complex, and sometimes contradictory, materials; to write and defend their opinions about these materials intelligently; and to apply their knowledge in creative and productive ways. These are all skills that will serve them well in later years.[6]

Unlike other gauges of academic achievement, AP is subject specific and can be taught and studied for, not an after-the-fact accolade that simply appears, deus ex machina. Its scores denote actual knowledge and skills that a student demonstrates in connection with a subject, not some curriculum-agnostic abstraction like "ability."

Because no good deed goes entirely unpunished, however, the very fact that AP is linked to a detailed framework and can be studied for carries the risk that "teaching to the test" will overpower sound pedagogical practice, and that kids will grub for exam scores rather than the thrill of insight, originality, and intellectual growth. While it's not possible to block all such deviations by instructors and pupils, the "new AP" course frameworks do pretty well at focusing on deep understanding, not just recall, and the open-response, essay-style items on today's AP exams can't really be mastered through rote learning. Top-notch teacher preparation and professional development also make a difference, although the faster the program grows the harder it is to ensure that all those placed in front of AP classrooms will have benefited from such opportunities.

Other distinct advantages of Advanced Placement, when viewed alongside alternative sources of high-level academic achievement and recognition, are that it's undertaken by individual pupils, not just a sampling of them, and that one's results are attached to oneself, not averaged with others or associated with a faceless group of "Tennessee students" or "eleventh grade girls." Its expectations are transparent and its scoring system is uniform across the land. At least some of its benefits for participants are tangible, even calculable in dollars and time spent, unlike such nebulous educational desiderata as "social-emotional learning." It's not perfect but, along with the much smaller IB program, AP comes closer than anything else in American secondary education to an academic gold standard. So long as its thousands of participating schools and school systems heed the cautions noted above, it can—and should—continue to attract more youngsters in more communities across the land.

GOLD FOR THE MANY

All students who are willing to accept the challenge of a rigorous academic curriculum should be considered for admission to AP courses. The Board encourages the elimination of barriers that restrict access to AP courses for students from ethnic, racial, and socioeconomic groups that have been traditionally under-represented in the AP Program. Schools should make every effort to ensure that their AP classes reflect the diversity of their student population.
—EQUITY STATEMENT OF THE ADVANCED PLACEMENT PROGRAM

The gold contained within the AP program's thirty-eight courses and exams is gradually entering the education strongboxes of millions of young people without regard to their personal circumstances, the varying standards of their states and districts, or the idiosyncratic practices of their schools. Although access to it and the benefits that may flow from it remain far from evenly distributed, it has undergone a seismic change. When AP emerged in the 1950s, and for decades thereafter, poor and minority youngsters had limited access to the best that American education had to offer, and those limits were part of what kept them—and often their children and grandchildren—poor. Today, however, AP's rich curriculum, sophisticated pedagogy, and rigorous expectations are coming within reach of many girls and boys from disadvantaged circumstances, thanks in no small part to the College Board's wholehearted embrace of that additional mission as well as the hard work and support of policy makers, educators, and philanthropists.

But what a tough mission to carry out successfully! Journalist Alina Tugend caused a stir in September 2017, as Mayor de Blasio's "AP for All" initiative was revving up in New York City, when the *New York Times Magazine* published her long article suggesting that the big national push to enroll more poor kids in Advanced Placement classes has been an expensive failure because few such kids succeed on the exams and there's no proof that the AP experience does anyone much good in the absence of a qualifying score. "Is it effective," she asked, "to be investing the time and resources in a program whose benefits seem so difficult to pin down? And allocating funds in this way can have perverse consequences. If only a small number of students are truly prepared for Advanced Placement, then students who are either unprepared or unmotivated to be admitted have to fill out the class." She quoted a Florida AP teacher who complained that "now you put thirty kids in a classroom and fifteen have no business being there. And the kids who don't want to be there, they become disruptive."[7]

Although causal connections are hard to prove, successful completion of AP classes and qualifying scores on the ensuing exams are undeniably associated with success in college, and bringing this potentially life-changing benefit to more poor and minority youngsters is a laudable undertaking. At least as valuable is direct exposure to high expectations, rigorous standards, and serious learning of important content in realms that matter as much for good citizenship and effective participation in adult society as for college and career.

Yet desirable as it is to open AP-level academics to more kids in more schools and thereby help level the playing fields of life, the reason this is hard to make happen, especially at scale, is that genuine success requires so many other things to move in sync, both in school systems and in the lives of kids.

Some of those moves are partially within the College Board's control. The new suite of pre-AP courses, for example, is a purposeful attempt by the Board to leverage the ninth grade curriculum (and indirectly influence what happens in middle school) so as to pave the way for later AP success. Professional development opportunities for thousands more teachers, while demanding and costly, are something that program leaders know how to provide.

AP leaders have also scrambled to beef up the student and teacher supports that they are rolling out in 2019, including more formative assessments, feedback loops during the school year, and access to competent (and free) sources of help for struggling kids and their instructors.

But the College Board can't do it all alone. The AP program has scant leverage on what happens before ninth grade, and disadvantaged youngsters drag many anchors with them into high school, including the wretched academic preparation that many received beforehand. Although well-functioning secondary institutions such as New York's Urban Assembly School for Law and Justice (see chapter 5) can take forceful steps to undo the damage with their ninth graders and ready many of them to tackle AP (and similar advanced classes) in later years, this is a very heavy lift.

High schools, too, present inherent challenges. They're stubborn, complex institutions with deep-set routines and traditions as well as attitudes and cultures. They're subjected to multiple concurrent reforms and innovations—dual credit often among them—which sometimes tug in different directions. This can easily frustrate and exhaust their leaders and instructors, sometimes turning them into cynics. Yet if teachers, counselors, and administrators, many with tenure and long years of experience in their present roles, are unaccustomed to ushering poor and minority kids—and kids with so-so grades but a spark in their eyes—into AP classrooms and then doing their utmost to help them succeed, the AP program itself has limited power to alter the situation (although catalyzing such changes is the mission of many admirable outside groups). And if the educators who work in a school don't expect (and may not really want) AP to encompass more students, it's unlikely that many of their pupils and parents will expect or see the value of it, either.

Even when all those stars can be aligned, perhaps with the help of interveners such as NMSI and EOS, there remains the problem of mediocre feeder schools, which are beyond the power of high school people to change, as well as the problem of district policies, state standards, and assessments that encourage educators and kids to settle for basic "proficiency" rather than posing the intellectual challenges and academic expectations—and mustering the instructional resources to match—that must undergird widespread success with college-level courses. Amplifying the challenge are educator-preparation programs that pay scant attention to "gifted" students, much less to the special challenges of gifted-but-disadvantaged youngsters, and policies (federal, state, local) that discourage acceleration, that consign every student in a given grade to the same (often low) standards of achievement, and that view souped-up classes for some kids as inherently elitist and discriminatory.

Many disadvantaged youngsters, including the brightest among them, face hurdles outside school, too. Although low-income and minority communities contain plenty of well-functioning families with reserves of social capital, that's far from universal in the populations that AP is now striving to engage. Family obligations and jobs often consume time and energy. Disruptions at home and neighborhood can make it hard to concentrate on brain-racking homework. Parents lacking college experience may not be much help with that homework and may have trouble getting their kids to Saturday study sessions and such. Even the most committed high school teachers, advisors, and external boosters can only do so much if students' lives beyond the school building press in the opposite direction.

Those striving to make AP accessible to more kids in more places must also grapple with the paradox of participation rates that go up while success rates go down, particularly among minority youngsters. That was the thrust of Tugend's provocative piece and kindred criticisms: How much good does AP do kids who fail to get qualifying scores on the exams? We heard many positive anecdotes—possibly self-justifying—from teachers, yet conventional research has not definitively shown that AP participation has value in the absence of passing scores. The program's democratization has meant that thousands more minority pupils *are* getting higher scores, which is indisputably a good thing for them. But is it a good thing that even more thousands of their peers sit in the same classrooms and then get 2's and 1's on the exams while traditional AP students rack up most of the 4's and 5's? If Advanced Placement is indeed to function as an important lever in closing achievement and excellence gaps and thereby narrowing other big gaps in American society, how do we explain the widening of some gaps as the program casts a wider net?

This is truly fraught, especially when we see other parents and teachers—also mindful of their own interests—suggesting that it dilutes what's learned by traditional AP students (that is, motivated kids from supportive middle-class homes and solid middle schools) when they're joined in class by lots of ill-prepared pupils, some of whom had to be persuaded to be there. There are signs of political backlash from advocates as well as parental unrest and resistance from veteran AP teachers.[8]

After thoroughly examining the relevant research, the University of Southern California's Suneal Kolluri offered this judicious summary of the situation:

> The AP program is yet to achieve its dual goals of equitable access and effective college-level skill development. Although more students from groups traditionally underrepresented in AP are now taking at least one AP course, schools in wealthier neighborhoods have significantly increased AP opportunities for their students . . . . [T]he increase in access to AP in the context of entrenched social and educational inequities is noteworthy. However, the case may be that more AP participation is not necessarily beneficial. Today, students appear less likely to experience enhanced college-going outcomes tied to their participation in AP. This trend may be tied to the fact that greater percentages of students, particularly those from marginalized populations, have failed AP exams.[9]

As is true of every other education reform, it's infinitely easier to usher more kids from more varied backgrounds through the doors of Advanced Placement classrooms than to ensure that many of them emerge with the exam scores that denote success. Not even trying to make this happen, however, would be akin to not sending out-of-shape youngsters into phys ed classes on grounds that too few will be able to do push-ups and chin-ups when they come out. Sticking with such a regimen, it's fair to say, will cause gym teachers eventually to adapt their methods so that more kids get fitter, and even those who still can't quite reach the chinning bar will have stronger muscles and be better prepared for healthier lives.

Sticking with the regimen—and the analogy—also means that more PE instructors will be needed and their own preparation will have to change. Perhaps it will mean that others responsible for those children—parents, previous teachers, scout leaders, and such—will take fitness more seriously. And the schools and colleges that subsequently receive those fitter young people will also need to adapt by recognizing what they're now capable of and not making them repeat the exercises that they've already mastered.

In sum, opening the AP door to more kids is a good thing to do, not only for the benefit of those immediately affected but also because its implications should reverberate through what precedes and follows it. And *not* expanding access, even if the price is a period of declining pass rates, would wall off an important path to upward mobility and make AP more culpable of preserving societal inequities by conferring additional advantages only on the advantaged.

BASTION OF LIBERAL ARTS

AP's role as a bulwark of liberal learning is notable, as are today's mounting threats to such education. With rare exceptions, the program has rebuffed demands that it incorporate more applied and career-oriented subjects as well as those linked to ethnicity, gender, and ideology. Its course catalog resembles the curricular offerings of a traditional liberal-arts college. Indeed, it's more traditional than many such institutions in 2019. (Grinnell College, for example, offers courses in "Gender, Women's and Sexuality Studies" and "Peace and Conflict Studies." Kenyon College—a parent of AP—now has departments of "African Diaspora Studies" and "Public Policy" as well as "Women and Gender Studies.")

At a time of deepening politicization of university curricula, pragmatic careerism among college students, and mounting interest in career and technical education (CTE) among policy makers, AP still mostly flies the banner of "arts and science" education in the high schools and supplies a ladder for students climbing toward that kind of college degree. In key fields such as history, civics, and literature, AP continues to signal the central importance of seminal documents and classic works. But for how long can it plug holes in an ever-leakier dike? What if fewer college students want such degrees, believing that BA's in English or history or philosophy won't pay off in the world of adult jobs? And what if the bloom is off the rose of "universal college attendance" among K–12 policy makers? Maryland legislators, for example, recently set as a goal that 45 percent of the state's high school graduates will have concentrated in CTE. Campaigning in 2018, Ohio's new governor— Mike DeWine—made a much bigger deal of career education than conventional academics. Other jurisdictions and policy leaders will surely follow. Although much of modern CTE also entails college study—and some high schools manage expertly to combine specialized career preparation with AP[10]—the fact remains that AP was designed for, and holds the most straightforward benefit for, young people who are bent on a fairly traditional four-year college education. Indeed, as we discussed in the previous chapter, AP in its way is a staunch ally of liberal education, which gives it added value for students who conclude—and there's recent evidence suggesting that more of them would be wise to recognize—that a degree in English may actually do them greater good in the modern job market than a major in culinary services or law enforcement.[11]

Still, if fewer young people pursue arts and science studies in college, it's more important than ever that their K–12 schools construct a solid foundation. Well-taught AP courses in subjects like history, government, language, and literature are valuable preparation for citizenship, not just college. So, too, are classes in economics, art history, environmental science, computer science, and psychology, plus the many languages spoken in the United States and beyond. Precisely because the AP catalog *does* embody a liberal education at a time when many are moving in different directions, its worth as a curricular anchor in high school is amplified. Policy makers pushing for more CTE in their schools ought not forget that career (and college) readiness, valuable as it is, isn't the same as preparation for responsible adulthood. High schools need to embrace both.

The College Board is open to incorporating into AP subjects that are less "liberal artsy" and will do so if both schools and colleges signal sufficient demand for them, so long as those subjects also possess a respectable body of serious content that can be taught at a high level and is amenable to AP-style assessment. In addition to their embrace of computer science, they've previously explored engineering and anatomy-physiology suited to the health professions, and no doubt they'll consider others. The sheet that Trevor Packer hands to advocates for additional AP courses is explicit: They must demonstrate that their course is already being taught in a number of colleges; that it leads to more advanced study in the same field; that if taught in high school it would enhance students' knowledge, skills, and abilities— and that colleges are prepared to confer credit on those who master all that before arriving. That's a high bar, but computer science cleared it, and in time other practical subjects doubtless will. Those in charge of AP are sensitive to brand dilution, however, and hesitant to place the imprimatur of Advanced Placement on things like marketing, entrepreneurialism, and journalism. It's no surprise that partisans of such fields would love to shelter in the AP tent— but there are and should be limits to how far and in what directions that tent extends.

Hyper-vocationalism is not the only threat to liberal learning in today's America. AP leaders must also grapple with waves of political correctness and culture wars in the curriculum as well as widening gaps between K–12 and college when it comes to what's important to learn.[12] The College Board has been intentional about aligning AP content, pedagogy, and exams with today's changing emphases in college instruction. But particularly in the battleground realms of humanities and social studies, what society properly expects its young people to learn during their compulsory education is ever more distant from what many college faculty in those fields want to teach, even in introductory courses. So maintaining a sturdy bridge—which AP must forever do if it's to fulfill its mission of bringing college-level academics into high school—is bound to get harder.

MANUFACTURER OF CHOICE

Although seldom viewed through this lens, Advanced Placement is a valuable source of choice in American secondary education, not just because it's taught in all sorts of schools—district, charter, private, parochial, virtual, even at home—but also because it enables individual students and their families to customize curricula to match their own interests, capabilities, and prior attainments. In this way, it also aligns admirably with today's push to "personalize" children's educational experiences and to enable them to move through those experiences at differing velocities.

Another key element of choice that AP embodies is volition. Kids only partake when they want to or when they choose a school where it's part of the core curriculum. That does not, however, mean it's equally available to all who might want or benefit from it. Although the program is approaching ubiquity across the United States, roughly three out of ten high schools do not now offer it. It's especially scarce in small rural schools and urban neighborhoods. It's ebbing in some snooty prep schools. And because some schools restrict entry into advanced classes, or cannot supply enough to match the demand, not all of their students can participate even when the school itself is one that "offers" AP.

Most discussions of choice in education focus on picking one school rather than another, but AP functions primarily as a supplier of "course choice" within schools.[13] As with choosing schools, however, the options are finite. The thirty-eight subjects in the AP catalog are more than any given school can deliver. Although a few big high schools serving college-obsessed constituencies come close to serving the full menu, in most of them only a sampling is on offer. Resources—budget, teachers, classrooms, labs—and enrollments are common constraints, forcing educators, policy makers, outside organizations, and funders to set priorities. STEM courses are in vogue in many places. Other schools cherry-pick the subjects they believe will do their students—and perhaps local employers and economies—the most good. For example, the impressive uptake for the new Computer Science Principles course was spurred by the belief that it will both attract more students (especially girls and minorities) to AP and draw them into careers that benefit them and their communities.

Other schools align their AP course offerings with their curricular focus: a science and math school goes big for STEM courses while one that concentrates on the humanities or social sciences (for example, New York's School for Law and Justice) may shun physics and calculus in favor of economics, history, and English. This makes sense for the school but again limits the choices for its students.

Online offerings are a boon to small rural schools that lack the capacity to offer many teacher-taught AP courses, and they can also expand the options for individual students no matter where they live. (The same is true for online dual-credit offerings.) Yet it's hard to navigate the cyber-seas on one's own, and those who manage it are apt to have support at home as well as school. Just picking the right course from a quality vendor can be tricky, as not every online source is equally sound. Some carry hefty price tags. Because states and districts have graduation requirements, a student who wants an online AP course to count toward her diploma will need to steer around those corners, too. If she hopes to obtain college credit, she'll need to determine which colleges offer what kinds of credit for what level of scores on that exam. She'll need to obtain textbooks and materials as well as access to suitable technology, and must then show up in person for a properly proctored exam on a fixed date and time. If she's carrying a full load of regular classes and activities at the school itself, she may find it hard to muster the hours and self-discipline to persevere with an online course. And where will she turn if she runs into trouble grappling with the material? Some online providers are good about providing such help but others leave students pretty much to sink or swim.

While the College Board already reviews the syllabi of online AP providers and supplies substantial online material to assist AP students and their teachers, it still seems to regard online courses as a sideshow and concentrates the overwhelming majority of its effort on traditional instructors in brick-and-mortar classrooms. Surely this must evolve in the decades to come, if only to keep pace with technology and technology-based schooling, but also to further the Board's equity goals and make more "gold" accessible to more of the youngsters whose education it may enrich.

RESOURCE FOR SMART KIDS

AP began as a fast-moving escalator for high-achieving pupils, one that sped them to more advanced courses in subjects where they had outstripped their schools' conventional curricula and helped them avoid the college drudgery of repeating stuff they had already learned.

In thousands more places today, AP is the finest and most treasured expression of gifted-and-talented education at the high school level. (Schools' own "honors" courses are more widespread but, like dual credit, they lack any common standard or external validation.)

That doesn't mean everyone taking AP is a young Einstein—many are motivated hard workers with reasonable ability—and the proliferation of AP subjects means that the program can do well by more diverse kinds of talent and achievement. (The kid who shines in AP Studio Art: Drawing is probably not the same one who's excelling in AP Chemistry.) Indeed, AP in many high schools today is more open and accepting than the gifted-and-talented programs in earlier grades, based as they often are on IQ tests or limited to kids with teacher recommendations or scrappy parents. But that doesn't make it any less valuable for hundreds of thousands of high-achieving young people who otherwise would be confined to their schools' standard offerings and lockstep progression through course sequences. That those high achievers now hail from more varied backgrounds and attend more different schools than in Finn's day is cause for celebration. But continuing to narrow the "excellence gap" with AP's help carries major implications for the offerings of America's elementary and middle schools, for it's crazy to wait for high school to tap into and cultivate this additional human potential. It must therefore be the responsibility of states, districts, and schools to do far better than most have at early identification of talent and interest across the demographic spectrum and at providing the curricula, instructional capacity, and individualization that best serve those who get identified.

AGENT OF EDUCATION REFORM

Advanced Placement is legitimately viewed as an engine of education reform at both the system and school-building levels. It's not anti-system like vouchers and charters and it's not top-down like the Common Core standards but, when properly implemented, it meshes smoothly with many elements of today's reform agendas. Besides better serving smart kids and conferring additional choices, it contributes to revitalizing high schools; raising—and universalizing—academic standards, rigor, and criteria for student performance; attracting and retaining eager, knowledgeable teachers; and developing curricula and assessments that can be compared across districts and states without being blown away by the political tempests that roil government initiatives in the realm of standards and testing. Above all, AP has become a serious player in the national effort to enhance educational opportunities—and a real shot at mobility—for disadvantaged youngsters. It also wields enormous influence over what's taught and learned by millions of high school students—and how the achievement of those students is judged—in scattered schools and far-flung districts in every state.

Because it fits into so many disparate agendas, however, AP-as-agent-of-reform is also something of a blind man's elephant, appearing differently (and attracting/repelling differently) according to the policy frame one puts around it. Yes, it's versatile. Yes, it's true—as we heard from superintendents and principals alike—that a well-functioning AP program can lift other boats in a high school while altering expectations among staff, students, and families. That, however, doesn't make it easy to install a robust AP program in a school, much less throughout an entire district or state. Even when a high school's curricula and culture can be changed, needy students will still pour in from middle schools that did a woeful job of preparing them for advanced academic challenges, and veteran staffers in the receiving school may not have had the training that best equips them to turn those needy newcomers into star performers.

Expanding (or initiating) AP also poses resource trade-offs and priority issues for schools and districts. Should they instead do more for low achievers? Upgrade their CTE offerings rather than trying to push more kids into college? Focus on dual credit instead? Can they muster the human resources to do AP well, including teacher buy-in and committed school leadership? Mandates from the mayor or superintendent may set policy wheels in motion, but that doesn't mean there will be swift and responsive movement on the ground.

Abundant Dilemmas

Besides the challenges inherent in the half-dozen AP roles and missions described above, four additional dilemmas loom as we consider the future of the Advanced Placement program.

COMPETITORS AND QUALITY CONTROL

AP no longer has a near monopoly on the provision of challenging, college-level academics during high school. Students and schools seeking such opportunities—and the rewards that may attach to them—have at least four other programmatic locations to which they can turn, in addition to whatever their own teachers may develop.

Among the available alternatives in 2019, however, the only one big enough to pose serious competition to Advanced Placement is dual credit in its many forms, which may (depending on one's data source) already rival AP in its high school penetration and student participation. This boils down, in essence, to colleges offering their own courses to high school pupils rather than high school instructors teaching college-level material to those students.

Dual credit has notable pluses. It offers a direct and comparatively easier route to more certain credit, introduces high school students at little or no cost into a college-bound culture as well as supplying experience with college-level academics, expectations, and practices. The credit that it yields can shrink the time and money one must devote to college itself. Diverse and decentralized as it is, we've encountered sterling examples of dual credit in action and can point to reasonable coherence within the subspecies known as "early college" and "P-TECH" schools.

Successful harvesting of credit via this route, like AP success, is associated with a superior track record in college. That evidence grows stronger when the dual-credit course is delivered by college instructors on their own campus, with full-fledged college students sitting in the same classrooms—and particularly when a four-year college is responsible. Yet that combination of conditions is rare within the dual-credit universe. And even when they're all present, it's hard to know whether harvesting credit this way causes or simply correlates with the benefit that follows.

Dual credit is also more immediately amenable than AP to career-oriented and technical courses in addition to traditional academics, a difference that's both good and bad. Good because it diminishes nose-to-nose competition between the two programs, further widens one's options, and points policy makers and educators toward useful roles for both. Not so good if it portends five-star opportunities for more privileged kids and thinner gruel for poor kids—and definitely not good if occupationally focused dual-credit courses put the squeeze on preparation for adult citizenship.

The biggest downside to dual credit is its rickety quality control. Harking back to the three questions that we posed in chapter 8, dual credit in the United States today has only a shaky response to, "Is it really college quality?" The answer turns out to depend on the course, the instructor, the college it's associated with, and the high school that's party to it.

On the fiscal front, dual credit's cost challenge is that its price tag for taxpayers—who often pay both the high school and the college—exceeds that of the same course when taken in college. On the other hand, this may yield savings for students who can ease their tuition burden and perhaps also make it up to taxpayers by not lingering as long in a publicly supported college.

AP, by comparison, does a commendable job of assuring college-level quality. It's consistent, it employs a widely understood and time-tested national standard as well as uniform metrics, and several forms of benefit usually accrue to those who do well at it, although here again, the causal connection is murky. On the downside, despite the substantial investment of time and effort by students and teachers that is required for AP success, one cannot be sure of harvesting credit once enrolled in college.

Advanced Placement poses fiscal issues, too. Its price tag for schools may be sizable, particularly when institutional opportunity costs are weighed, although the only out-of-pocket costs for students are apt to be exam fees and related charges, which may be covered by school, state, or philanthropy. As for the colleges, they pay nothing for AP per se but lose revenue when it leads to speedier college students who pay less tuition and generate less in state subsidies.

The deservedly well-regarded International Baccalaureate program is closer kin to Advanced Placement than is dual credit—and, as we've seen, some students take both, or even all three—but it remains a boutique-size offering in US education while AP is more like Nordstrom.

Having multiple options, however, is good for students, educators, families, and policy makers. If AP were still flying solo in the provision of college-level work to high school pupils, it would be subject to unmanageable pressures. It would be pushed into too many curricular niches and lobbied hard to relax its standards. It would lack the capacity to grow as swiftly as the demand—and politicians—would want. And it wouldn't be able to take as many chances, experiment with innovations, pilot-test new courses, and generally tend its own vineyard. Competition brings problems, to be sure, but it also holds advantages that may count for more.

CREDIT OR NOT

While simply enrolling in a dual-credit class comes close to ensuring some sort of credit on arrival in college, some of the young people embarking on AP are encountering diminished returns when it comes to securing the credit they want as elite private colleges (and a few others) up the ante on awarding such credit. But the population of AP course takers appears to be rising faster than the number of credit-averse universities. That's partly because College Board lobbyists are doing their darnedest to safeguard 3 as a credit-worthy score on public campuses and partly because "elite" turns out to be a relatively short list. When one gets to number seventy-eight on *U.S. News*'s ranking of "national universities" (Baylor), one finds that 3's still suffice in many subjects on many hundreds of campuses.[14] Still, that short list is not unimportant, given the eminence of the institutions on it that now demand 5's.

We recognize that academic standards and course content vary from campus to campus, yet we've become cynical about the motives behind this score escalation at most of the colleges that now engage in it (and about AP avoidance by some prep schools). Yes, there are examples of true mismatches between what AP expects by way of content and/or student performance and what a university's professors seek or a private school's faculty prefers to teach, but far more widespread is an unattractive blend of academic snobbery, revenue maximizing, and avoidance of the institutional hassles that follow from generous conferring of credit or waiving of introductory courses for incoming students.

In terms of actual numbers, it won't matter much, because a tiny proportion of US students attend the institutions that are making AP-based credit and course waiving harder to get—and an even smaller fraction enroll in the prep schools that are shunning AP. Still, when Ivy League and other high-status universities thumb their noses at scores of 3 and even 4, or simply insist that everyone must take a full four-year complement of courses from their own faculty, it undermines the claim that a 3 should qualify one for credit or course skipping, and it weakens the expectation among high school students and their parents that one can shorten one's time to degree and save some money with the help of AP.

Pushing back, the College Board has successfully pressed nearly half the states to require their public campuses to grant credit for 3's, and the vast majority of students matriculate at such institutions. Still, we can foresee a divide emerging as one sort of university makes it harder to get AP credit while another makes it (relatively) easier—and we can detect hints that legislatively forcing colleges to award credit discomfits some faculty members and could produce its own AP backlash, especially among those with a professorial aversion to letting high school teachers handle courses that would otherwise be their own.

With AP's primary markets—at both the secondary and postsecondary levels—growing larger and more diverse, the program can certainly continue to thrive, albeit perhaps with slightly diminished luster, if big-name colleges and prep schools limit their involvement or spurn AP entirely. In hindsight, though, the emergence of such limits might have been foreseen, for AP was once a badge that marked schools and colleges—not just students—as special. But special always dims in the shadow of universality—and those who insist on being special may need to retrieve that status in other ways. Thus Kolluri writes of elite populations that contrive to maintain their cultural capital and distinctiveness by dissociating themselves from anything that's too inclusive, which causes one to wonder whether something else may yet take AP's place for those elites, their tree-shaded academies, and their impossible-to-get-into colleges. Might it be the International Baccalaureate? Initiatives (such as the Harvard faculty approved in principle) to admit students into combined BA/MA programs? Perhaps the rejection of all grades, tests, and transcripts—which may be seen as the academic equivalent of becoming vegans while ordinary folk chomp flesh. We're more mindful than when we started of the inherent conflict in balancing AP's quondam role as a prize for the few with its newer role as opportunity enhancer for the masses.[15]

UNCERTAIN RESULTS

How much good does AP actually do for young people who put themselves through its challenging classes and exams?

The College Board highlights four categories of benefit that may follow from AP success: improved college admissions, credit on arrival, skipping introductory classes, and gaining skills that help one do well in college. Those are also the reasons we heard—in different combinations and with differing emphases—from high school students explaining why they take AP courses today.

They're not wrong. Good grades in AP classes on one's transcript and high scores on AP exams may indeed assist with admission, the more so if one is applying from a little-known high school. Degree credit based on robust AP scores is available on the overwhelming majority of college and university campuses, although the scores needed to reap it differ, as does the type of credit to be had. The same goes for placing out of 101-level courses in various subjects. And there's no gainsaying that most kids acquire valuable skills and knowledge if they successfully weather AP classes during high school.

Without true experiments, it's not possible to be certain whether AP *causes* greater success than these young people would otherwise realize. But that, in turn, depends on how one gauges success and construes causation. We're so accustomed to judging education innovations and interventions by whether they raise some test score that we easily overlook the collateral benefits that can come from challenging oneself with a more rigorous course or two (or five). Yes, kids can over-enroll and over-stress themselves, but on the whole it's a fine thing to strengthen their college-admissions prospects via buffed-up GPAs and transcripts—the more so if it means that young people from ordinary high schools get more favorable consideration by selective colleges. This diversifies the pool of visibly "eligible" college students—and counters the undermatching problem by extending the list of imaginable colleges in the students' eyes as well. And if AP success among populations that didn't previously have much of it, and among tens of thousands of young people who didn't previously enjoy it, results in more such kids who *go* to college and predicts greater success among those who do, this is a good thing. As for the skills, that's a no-brainer: the more one comes out of high school with, the better off one will be in college and in life.

It's good, too, if AP curbs senioritis and proffers intellectual challenges to high-achieving, high-ability young people that their schools' standard offerings cannot deliver. It's really good if what you learn in an AP US Government class helps ready you for responsible adult citizenship or if what you learn in Art History or English Literature gives you some understanding of Western culture—and perhaps a clearer eye for beauty. The increasing diversity within one's AP classroom may also increase one's familiarity with kids who don't look much like oneself yet turn out to be at least as able. New friendships may form. It might even foster tolerance!

Repeatedly in these pages, we have asked whether it matters more to elevate the number of kids who get qualifying scores on AP—the surest shot to long-term advancement for them—even as far larger numbers of those entering AP classrooms and exam rooms fail to get those scores, or to boost the rate of success among AP participants and minimize the number of young people who fruitlessly embark on it.

We've stopped asking because we have reached an answer: it's right to increase the absolute number of young people who succeed with this, even if the success rate sags—so long as that sag doesn't get accepted as a permanent inevitability, particularly when it's the exam results of disadvantaged and minority test-takers that appear to cause it. Were that to persist, the "excellence gap" will have wobbled a bit but it won't actually shrink.

Although we're persuaded that AP participation does *some* good for many of the young people who don't make it to the qualifying score threshold on exam day, escorting more poor and minority kids to that threshold is the foremost challenge ahead—and it's one that policy makers and education leaders should join the College Board in meeting. Today, far too many of the black and Hispanic girls and boys who enter Advanced Placement classrooms wind up getting 1's on the exams—and far too many of the country's 1's are associated with poor and minority youngsters. Although increased access is bound to bring a decline in passing rates for a time, and the AP scoring system means that 1's and 2's will never vanish, it would be a huge mistake to settle for such discrepant results over the long haul. That doesn't mean standards should slacken, that traditional AP students should have their experience diluted, or that access should be curbed. Rather, it calls for redoubled efforts both before—long before—and during the AP cycle to build the skills that translate into qualifying scores among the young people who are being most strongly encouraged to enter that cycle. It also calls for redoubled efforts to ensure that the adults in their schools are well prepared to escort them on this arduous journey.

Note, too, that dual credit may contain a kindred challenge: young people who engage in it and, after achieving passing grades from their instructors, do in fact obtain credit as a result, yet who by most other measures—state assessments, National Assessment, SAT, ACT, and so on—were not actually "college ready" when they entered the dual-credit classroom and who may well not be college ready when they emerge from it. Yes, they'll be admitted to open-access postsecondary institutions—community colleges and others—but may be sent for remediation when they get there. How much good did dual credit actually do them—and don't its proponents have some obligation to tackle this quality-control problem alongside the access challenges? We suggest that it's as important to ensure that those who participate in dual credit are truly able to benefit from the experience as it is to close the "excellence gaps" that are manifest in today's AP results.

MISSION VERSUS MARGIN

Inside the College Board's sprawling offices in a grand high-rise near Ground Zero in lower Manhattan, we hear that the organization's several programs, AP among them, are routinely discussed in terms of "mission and margin," referring to the Board's twin motives to do good—for kids, schools, colleges, and education—while also doing well enough to support its own comfortable operation in New York and at least ten other outposts as well as investing in new initiatives and subsidizing programs that don't pay for themselves. Like its frequent partner, the Princeton-based Educational Testing Service, the College Board is a nonprofit organization, but it has big overheads, a well-paid team, lots of events, and a reputation to uphold. And AP has become its premier revenue pipeline.

We believe Board hierarchs when they say they don't make programmatic decisions just to maximize income and when they note that, if revenue were their foremost goal, they would welcome other potentially lucrative subjects into the AP fold and perhaps banish some—such as Latin and Japanese—that today have few takers. Like a university that sustains its classics and comparative philology departments though they cost more than they bring in, the AP program is proud of the intellectual integrity and disciplinary balance of its subject list and has resisted dilution. It has shouldered the sizable development costs of worthy new courses, the redevelopment costs of overhauling frameworks and exams, and the start-up costs of many new student- and teacher-support materials. It has striven to find operational economies that let it raise AP exam fees more slowly than the inflation rate. It invested $80 million in the program enhancements scheduled for fall 2019 (see chapter 3), and it's difficult to imagine the Board seeing much of a monetary return on this hefty outlay.[16] Even so, there's no denying that the College Board is widely viewed as a self-absorbed "money machine" and that its lobbyists are hard at work in state capitals to get AP credits more widely accepted and to encourage the spread of AP courses and exams into more high schools and student populations. For long-term credibility and trust, it's going to have to find better ways of showing how pursuit of its mission requires such a generous margin.

Stealthy No More

Advanced Placement today is far too large and aggressive to remain under anybody's radar. What for several decades was a scarcely visible path by which a handful of savvy, well-connected kids could quietly accelerate their access to college-level academics and thereby get a head start on college itself has widened into a major thoroughfare within American secondary education and a much-trafficked route from there into postsecondary education. In so doing, it has also evolved from a luxury good—a fringe benefit, as it were, of enrolling in places like Stuyvesant, Andover, Evanston Township High School, and Wellesley High School—into an engine of upward mobility and education reform for millions of young people and thousands of schools.

That's indisputably a good thing, but—as any entertainer, artist, athlete, or politician who has moved from tributary to mainstream can attest—the hazards multiply with the rewards. AP has already drawn competitors, experienced rejection from former lovers, and been assaulted by culture warriors. How long before it also falls prey to critics of the sort that challenged Common Core and other attempts at national standards, curricula, and testing? It's doubtful that its private auspices can forever shield it from partisans of local control and state educational sovereignty—or from those who contend that American schools suffer from excessive standardization, way too much testing of every sort, and a dangerous obsession with test-prep instruction.

What some—ourselves included—laud as a respect-worthy national benchmark of liberal learning and intellectual rigor, a rare source of "tests worth preparing kids for," others see as a straitjacket on creative teaching, a pusher of antiquated and inutile content, a perpetrator of the myth of a common culture, and a co-conspirator in the college-admissions rat race.

Every education reform gathers enemies (and envy) as it grows—the more so if it appears popular and successful. Advanced Placement today is vulnerable to charges that it diverts scarce resources to smart kids and those who "would do fine anyway" rather than concentrating those resources on the neediest. It invites allegations that it must be discriminatory, else black and Latino youngsters would fare as well on its tests as white and Asian kids, leading to the conclusion that it must need some sort of midcourse correction. Easier standards, maybe, or different scoring metrics? Perhaps some form of affirmative action?

Because it bridges both high school and college—and its ability to bring thousands of professors and teachers into the same rooms in pursuit of colleagueship, shared learning, and common purpose remains awesome—AP faces additional vulnerabilities as interests, priorities, and resources shift on both sides of that span and as tall vessels sailing downstream threaten to bang into it. Revenue-maximizing colleges are less willing to grant credit for work done before getting there—or insist on themselves serving as the source of such work. High schools have budget worries—and institutional pride—of their own as well as curricular, pedagogical, and staffing rigidities, plus influential unions with jobs to defend.

The College Board cannot overcome all these challenges on its own, which is why political leaders, philanthropists, and education influencers need to pitch in. At the same time, AP has ample assets, not just its size, reputation, and the depth of its penetration into many institutions and people's minds. Thanks in no small part to the program's expert leadership, particularly in the hands of the intrepid and tireless Trevor Packer, AP also displays a level of nimbleness, responsiveness, *and* proactivity that's rarely seen in complex, large organizations with long histories, hoary traditions, and a zillion alums. It didn't have to launch Capstone, Computer Science Principles, the new pre-AP offerings, or the "AP Potential" device to help high schools identify promising young people before they arrive. Nobody forced it to equip teachers and students with troves of additional study material, feedback loops, and guides for the perplexed. Nimbleness and responsiveness also characterize the Board's willingness to revise its history frameworks in light of criticisms, although it often does a better job of responding than of initial messaging.

It's not easy to get out in front of the doubters and critics, however. Board leaders possibly had a chance in February 2019 when they made public a new requirement that students must henceforth register by November for their May AP exams, or pay a penalty. This preregistration brings several benefits: It saves kids time on test day; it gets their scores more rapidly to their schools, the colleges they're applying to, and themselves; and it shows the AP program where to send those formative assessments and links to sources of help during the year. (Heretofore, AP hasn't known which students are sitting in its classes until they take the exams in May.) The $40 penalty fee for registering late is intended to incentivize kids not to be late—and in pilot runs that seemed to work well. Yet within hours of the announcement, critics pounced, with—for example—a New Jersey guidance counselor telling the *Washington Post* that the fees amount to "usury" that "benefit no one except the College Board." As the weeks passed, the objections continued to mount.[17] By contrast, a New Mexico AP teacher who took part in the pilot declared herself pleased with the change because "fall registration has been a great way to build a culture in AP where everyone was on board,"[18] but there's no denying the wider impression that the Board is just being greedy.

The AP program would clearly benefit from better public relations, but it's robust enough to withstand bad press and critics. For the most part, it enjoys an enviable reputation for integrity, rigor, and a commitment to educational excellence. In the end, sadly, the biggest challenge to what it seeks to do for more kids in more places is one that doesn't emanate from critics, rivals, or enemies.

No, the foremost challenge arises from the parlous state of American K–12 education in general, not just our flatlining high schools but also the wholly inadequate learning that's taking place in so many elementary and middle schools. In 2017, only one-third of US eighth graders attained (or exceeded) the "proficient" level in math on the National Assessment of Educational Progress, as did a meager 36 percent in reading. It's a safe bet that most youngsters who haven't managed to reach proficient will be unready (to say the least) to thrive in AP classes and exams.[19] (Neither will they get a whole lot from dual credit.)

Unsolved, this can only mean that a great many kids with the intellectual firepower to succeed in college-level work during high school won't have the educational foundation that makes such success a reality. Excellence gaps will remain. Disadvantaged kids will continue getting too many 1's on AP exams—and there's a growing number of such kids, as US student demographics change, as fewer young people have strong family supports, and as other societal and political divisions worsen.

Stealthy though it no longer is, Advanced Placement is here to stay, and we applaud its capacity and determination to draw more girls and boys of every background into its lofty orbit. It already escorts millions of them to doors that open to a brighter future. It could do that for many more. But it cannot compensate for an entire system that fails far too many millions before they ever get close to high school.

Notes

1. John Tierney, "AP Classes Are a Scam," *The Atlantic*, October 13, 2012. https://www.theatlantic.com/national/archive/2012/10/ap-classes-are-a-scam/263456/.

2. Amanda Zhou, "More Students Are Taking AP Exams, but Researchers Don't Know If That Helps Them," *Chalkbeat*, August 3, 2018. https://www.chalkbeat.org/posts/us/2018/08/03/more-students-are-taking-ap-exams-but-researchers-dont-know-if-that-helps-them/.

3. Diane Ravitch, quoted in Alina Tugend, "Who Benefits from the Expansion of A.P. Classes?" *New York Times Magazine*, September 7, 2017. https://www.nytimes.com/2017/09/07/magazine/who-benefits-from-the-expansion-of-ap-classes.html.

4. Jay Mathews, "The Triumph of Advanced Placement," *Washington Post Magazine*, October 23, 2018. https://www.washingtonpost.com/news/magazine/wp/2018/10/23/feature/meet-the-man-who-made-advanced-placement-the-most-influential-tool-in-american-education/?utm_term=.61b73fb6b085.

5. Nat Malkus, *AP at Scale: Public School Students in Advanced Placement, 1990–2013* (Washington, DC: American Enterprise Institute, 2016), 1. https://www.aei.org/wp-content/uploads/2016/01/AP-at-Scale.pdf.

6. Sheila Byrd and others, *Do They Deserve Gold Star Status?* (Washington, DC: Thomas B. Fordham Institute, 2007), 6.

7. Tugend, "Who Benefits."

8. Steve Farkas and Ann Duffett, *Growing Pains in the Advanced Placement Program: Do Tough Trade-Offs Lie Ahead?* (Washington, DC: Thomas B. Fordham Institute, 2009).

9. Suneal Kolluri, "Advanced Placement: The Dual Challenge of Equal Access and Effectiveness," *Review of Educational Research* 88, no. 5 (2018): 698.

10. *Advanced Placement and Career and Technical Education: Working Together* (New York: College Board, 2018).

11. Melissa Korn, "Some 43% of College Grads Are Underemployed in First Job," *Wall Street Journal*, October 26, 2018. https://www.wsj.com/articles/study-offers-new-hope-for-english -majors-1540546200.

12. Emmanuel Felton, "More AP Courses Slated for Major Overhaul," *Hechinger Report*, October 20, 2014. https://hechingerreport.org/ap-courses-slated-major-overhaul/.

13. Michael Brickman, *Expanding the Education Universe: A Fifty-State Strategy for Course Choice* (Washington, DC: Thomas B. Fordham Institute, 2014).

14. *U.S. News and World Report*, "Best Colleges, 2019," accessed November 9, 2018. https:// www.usnews.com/best-colleges/baylor-university-6967.

15. Kolluri, "Advanced Placement," 701.

16. College Board, "Student Participation and Performance in Advanced Placement Rise in Tandem," press release, February 6, 2019. https://reports.collegeboard.org/ap-program-results /2018/press-release.

17. Scott Jaschik, "Will AP Changes Give More of an Edge to the Wealthy?" *Inside Higher Ed*, March 11, 2019. https://www.insidehighered.com/admissions/article/2019/03/11/anger-grows -over-changes-ap-registration-deadlines.

18. Valerie Strauss, "The College Board Is Changing Sign-Up Rules for AP Tests: Critics Say It's an Undue Burden on Students," *Washington Post*, February 7, 2019. https://www.washingtonpost .com/education/2019/02/07/college-board-is-changing-sign-up-rules-ap-tests-some-counselors -are-livid/?utm_term=.c13757a2b3f4.

19. Of course, there are exceptions. Students who struggle in one subject but excel in another, those whose English literacy may be so-so but who are accomplished in another language, who may not be great at reading or math but have outstanding skills in one of the arts, and so on.

Cui Bono? Weighing the Benefits of Advanced Placement and Dual Credit

The research literature on Advanced Placement has traditionally been dominated by the College Board. On the whole, its bottom-line findings appear clear-cut and emphatic: Succeeding at AP (scoring 3 or above on an AP exam) correlates with—in everyday language, "predicts"—more positive postsecondary outcomes, particularly when students go on to major in a discipline related to their AP experiences (notably in STEM subjects). Although the evidence is weaker, there may also be benefits associated with scores of 1 or 2, possibly just from taking the course. The Board's research has been criticized, however, for underplaying important limitations, notably the "selection effect" of taking AP in the first place, due to the fact that more motivated and hardworking students are likelier to do that, and such students are already likelier to be on track toward successful college outcomes.

Non–College Board research is skimpier. These studies generally downplay the singular significance of AP as a causal factor in predicting positive outcomes, but some also report positive results for students with qualifying scores, particularly—again—when those scores are earned in subjects that they go on to major in during college (or, more generally, in STEM subjects).

At the same time, a growing body of studies also points to benefits associated with successful completion of dual-credit courses, notably increased rates of high school graduation, college enrollment and persistence as well as more robust college GPAs and four-year graduation—much like the enhancements associated with AP. But this research has also been skimpy to date and comes with important limitations: The dizzying variety of dual-credit forms and formats makes it impossible to generalize, as outcomes often differ depending on where a class is taken, what subject is taught, which instructor teaches it, and the like.

Like AP, dual-credit analyses are also plagued by selection effects. And although the research comparing the two approaches is skimpier still, what's available generally shows AP students faring somewhat better in college than their dual-credit peers. These findings, however, continue to be hampered by the limitations already noted.

As we discussed in chapter 8, dual credit is not the only alternative to Advanced Placement. A small but growing body of research attests to the benefits of the International Baccalaureate program[1] and of Cambridge's AICE exams.[2] As we showed in that chapter, however, both alternatives pale in size (in the United States) next to AP and dual credit, so here we focus on the latter two. We review the available research on both, seeking to compare potential benefits, highlight key limitations, and note important issues that would benefit from further study.

AP Evidence and Outcomes

Multiple College Board studies have shown that students who earn qualifying scores on AP exams are likelier to score higher than their non-AP classmates on standardized tests; to enroll in college; to enroll in selective institutions; to earn superior grades while there; to graduate from college—and to do so within four years (without transferring to another campus). Students who take an AP exam do better at college retention, too, a finding that also applies to low-income students (compared to non-AP students with similar backgrounds), although that study was limited in that those who earned qualifying scores and those who did not were grouped together.[3]

That's serious stuff, not to be pooh-poohed. The College Board research oeuvre also shows that students who score 3 or higher on an AP exam are more likely than their non-AP classmates to major in a discipline related to that exam; to perform well in subsequent college courses in that discipline (and/or related fields); and to take more credit hours in that or related subjects, particularly STEM subjects.[4]

It's harder to isolate the effect of just sitting in an AP classroom or taking the exam without earning a qualifying score. The College Board reports that scoring a 2 may be associated with better postsecondary outcomes than non-AP students, though the margin (not surprisingly) is less than for those who earned qualifying scores.[5] One 2008 study found (in Texas) that students who took an AP course and exam performed better than students who took only the course or did not participate in AP at all, in terms of higher college GPAs and four-year graduation rates.[6] Another found that students with similar class rank or SAT scores ended up with higher college grades if they scored a 2 in certain subjects (math, history, English, or world languages), though these results were again less positive than for students with qualifying scores.[7] Others found that students who earned 1 or 2 fared better than those with no AP involvement with respect to college enrollment, retention, and graduation.[8] But there is much need for further research in this area, particularly from independent scholars, as well as studies that better control for selection biases and that distinguish between scoring 1 or 2 on an AP exam.

Another underdeveloped area is research probing differences among students who score 3, 4, or 5. A few recent College Board studies show links between higher scores and the likelihood of choosing the same subject as a college major, and between higher scores in science subjects and higher first-year GPAs.[9] Other studies differentiating between scores have found mixed results.[10] In most extant research, however, students are simply grouped into "qualifying" (scoring 3, 4, or 5) or "not qualifying" (scoring 1 or 2). Further deconstructing results by score would be informative, the more so as some universities now require the loftier scores before granting credit. On the other hand, AP instructors, particularly those who teach disadvantaged pupils, seem convinced that those who score 2 are better prepared to succeed in college than those who don't. It may be that benefits such as persistence in college and experience tackling advanced academic work are robust even in the absence of credit-worthy exam scores.

As might be expected, some critics complain that because the College Board has an obvious interest in validating its own program, AP research undertaken—or commissioned—by it must be viewed skeptically.[11] Fortunately, a growing number of external researchers have begun to study the program, mostly since 2000, and their findings, though generally positive, have been somewhat more mixed. For example, a 2004 study in California showed that after controlling for a student's socioeconomic status and prior academic variables, the number of AP courses taken was unrelated to a student's freshman college GPA (but researchers grouped AP, dual credit, IB, and honors courses together), and "has little, if any, validity with respect to the prediction of college outcomes," before—confusingly—adding that "AP *examination scores* are among the very best predictors" (emphasis added).

Some external studies have shown little or no relationship between AP participation and subsequent college outcomes such as freshman GPA and sophomore retention, or five-year degree attainment, although some positive outcomes were associated with passing AP exams.[12] Others have shown that AP students are likelier to have higher incomes after college and/or likelier to obtain advanced degrees (although those studies rely on descriptive survey data and have no controls).[13] One 2017 study from the Education Commission of the States shows that rural students who earn scores of 3 or higher have similar rates of two- and four-year college enrollment as do urban and suburban students, although (as we note in chapters 3 and 4) the latter far exceed their rural peers in AP participation.[14]

Other independent studies have reported results that resemble those from the College Board. They find, for example, that AP participation and exam success are associated with loftier college entrance exam scores, more robust GPAs and graduation rates, and greater likelihood of obtaining advanced degrees. The major difference appears to be that, as more variables are considered in an effort to isolate the causal impact of AP, that impact often diminishes or proves statistically insignificant. Rigorous independent studies that try to control for multiple covariates show that the strongest results associated with AP appear when students obtain qualifying scores, particularly in science and math subjects. This mirrors College Board research, though with smaller effect sizes.[15]

An important 2018 study by economist David Troutman, focused on students matriculating into the University of Texas system, suggests that credit earned via AP predicts a number of positive outcomes related to college persistence and graduation (see more on this study below).[16] A Tennessee study found that students awarded college credit via AP persisted longer in college and earned better grades than other students, although this effect was later shown to be insignificant when background variables such as family income and parental education were controlled for.[17] This study, and another in Texas, also showed no correlation between AP participation and degree attainment within five years or between AP participation and college GPA.[18]

A conservative interpretation of both College Board and independent research is that, while no causal effect can yet be isolated, it's reasonably clear that AP students who achieve qualifying scores on the exams tend to fare better in college, and those who continue in subject areas related to their AP exams are even likelier to enjoy college success.

We don't subscribe to the view that College Board studies should be discarded because of the sponsor's close association with the program. To its credit, the Board's recent studies take pains to explain their methodologies. They do not hide their limitations (although, as is typical of education research, the limits are apt to be spelled out in an appendix like this, not in the "executive summary") and they're open to criticism, while also game to push back when they think it necessary.

The biggest limitation—and source of most frequent criticism—is that College Board research (as well as most independent research) into AP inadequately controls for selection effects: the likelihood that more motivated and hardworking students opt to participate in AP in the first place and that these young people are probably already on track toward successful education outcomes; that students who typically have access to AP may attend better-resourced schools in better-off communities; and that AP classes may be taught by abler, more knowledgeable, and more dedicated teachers.[19]

Controlling for such factors is extremely difficult due to the scarcity of true experimental studies that isolate the actual impact of a "treatment" from the many other factors that may influence its apparent outcome. This the College Board acknowledges:

> Random assignment is generally not feasible or practical due to the real-world benefits and burdens related to AP and DE [dual enrollment] participation (e.g., having unprepared students assigned to an AP or DE program, having motivated and able students being precluded from participation).[20]

Trevor Packer elaborates further:

> AP predictive validity studies . . . are the most traditional of all AP research studies. . . . These are not, nor are they designed to be, causal/impact studies; in other words, these studies do not claim that AP courses cause students to do better than other students in the sophomore-level college course where they are placed. They simply show that the scores do predict, as an SAT score does, how well a student will perform—hence, "predictive validity". . . .
>
> In the same way that we don't claim that taking the SAT "causes" students to do better in college, but instead predicts, these traditional AP studies, different from the newer wave of research that attempts to isolate AP's impact on outcomes like four-year graduation rates and freshman GPA, simply demonstrate the validity of using AP scores for course placement decisions on campus.[21]

Some recent studies by the Board attempt to control for selection-related factors by matching AP and non-AP students on prior academic achievement (for example, SAT scores), poverty, and other demographic characteristics. They employ statistical modeling and other well-regarded analytic methods to incorporate control variables, or they use quasi-experimental methods (for example, regression discontinuity or difference in difference[22]) in an effort to block the selection effects of AP and other acceleration programs such as dual credit.[23] Yet the best of the Board's research—and almost all other AP research—remains quasi-experimental.

One forthcoming multiyear study seeks to buck this trend. Undertaken by Mark Long and Dylan Conger, in collaboration with the College Board and with support from the National Science Foundation, it examines the impact of AP Biology and Chemistry classes on high school students by looking at outcomes in terms of college enrollment, persistence, and measures of science skill and STEM interest, and it employs a randomized experimental design. When released, this will mark perhaps the most rigorous study to date of the AP program. Preliminary results suggest substantial causal impacts from taking an AP science course on most of the outcomes noted herein.[24]

Evidence of postsecondary benefits is a key pillar of the claim that AP saves college students time and money by enabling them to earn credit before they walk through the ivy gates (or gain other advantages such as skipping introductory courses). Some of the College Board research previously cited points toward cost savings for students.[25] AP students are shown in one study to reduce their time to graduation, which could yield tuition savings, though these findings relate only to students earning qualifying scores—and the same study found that those who *failed* an AP exam had *lower* graduation rates than those who took no AP exam.[26] But a 2010 independent study in Texas found that AP was unlikely to save taxpayers money, and the average time to degree for AP students was not significantly shortened.[27]

It may be that AP-related savings of time and money for college students is rarer than generally assumed because few students pass enough AP exams—and are granted enough credit by their colleges—to skip entire semesters, much less full years.[28] This is of course complicated by the myriad ways in which universities do and don't grant credit for AP scores as well as whether one's AP exam matches what one then opts to study in college. It's also the case that many students—even among those eligible to receive credit—choose to repeat the course once in college.[29]

Future research on the efficacy of AP should include key questions that have been inadequately examined so far but are increasingly pertinent for policy makers and practitioners: What are the differences between taking AP in urban, suburban, and rural environments? What school-level conditions are most conducive to AP success? What state and district policies are most effective in increasing AP access for marginalized groups? And which practices best equip schools to help students succeed in AP?

It's also important to probe deeper into the nuances and subtleties of "selection effects." It seems possible, even likely, particularly as more poor and minority students participate in AP (and dual credit—see below), that what they learn in an AP classroom (and demonstrate on the exam) may not *cause* them to do better in the years that follow, yet the experience itself—and the fact of having been encouraged to undertake and endure it—causes them to "select into" a more successful population than they otherwise would have, perhaps to attend a college that they would not otherwise have considered (or been admitted to), perhaps to arrive with the confidence that they belong there, and so forth. They may always have had the potential to succeed on a faster track but the entrance to that track hadn't been unlocked for them. In that sense, participation in the program had a positive effect, a causal effect—it liberated a positive change in young people's education trajectories and life prospects—even if that effect had little to do with differences between what was taught in their AP classrooms versus what was happening down the hall in regular high school classes.

Dual Credit Evidence and Outcomes

As we discussed in chapter 8, national data on dual credit (DC) are sorely limited, because policies and programs are so diverse and because there's nothing like the College Board to drive, track, and organize such information. The federal National Center on Education Statistics last surveyed dual-credit participation en masse in 2011, and its 2019 release of limited class of 2013 participation data leaves plenty of questions. The federal Office for Civil Rights (OCR) invited districts to report dual-credit data in 2013, but this only became a mandatory survey question in 2015. As noted in chapter 8, initial analyses of that first attempt at a comprehensive OCR tally reveal discrepancies in how dual-credit participation by students is reported by districts, making it difficult to grasp the scale and scope of the program as a nationwide phenomenon—insofar as DC can even be termed a "program," for it lacks any standard definition or uniform format.[30] The variability and decentralization of dual credit make it hard to determine whether one example can even be compared with another and practically impossible to generalize about DC's efficacy as a large-scale education intervention.

Partly for these reasons, research on the impact of DC often focuses on specific geographic or institutional settings. Here we often see positive findings, albeit shadowed—like AP research—by issues such as selection bias. Taking dual-credit courses has been associated with higher four-year college enrollment rates and stronger levels of persistence than are found among non-DC students.[31] In New York City, Iowa, and Texas, among other places, DC students have also shown superior rates of high school graduation, better college grades, and greater degree completion. In New York and Florida studies, they entered college with an average of fifteen more credits than non-DC students, which implies at least the potential for tuition savings and speedier degree completion.[32]

A growing body of evidence suggests that earning some form of dual credit is associated with superior rates of college persistence and graduation.[33] Mounting research also indicates that students earning credits in this way are likelier to matriculate in the first place, to obtain a higher first-year GPA, and to graduate within six years.[34] Yet most DC research suffers from the same kinds of methodological limits as AP research. Findings are generally correlational or predictive at best and analysts have not controlled for many variables that may affect pupil outcomes. Students who take part in DC may self-select, just like AP students.[35] DC's effects may also depend on the subject being taught as well as the attributes of those doing the teaching and those being taught. Lower-income students appear to benefit more than higher-income students from DC courses in one context while minority students are shown to benefit disproportionately from DC in another.[36]

A 2017 study from the Texas Higher Education Coordinating Board and RAND found that DC students in Texas had better college outcomes than non-DC high school graduates: higher matriculation rates, higher grades in subsequent courses in the same subjects, and greater likelihood of persisting in and completing college. Yet a 2018 follow-up was tempered with caution. For example, potential self-selection biases appear to have caused much of the observable differences between DC participants and nonparticipants when it came to high school completion, college enrollment, and completion. Additionally, the most positive outcomes were shown for traditionally advantaged groups (for example, white students) while there was no increase in two- and four-year college completion for black and Hispanic students (though there were some participation benefits at two-year colleges). There were also negative effects on many postsecondary outcomes for DC students who were eligible for subsidized lunches, which the study's authors say may be a consequence of weaker academic preparation among low-income students. This research, too, has been hampered by familiar issues, namely, the variability in just about every element of DC, including instructional quality, instructor qualifications, eligibility criteria, advising practices, and resource levels.[37]

Perhaps the soundest and most persuasive DC studies have focused on the relatively homogeneous realm of Early College High Schools (ECHS). Highlighted in a rigorous 2017 review by the federally supported What Works Clearinghouse (WWC), these analyses made use of lotteries to determine entry into ECHS programs—in essence an experimental design—and reported strong positive short- and long-term academic outcomes for participants. Thirty-five studies were reviewed, but only two met WWC's exacting standards for showing causal effect on student outcomes without reservations.[38] Three more met those standards with some reservations.[39] But it's difficult to generalize from the ECHS experience to dual credit more generally, and extremely difficult to make well-supported claims about its effects. It would be more accurate to treat these studies as examples of the impact of ECHS rather than applying them to DC as a whole.

The WWC report has also been faulted for including (in its five highlighted studies) two that focused on Texas. The conditions under which DC has burgeoned in Texas (see chapter 8) have been unique—as in the case everywhere. There are obvious issues when trying to apply state-specific findings to a national endeavor. But it's not just state differences that matter here. A major limitation of DC research to date is the nebulousness of the "intervention" being studied. For example, it seems to matter whether the courses are taught in the high school, on the college campus, or online. Some studies suggest that DC is related to increased college enrollment only when the classes take place on college campuses—and only in specific subjects.[40] DC's impact may also be affected by whether the course was taught by a high school teacher or a college instructor, though a 2018 Texas study found "more similarities than differences" between academic outcomes by instructor type.[41]

The WWC report illustrates other problems encountered in dual-credit research. Unsurprisingly, positive student outcomes are associated only with earning such credit in core academic subjects; the majority of gain was for students who took two DC courses and there was little added benefit from taking more; the samples did not (of course) account for differences related to unobservable characteristics between DC and non-DC students; and at least one of the Texas studies looked at college outcomes in 2004, though dual credit was tiny in the Lone Star State back then and much has changed since. A final issue: Researchers could not track students who went out of state for college.

Research on the cost-benefit of dual credit is also mixed. Texas-based analysts estimated that the cost in 2016–17 of providing dual-credit instruction was about $111 per semester hour for each participant, or $122 million statewide, but tuition and fees varied widely by location and by the type of DC instructor (community college, four-year college, or high school). Broadly speaking, however, the quantifiable benefits of DC—when gauged in savings to the state—outweighed the costs. Analysts estimated that:

> The short-term benefits (e.g., lower state expenditures for higher education) related to reduced time to degree were 1.18 times the cost of dual credit. In other words, each dollar invested in dual credit returned $1.18 from students spending less time in college and entering the workforce earlier. Long-term monetary benefits (e.g., tax revenues) associated with a greater number of college graduates were almost five times the estimated cost of dual credit.[42]

By contrast, a 2017 analysis by Georgetown University's Marguerite Roza looked at data from Georgia, Ohio, and Florida, and found that dual credit doesn't save states money, that "the public cost for a high school student to take a three-credit class via dual enrollment was actually higher than if the student waited" to take it in college, as the state ends up paying both the high school and the college. This recalls the "double-funding" issue we saw on the ground in Texas (chapter 8). Further, reported Roza, "the data show that the cost implications vary substantially by state, program, and funding details inherent in a state's dual enrollment design and state education funding formulas," suggesting that there's no broadly generalizable evidence that dual credit saves states money.[43]

In his 2018 University of Texas study, economist David Troutman also found little difference between DC and non-DC students concerning student debt if they graduate within four years, although among those who take five years he found a modest debt reduction ($500 to $600) for students who started with over fifteen credit hours from dual credit.[44]

The benefits from dual credit, in other words, are more likely to accrue to successful students than to taxpayers and budget makers. The extant literature on dual credit shows it to be, by and large, a positive thing for kids in certain contexts. Opting for DC instead of AP may also have an advantage in terms of the likelihood of establishing credit at a partner institution, the more so if the state supports dual credit in its community and four-year colleges. But it's not clear how useful this is to students choosing to attend non-partner colleges or go out of state. Moreover, research suggests that the more intensive model of dual credit found in ECHS's has the best results, though such schools represent just a small part of the DC universe.

Ultimately, the studies cited here suggest that selection biases are as relevant to DC research as in AP research, and that we don't yet fully understand what kinds of dual credit benefits which students under what conditions.

Comparing AP and Dual Credit

Although some tantalizing studies are underway, we can find no definitive national research on the comparative benefits of the two approaches to bringing college-level coursework to high school students. College Board comparisons usually portray AP in a more favorable light.[45] For example, a 2015 study reported that AP students scoring 3 or above showed more positive college outcomes (enrolling in four-year institutions, first-year grades, persistence in college, graduating in four or six years) than did students who took at least one dual-credit course affiliated with either a two- or four-year institution. Even students scoring below 3 on an AP exam performed better than DC students affiliated with two-year colleges, though the results were inconclusive when compared to DC students affiliated with four-year colleges.[46] But such studies are—once again—limited by the difficulty of differentiating among DC models, isolating DC course participation from other non-AP college-level courses (including AP course-taking that doesn't lead to exam-taking), and not controlling for differences in credit-granting policies across postsecondary institutions. The 2015 study cited here was also unable to remove from the DC sample those students whose dual-credit courses had a career-and-technology focus (very different from AP), and it focused only on four-year college outcomes, though most DC involves courses given by—and subsequent enrollment in—two-year institutions.

On one key (if obvious) indicator, dual credit clearly trumps AP: Students taking DC courses are far likelier to actually earn college credit at the end of them. The 2011 NCES survey showed that about 93 percent of students enrolled in DC courses did receive such credit. Although it varies somewhat by subject, the College Board's own research suggests that more than 90 percent of students earning C's or better in dual enrollment courses obtain credit, versus about 56 percent of matched students who score 3 or above on an AP exam.[47]

Troutman's aforementioned 2018 study compared Texas students who entered the UT system with credit from DC, AP/IB, or both. He reports positive benefits for dual-credit versus non-dual-credit students, but he also reports that AP/IB students generally fare better than DC students on a number of metrics: GPA, subsequent course completion, persistence, and four-year and five-year graduation. For example, AP/IB students were three times likelier than peers with no AP, IB, or DC to remain for the second year of college. (Dual-credit students were twice as likely.) The very strongest performance, however, was shown by those who arrive at UT with credit from both AP/IB and DC. Which brings us back to selection bias, as those young people are apt to be exceptionally motivated and discerning learners while in high school and there's no reason to expect such traits to vanish once they enter college.[48]

We see a similar pattern in recent data from Indiana. A review of the 2015 Hoosier high school graduating class found that DC students were significantly less likely than non-DC (and non-AP) students to need remediation in college, were significantly more likely to enroll in college, to have higher freshman GPAs, and to persist at least into their sophomore year. On all of those metrics, however, AP students (with scores of 3 or higher) performed significantly better than DC students, and—as in Texas—those who earned credit from both fared better still.[49]

Other analysts have shown that DC students have similar or better outcomes than their AP peers (though one shows positive benefits for DC community college students only).[50] But another recent look—this one by the College Board—uses data from the internationally administered TIMSS assessment to compare DC, IB, and other advanced students in calculus and physics. They find that DC students have more experienced and confident teachers (perhaps because most are college faculty), more parents with college degrees, and more books in their homes. Among AP students, parents are less likely to have high school diplomas, more likely to be black or Hispanic/Latino, and more likely to be second language English learners. Despite these differences, AP Calculus students far outperformed the international median while DC calculus students underperformed it.[51]

Summary

Research comparing AP directly with DC remains limited in scope and applicability, and its results are complex and often inconsistent. Both approaches seem to show benefit—inextricably entangled with selection effects—though several recent studies find somewhat stronger benefit from AP and even stronger benefit for those young people who emerged from high school with both. Yet we still have major unresolved questions: Does participation (and/or success) in the program itself (whether AP or DC) actually *cause* students to have better outcomes than their non-participating peers? Are there tangible longer-term benefits—such as employment, earnings, and such—for students who take and pass AP or DC in high school? (Long-term tracking data on post-college individuals is lacking in almost all education research.) What student populations derive greater benefit from which program, and under what circumstances?

We don't anticipate ever seeing a "final" answer as to whether one program is superior to the other. As we note in chapters 8 and 12, the extant literature on dual credit and AP suggests that either (or both) can do good things for students in certain contexts. The model of instruction is important, as is the commitment of the school leadership and teaching staff and the quality of support given to students.

As to which program serves low-income and minority students better, the answer may again be either or both. It cannot be an accident that some of the best DC results are seen in intense, long-term, and whole-school intervention models such as Early College High Schools. We also observed, time and again, in the course of our research that the best results for low-income students taking AP emerge when all these qualities are present—and persistent—as part of systematic school-wide efforts to improve outcomes for these kids. Similar observations emerged from a large body of qualitative research at the University of Virginia: "When consistent and widely endorsed support structures are in place over a lengthy period of time, talented students of diverse backgrounds can overcome deficits in requisite study skills, background knowledge, and language."[52] The importance of such long-term models for low-income and minority students, including a focus on what happens to them prior to high school, cannot be overstated.

We conclude, once again, that it's valuable to have several high-quality options, not just a single route to obtaining college-level academics for high school students who are ready for such challenges. While young people in Texas—or Ohio or New Jersey, or wherever—may benefit from a widening array of AP options at their school, they—or some of their classmates—may also benefit from bona fide dual credit carried out with intellectual integrity and college-level rigor. Either way, the quality of AP or DC instruction must be high and the judgment must be valid as to whether the student's work is truly college level. AP so far has a clear advantage in this area, but both programs would benefit from more rigorous research into the mechanics of what actually makes them work for students.

Notes

1. For studies showing that IB participation may be associated with positive rates of college persistence, see Liz Bergeron, *Diploma Programme Students' Enrollment and Outcomes at US Postsecondary Institutions, 2008–2014* (Bethesda, MD: International Baccalaureate Organization, 2015); Vanessa Coca and others, *Working to My Potential: Experiences of CPS Students in the International Baccalaureate Diploma Programme* (Chicago: Consortium on Chicago School Research, 2012). Research showing that IB participation is associated with matriculation in more selective colleges includes Coca et al., *Working to My Potential*. Research associating IB participation with higher academic achievement includes G. Harold Poelzer and John F. Feldhusen, "An Empirical Study of the Achievement of International Baccalaureate Students in Biology, Chemistry, and Physics—In Alberta," *Journal of Advanced Academics* 8, no. 1 (1996): 28–40; Elizabeth Shaunessy and others, "School Functioning and Psychological Well-Being of International Baccalaureate and General Education Students: A Preliminary Examination," *Journal of Secondary Gifted Education* 17, no. 2 (2006): 76–89. Research suggesting that IB participation is associated with stronger academic motivation includes Rira R. Culross and Emily T. Tarver, "Perceptions of the International Baccalaureate Program: A First Year Perspective," *Journal of School Choice* 1, no. 4 (2007): 53–62. Studies have also shown that IB students are more likely than non-IB students to report that their classroom atmosphere is positive; see Regan Clark Foust, Holly Herthberg-Davis, and Carolyn M. Callahan, "Students' Perceptions of the Nonacademic Advantages and Disadvantages of Participation in Advanced Placement Courses and International Baccalaureate Programs and Others," *Adolescence* 44, no. 174 (2009): 289–312.

2. By all accounts, Cambridge's AICE program is a rigorous academic program at the level of AP or IB. But few studies directly compare its outcomes with its more popular alternatives in the United States. One 2011 study compared IB, AICE, and AP students and found that AICE and AP students earned higher first-year GPAs than their IB peers but that all performed better than their non-AP/AICE/IB peers. Stuart Shaw and Claire Bailey, "Success in the US: Are Cambridge International Assessments Good Preparation for University Study," *Journal of College Admission* 213 (2011): 6–16.

3. For studies showing that AP success is correlated with higher scores on standardized tests, see Maureen Ewing, Wayne J. Camara, and Roger E. Millsap, *The Relationship between PSAT/NMSQT Scores and AP Examination Grades: A Follow-Up Study* (New York: College Board, 2006); Krista D. Mattern, Emily J. Shaw, and Xinhui Xiong, *The Relationship between AP Exam Performance and College Outcomes* (New York: College Board, 2009); Mary E. M. McKillip and Anita Rawls, "A Closer Examination of the Academic Benefits of AP," *Journal of Educational Research* 106 (2013): 305–18. For studies showing that AP students who earn 3 or above enroll in four-year college at higher rates, see Michael Chajewski, Krista D. Mattern, and Emily J. Shaw, "Examining the Role of Advanced Placement Exam Participation in Four-Year College Enrollment," *Educational Measurement: Issues and Practice* 30, no. 4 (2011): 16–27; Kelly E. Godfrey, *Exploring College Outcomes for Low-Income AP Exam Takers with Fee Reductions* (New York: College Board, 2016); Jeffrey N. Wyatt, Brian F. Patterson, and Tony F. Di Giacomo, *A Comparison of the College Outcomes of AP and Dual Enrollment Students* (New York: College Board, 2015). For research showing that successful AP students enroll at selective institutions at higher rates, see Mattern, Shaw, and Xiong, *Relationship between AP Exam Performance*. Studies that show successful AP students enrolling in college at higher rates include Chajewski et al., "Examining the Role of Advanced Placement"; Jeffrey N. Wyatt and Krista D. Mattern, *Low-SES Students and College Outcomes: The Role of AP Fee Reductions* (New York: College Board, 2011). Research showing that successful AP students may earn higher grades includes Leslie Keng and Barbara G. Dodd, *A Comparison of College Performances of AP and Non-AP Student Groups in Ten Subject Areas* (New York: College Board,

2008); Rick Morgan and John Klaric, *AP Students in College: An Analysis of Five-Year Academic Careers* (New York: College Board, 2007); Daniel Murphy and Barbara Dodd, *A Comparison of College Performance of Matched AP and Non-AP Student Groups* (New York: College Board, 2009); Brian F. Patterson, Sheryl Packman, and Jennifer L. Kobrin, *Advanced Placement Exam-Taking and Performance: Relationships with First-Year Subject Area College Grades* (New York: College Board, 2011); Emily J. Shaw, Jessica P. Marini, and Krista D. Mattern, "Exploring the Utility of Advanced Placement Participation and Performance in College Admission Decisions," *Educational and Psychological Measurement* 73 (2013): 229–53. Studies showing that successful AP students have higher four-year college graduation rates include Krista D. Mattern, Jessica P. Marini, and Emily J. Shaw, *Are AP Students More Likely to Graduate from College on Time?* (New York: College Board, 2013); Chrys Dougherty, Lynn Mellor, and Shuling Jian, *The Relationship between Advanced Placement and College Graduation* (Austin, TX: National Center for Educational Accountability, 2006); Morgan and Klaric, *AP Students in College*. Another, showing that AP exam-takers have higher rates of second-year college retention, is Krista D. Mattern, Emily J. Shaw, and Xinhui Xiong, *The Relationship between AP Exam Performance and College Outcomes* (New York: College Board, 2009).

Another study showing that low-income AP students, in particular, have higher rates of second-year retention in college is Jeffrey N. Wyatt and Krista D. Mattern, *Low-SES Students and College Outcomes: The Role of AP Fee Reductions* (New York: College Board, 2011).

4. Studies showing that successful AP students perform better in college courses within the same discipline or subject area include Sanja Jegesic and Jeff Wyatt, *Postsecondary Course Performance of AP Exam Takers in Subsequent Coursework: Biology, Languages, and Studio Art* (New York: College Board, 2018); Jeff Wyatt, *Postsecondary Course Performance of AP Exam Takers in Subsequent Coursework* (New York: College Board, 2018); Morgan and Klaric, *AP Students in College*; Brian F. Patterson and Maureen Ewing, *Validating the Use of AP Exam Scores for College Course Placement* (New York: College Board, 2013); Murphy and Dodd, *Comparison of College Performance*; Kelly E. Godfrey, Jeffrey N. Wyatt, and Jonathan J. Beard, *Exploring College Outcomes for Low-Income AP Exam Takers with Fee Reductions* (New York: College Board, 2016); Brian F. Patterson, Sheryl Packman, and Jennifer L. Kobrin, *Advanced Placement Exam-Taking and Performance: Relationships with First-Year Subject Area College Grades* (New York: College Board, 2011); Pamela K. Kaliski and Kelly E. Godfrey, *Does the Level of Rigor of a High School Science Course Matter? An Investigation of the Relationship between Science Courses and First-Year College Outcomes* (New York: College Board, 2014); and Keng and Dodd, *Comparison of College Performances*. Research showing that successful AP students take more credit hours in college includes Murphy and Dodd, *Comparison of College Performance*. Studies showing that successful AP students are more likely to major in a related discipline include Krista D. Mattern, Emily J. Shaw, and Maureen Ewing, *Advanced Placement Exam Participation: Is AP Exam Participation and Performance Related to Choice of College Major?* (New York: College Board, 2011); Morgan and Klaric, *AP Students in College*; and Emily J. Shaw and Sandra Barbuti, "Patterns of Persistence in Intended College Major with a Focus on STEM Majors," *NACADA Journal* 30, no. 2 (2010): 19–34. Research showing that successful AP exam-takers in STEM subjects perform better in college STEM courses includes Kara Smith and others, *AP STEM Participation and Postsecondary STEM Outcomes: Focus on Underrepresented Minority, First-Generation, and Female Students* (New York: College Board, 2018); and Mattern, Shaw, and Ewing, *Advanced Placement Exam Participation*. Research also shows that successful AP students earn higher college grades; see, for example, Timothy P. Scott, Homer Tolson, and Yi-Hsuan Lee, "Assessment of Advanced Placement Participation and University Academic Success in the First Semester: Controlling for Selected High School Academic Abilities," *Journal of College Admission* 208 (2010): 26–30.

5. Linda Hargrove, Donn Godin, and Barbara Dodd, *College Outcomes Comparisons by AP and Non-AP High School Experiences* (New York: College Board, 2008); Dougherty, Mellor, and Jian, *Advanced Placement and College Graduation*.

6. Hargrove, Godin, and Dodd, *College Outcomes Comparisons.*

7. Patterson, Packman, and Kobrin, *Advanced Placement Exam-Taking.*

8. Dougherty, Mellor, and Jian, *Advanced Placement and College Graduation*; Wyatt, Patterson, and Di Giacomo, *A Comparison of the College Outcomes*; Mattern, Shaw, and Xiong, *The Relationship between AP.*

9. Christopher Avery and others, "Shifting College Majors in Response to Advanced Placement Exam Scores," (working paper, no. 22841, National Bureau of Economic Research, 2016); Kaliski and Godfrey, *Does the Level of Rigor.*

10. Jeff Wyatt, Sanja Jagesic, and Kelly Godfrey, *Postsecondary Course Performance of AP Exam Takers in Subsequent Coursework* (New York: College Board, 2018); Jegesic and Wyatt, *Postsecondary Course Performance of AP Exam Takers in Subsequent Coursework.*

11. Russell T. Warne and others, "The Impact of Participation in the Advanced Placement Program on Students' College Admissions Test Scores," *Journal of Educational Research* 108, no. 5 (2015): 400–416.

12. Non-College Board studies showing that AP course participation is linked with higher GPAs and retention include William R. Duffy II, "Persistence and Performance at a Four-Year University," in *AP: A Critical Examination of the Advanced Placement Program*, ed. Phillip M. Sadler and others (Cambridge, MA: Harvard Education Press, 2010), 139–63; and Kristin Klopfenstein and M. Kathleen Thomas, "The Link between Advanced Placement Experience and Early College Success," *Southern Economic Journal* 75, no. 3 (2009): 873–91. External research linking AP course participation with higher rates of degree attainment includes Duffy, "Persistence and Performance"; and Kristin Klopfenstein, "Does the Advanced Placement Program Save Taxpayers Money? The Effect of AP Participation on Time to College Graduation," in *AP: A Critical Examination of the Advanced Placement Program*, ed. Phillip M. Sadler and others (Cambridge, MA: Harvard Education Press, 2010), 189–218. Klopfenstein also links AP exam participation with higher rates of degree attainment.

13. For a limited descriptive study linking AP students with higher incomes after college, see Lamont A. Flowers, "Racial Differences in the Impact of Participating in Advanced Placement Programs on Educational and Labor Market Outcomes," *Educational Foundations* 22, no. 1/2 (2008): 121–32. External studies showing positive links between AP students and their likelihood of earning advanced degrees include April Bleske-Rechek, David Lubinski, and Camilla P. Benbow, "Meeting the Educational Needs of Special Populations: Advanced Placement's Role in Developing Exceptional Human Capital," *Psychological Science* 15, no. 4 (2004): 217–24.

14. Sharmila Mann and others, *Advanced Placement Access and Success: How Do Rural Schools Stack Up?* (Denver: Education Commission of the States, 2017).

15. For a study that links AP exam taking and success with higher college-entrance exam scores and college GPAs, see Phillip L. Ackerman, Ruth Kanfer, and Charles Calderwood, "High School Advanced Placement and Student Performance in College: STEM Majors, Non-STEM Majors, and Gender Differences," *Teachers College Record* 115, no. 10 (2013): 1–43. Research showing that AP exam taking and success is linked with higher college graduation rates includes Robert H. Tai and others, "Advanced Placement Course Enrollment and Long-Range Educational Outcomes," in *AP: A Critical Examination of the Advanced Placement Program*, ed. Phillip M. Sadler and others (Cambridge, MA: Harvard Education Press, 2010), 109–18. For a study showing that AP exam taking and success are also linked with earning more advanced degrees, see Bleske-Rechek et al., "Meeting the Educational Needs of Special Populations." Other external research shows negative or negligible relationships between AP participation and college outcomes, although some of these studies show positive outcomes associated with earning 3 or above on AP exams: Klopfenstein, "Does the Advanced Placement Program"; Phillip M. Sadler and Gerhard Sonnert, "High

School Advanced Placement and Success in College Coursework in the Sciences," in *AP: A Critical Examination of the Advanced Placement Program*, ed. Phillip M. Sadler and others (Cambridge, MA: Harvard Education Press, 2010), 119–37; Saul Geiser and Veronica Santelices, *The Role of Advanced Placement and Honors Courses in College Admissions* (Berkeley, CA: Center for Studies in Higher Education, 2004); Randall E. Schumacker, "Graduation Completion amongst IB and AP Students in Postsecondary Education," *Multiple Linear Regression Viewpoints* 40, no. 2 (2014): 35–40; Warne et al., "Impact of Participation."

16. David R. Troutman and others, *The University of Texas System Dual Credit Study: Dual Credit and Success in College* (Austin: University of Texas System, 2018).

17. Duffy, "Persistence and Performance."

18. For more on the impact of AP course and exam participation on five-year degree attainment, see Klopfenstein, "Does the Advanced Placement Program." For more on the impact of AP course participation on college GPAs, see Duffy, "Persistence and Performance."

19. Several external studies unpack the limitations of AP research, including: unobservable selection biases (Klopfenstein, "Does the Advanced Placement Program); the likelihood that AP students attend better resourced schools (Kristin Klopfenstein and Kathleen M. Thomas, *The Advanced Placement Performance Advantage: Fact or Fiction?* [Nashville, TN: American Economic Association, 2005]); and the likelihood that AP students have more experienced teachers, Pamela L. Paek and others, *A Portrait of Advanced Placement Teachers' Practices* (New York: College Board, 2005).

20. Maureen Ewing, Kelly E. Godfrey, and Jonathan J. Beard, *Achieving College Success: What Do We Know about the Relationship between Acceleration Programs in High School and Subsequent College Outcomes?* (New York: College Board, forthcoming).

21. Personal correspondence.

22. Columbia University, Mailman School of Public Health, "Difference-in-Difference Estimation," accessed November 14, 2018. https://www.mailman.columbia.edu/research/population -health-methods/difference-difference-estimation.

23. Columbia University, Mailman School of Public Health, "Difference-in-Difference Estimation."

24. Mark C. Long and Dylan Conger, *AP Science Impact Study* (University of Washington, Evans School of Public Policy and Governance, forthcoming). https://evans.uw.edu/policy-impact/ap -science-impact-study. Provisional results cited here come from correspondence with the authors in August 2018.

25. For more on the potential cost savings of taking AP for students, see Mattern, Marini, and Shaw, *Are AP Students More Likely*.

26. Ackerman et al., "High School Advanced Placement." This study shows that there is reduced time to graduation for AP exam passers but longer time for exam takers who did not pass.

27. Klopfenstein, "Does the Advanced Placement Program."

28. Klopfenstein, "Does the Advanced Placement Program"; Kristin Klopfenstein, *The Effect of AP Participation on Time to College Graduation* (technical report, Richardson, TX, University of Texas, Dallas, 2008). https://www.utdallas.edu/research/tsp-erc/pdf/bk_klopfenstein_grad_time _technical_report_020810.pdf.

29. Sadler and Sonnert, "High School Advanced Placement."

30. As mentioned in chapter 8, a national accrediting body for dual credits exists—the National Alliance of Concurrent Enrollment Partnerships—but its reach to date has been quite limited.

31. Joni L. Swanson, *Executive Summary: An Analysis of the Impact of High School Dual Enrollment Course Participation on Post-Secondary Academic Success, Persistence, and Degree Completion* (Chapel Hill, NC: National Alliance of Concurrent Enrollment Partnerships, 2008); Ben Struhl

and Joel Vargas, *Taking College Courses in High School: A Strategy for College Readiness* (Boston: Jobs for the Future, 2012).

32. For New York, see Drew Allen and Mina Dadgar, "Does Dual Enrollment Increase Students' Success in College? Evidence from a Quasi-Experimental Analysis of Dual Enrollment in New York City," *New Directions for Higher Education* 2012, no. 158 (2012): 11–19. For New York and Florida, see Melinda Mechur Karp and others, *Dual Enrollment Students in Florida and New York City: Postsecondary Outcomes* (New York: Community College Research Center, 2008). For Iowa, see Katherine L. Hughes and others, *Broadening the Benefits of Dual Enrollment* (New York: Community College Research Center, 2012). For Texas, see, Matthew Giani, Celeste Alexander, and Pedro Reyes, "Exploring Variation in the Impact of Dual-Credit Coursework on Postsecondary Outcomes: A Quasi-Experimental Analysis of Texas Students," *High School Journal* 97, no. 4 (2014): 200–218.

33. Troutman et al., *University of Texas System*; Trey Miller and others, *Dual Credit Education in Texas: Interim Report* (Santa Monica, CA: RAND, 2017); Justine Radunzel, Julie Noble, and Sue Wheeler, *Dual-Credit/Dual-Enrollment Coursework and Long-Term College Success in Texas* (issue brief, Texas-ACT College Success Research Consortium, October 2014); Giani et al., "Exploring Variation"; James Appleby and others, *A Study of Dual Credit Access and Effectiveness in the State of Texas* (College Station: Texas A&M University Bush School of Government and Public Service, 2011).

34. Lawrence J. Redlinger and others, *Effects of Types of Early College Courses on Student Outcomes* (presentation, University of Texas, Dallas, June 1, 2017). https://www.utdallas.edu/ospa /files/Dual-Credit-RMAIR-FINAL.pdf; Michael U. Villareal, *The Effects of Dual-Credit on Secondary and Postsecondary Student Outcomes* (working paper, University of Texas at Austin, 2017); Karp et al., *Dual Enrollment Students*; Eric Lichtenberger and others, "Dual Credit/Dual Enrollment and Data Driven Policy Implementation," *Community College Journal of Research and Practice* 38, no. 11 (2014): 959–79; Robert D. Young Jr., Sheila A. Joyner, and John R. Slate, "Grade Point Average Differences between Dual and Nondual Credit College Students," *Urban Studies Research* 2013 (2013); Radunzel, Noble, and Wheeler, *Dual-Credit/Dual-Enrollment*.

35. Karp et al., *Dual Enrollment Students*; Josh Pretlow and Heather D. Wathington, "Expanding Dual Enrollment: Increasing Postsecondary Access for All?" *Community College Review* 42, no. 1 (2014): 41–54; Thomas Bailey and Melinda Mechur Karp, "Expanding the Reach of Dual-Enrollment Programs," *Community College Review* 75, no. 3 (2005): 8–11; Steven Chatman and Kandis Smith, "Dual-Credit Preparation for Further Study in Foreign Languages," *NASSP Bulletin* 82, no. 597 (1998): 99–107.

36. Giani, Alexander, and Reyes, "Exploring Variation"; Cecilia Speroni, *Determinants of Students' Success: The Role of Advancement and Dual Enrollment Programs* (New York: National Center for Postsecondary Education, National Center for Postsecondary Research, 2011); Melinda Mechur Karp and others, *The Postsecondary Achievement of Participants in Dual Enrollment: An Analysis of Student Outcomes in Two States* (New York: Columbia University, Community College Research Center, 2007).

37. Miller et al., *Dual Credit Education in Texas*; Trey Miller and others, *Dual Credit Education Programs in Texas: Phase II* (Washington, DC, American Institutes for Research, 2018).

38. *Transition to College Intervention Report: Dual Enrollment Programs* (Washington, DC: US Department of Education, Institute of Education Sciences, What Works Clearinghouse, 2017). Both studies shown to meet WWC's standards with no reservations include Julie A. Edmunds and others, "Smoothing the Transition to Postsecondary Education: The Impact of the Early College Model," *Journal of Research on Educational Effectiveness* 10, no. 2 (2017): 297–325; Andrea Berger and others, *Early College, Early Success: Early College High School Initiative Impact Study* (Washington, DC: American Institutes for Research, 2014).

39. The three WWC studies cited as having some reservations include Brian P. An, "The Impact of Dual Enrollment on College Degree Attainment: Do Low-SES Students Benefit?" *Educational Evaluation and Policy Analysis* 35, no. 1 (2013): 57–75; Giani, Alexander, and Reyes, "Exploring Variation"; Ben Struhl and Joel Vargas, *Taking College Courses in High School: A Strategy Guide for College Readiness; The College Outcomes of Dual Enrollment in Texas* (Washington, DC: Jobs for the Future, 2012).

40. Speroni, *Determinants of Students' Success.*

41. Miller et al., *Dual Credit Education Programs in Texas: Phase II.*

42. Miller et al., *Dual Credit Education Programs in Texas: Phase II.*

43. Marguerite Roza and Caitlin Brooks, *College Credit in High School: Doing the Math on Costs* (Washington, DC: Georgetown University, Edunomics Lab, 2017). http://edunomicslab.org/wp -content/uploads/2017/11/Dual-Enrollment-V2.pdf; Marguerite Roza, "States Be Aware: Cost Savings for Dual Enrollment Elude State Ledgers," *Brown Center Chalkboard* (blog), Brookings, November 30, 2017. https://www.brookings.edu/blog/brown-center-chalkboard/2017/11/30 /states-be-aware-cost-savings-for-dual-enrollment-elude-state-ledgers/.

44. Troutman et al., *University of Texas System.*

45. Studies showing that successful AP students (those scoring 3 or above) have higher four-year graduation rates than DC students include Wyatt, Patterson, and Di Giacomo, *Comparison of the College Outcomes*; Hargrove, Godin, and Dodd, *College Outcomes Comparisons.* Studies showing that successful AP students perform better than DC students in college include Wyatt, Patterson, and Di Giacomo, *Comparison of the College Outcomes*; Kelly Godfrey and others, *College Completion: Comparing AP, Dual-Enrolled, and Nonadvanced Students* (New York: College Board, 2014); Maureen Ewing and Jessica Howell, *Is the Relationship between AP Participation and Academic Performance Really Meaningful?* (New York: College Board, 2015); Kaliski and Godfrey, *Does the Level of Rigor.* Research showing that successful AP students perform better in specific college subjects than DC students include Kaliski and Godfrey, *Does the Level of Rigor*; Godfrey et al., *College Completion.*

46. Godfrey et al., *College Completion*, shows how students scoring below 3 on an AP exam performed better than dual enrollment students affiliated with two-year colleges. By contrast, Wyatt et al., *A Comparison of the College Outcomes*, show inconclusive results for students scoring less than 3 on an AP exam and for DC students affiliated with four-year colleges.

47. Godfrey et al., *College Completion: Dual Enrollment Programs and Courses for High School Students at Postsecondary Institutions: 2010–11, First Look* (Washington, DC: US Department of Education, National Center for Education Statistics, Institute of Education Sciences, 2011).

48. Troutman et al., *University of Texas System.*

49. *College Readiness Report Supplement: A Closer Look at Dual Credit Students* (Indianapolis: Indiana Commission for Higher Education, 2017).

50. Speroni, *Determinants of Students' Success*; Klopfenstein, "Does the Advanced Placement Program."

51. *Advanced Placement Calculus and Physics and TIMSS Advanced 2015: Performance Report* (New York: College Board, forthcoming). AP students are disaggregated from "other US Calculus students," who are defined in the study as "Dual Enrollment and IB students."

52. See Robin M. Kyburg, Holly Hertberg-Davis, and Carolyn M. Callahan, "Advanced Placement and International Baccalaureate Programs: Optimal Learning Environments for Talented Minorities?" *Journal of Advanced Academics* 18, no. 2 (2007): 205. See also Holly Hertberg-Davis, Carolyn M. Callahan, and Robin M. Kyburg, *Advanced Placement and International Baccalaureate Programs: A "Fit" for Gifted Learners? Research Monograph RM06222* (Storrs, CT: National Research Center on the Gifted and Talented, University of Connecticut, 2006); Holly Hertberg-Davis

and Carolyn M. Callahan, "A Narrow Escape: Gifted Students' Perceptions of Advanced Placement and International Baccalaureate Programs," *Gifted Child Quarterly* 52, no. 3 (2008): 199–216; and Regan Clark Foust, Holly Hertberg-Davis, and Carolyn M. Callahan, "'Having It All' at Sleep's Expense: The Forced Choice of Participants in Advanced Placement Courses and International Baccalaureate Programs," *Roeper Review* 20, no. 2 (2008): 121–29.

APPENDIX II

Additional Data

The tables and figures in this appendix augment the data and analyses in chapters 3, 4, and 8.

Chapter 3

TABLE A.1. Advanced Placement subjects and exams taken globally in 2018, public and private schools, with percentage shares and qualifying scores

AP subjects in 2018	Number of exams taken	Percentage share of all exams taken	Percentage of exams to earn a qualifying score (3 or higher)
English Language and Composition	580,043	11.4%	57.2%
United States History	501,530	9.9%	51.8%
English Literature and Composition	404,014	7.9%	47.3%
United States Government and Politics	326,392	6.4%	53.0%
Psychology	311,759	6.1%	65.6%
Calculus AB	308,538	6.1%	57.6%
World History	303,243	6.0%	56.2%
Biology	259,663	5.1%	61.5%
Statistics	222,501	4.4%	60.7%
Human Geography	216,783	4.3%	54.4%
Spanish Language	180,435	3.5%	88.3%
Physics 1	170,653	3.4%	40.6%
Environmental Science	166,433	3.3%	47.7%
Chemistry	161,852	3.2%	55.9%
Macroeconomics	146,673	2.9%	58.5%
Calculus BC	139,376	2.7%	79.8%
European History	101,740	2.0%	57.7%
Microeconomics	90,032	1.8%	67.9%
Computer Science Principles	72,187	1.4%	71.2%

Continued on next page

TABLE A.1. (*continued*)

AP subjects in 2018	Number of exams taken	Percentage share of all exams taken	Percentage of exams to earn a qualifying score (3 or higher)
Computer Science A	65,133	1.3%	67.8%
Physics C—Mechanics	57,399	1.1%	77.2%
Studio Art—2-D Design	36,249	0.7%	84.6%
Seminar	30,964	0.6%	82.8%
Spanish Literature	27,451	0.5%	70.3%
Physics 2	25,741	0.5%	63.1%
Physics C—E&M	25,074	0.5%	73.4%
Art History	24,964	0.5%	64.6%
Comparative Govt. and Politics	24,675	0.5%	63.3%
French Language and Culture	22,867	0.4%	77.2%
Studio Art—Drawing	20,853	0.4%	89.5%
Music Theory	19,018	0.4%	65.8%
Chinese Language and Culture	13,825	0.3%	91.3%
Research	9,640	0.2%	75.2%
Latin	6,409	0.1%	66.4%
Studio Art—3-D Design	5,777	0.1%	69.0%
German Language and Culture	5,053	0.1%	71.0%
Italian Language and Culture	2,926	0.1%	68.6%
Japanese Language and Culture	2,459	0.0%	77.8%
Total	**5,090,324**	**100%**	**59.0%**

Source: College Board

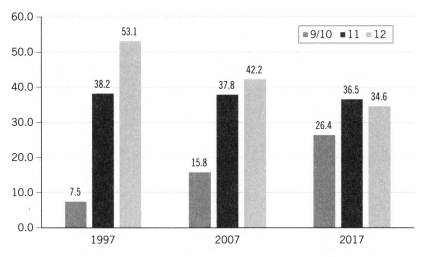

FIGURE A.1. Percentage of Advanced Placement high school students by grade level in US public and private schools, 1997, 2007, and 2017.
Numbers do not total 100 percent as some students take AP outside the grades shown here.
Source: College Board

TABLE A.2. Advanced Placement exams taken per 1,000 11th and 12th graders in the United States in 2017, public schools only, by state (and District of Columbia)

DC	1,017	New Jersey	641	Alabama	480	West Virginia	334
Maryland	943	Colorado	641	Minnesota	476	Alaska	299
Florida	869	**US**	**608**	Utah	455	Idaho	295
Texas	842	Nevada	573	Pennsylvania	454	Louisiana	295
Virginia	785	Wisconsin	551	Ohio	453	Nebraska	277
Illinois	756	Maine	550	Hawaii	432	Missouri	271
California	732	Kentucky	549	Arizona	420	Montana	267
Arkansas	723	Vermont	545	Michigan	420	Iowa	265
Massachusetts	710	Indiana	506	New Mexico	388	South Dakota	243
Georgia	692	Washington	501	Oklahoma	357	Kansas	229
New York	680	Delaware	496	Oregon	355	Wyoming	229
Connecticut	661	S. Carolina	496	N. Hampshire	341	Mississippi	224
North Carolina	643	Rhode Island	489	Tennessee	336	North Dakota	222

Sources: College Board and Applied Educational Research, Inc.

TABLE A.3. Percentage of 2018 graduating seniors, public schools only, who earned at least one qualifying AP score during high school, by state (and District of Columbia)

Massachusetts	32.9	Nevada	24.8	Delaware	19.6	Idaho	13.5
Connecticut	32.2	Washington	23.6	DC	19.6	South Dakota	13.3
Florida	31.7	**US**	**23.5**	Pennsylvania	19.4	Tennessee	13.0
Maryland	31.6	Georgia	23.2	Kentucky	18.5	Wyoming	12.9
California	31.3	Minnesota	23.0	Oregon	18.5	Montana	12.8
New Jersey	29.0	Rhode Island	22.1	Arkansas	18.1	Missouri	12.2
New York	28.7	Texas	21.9	Ohio	17.8	Oklahoma	12.1
Virginia	28.5	North Carolina	21.5	Arizona	17.2	North Dakota	12.0
Colorado	28.3	Michigan	21.2	Hawaii	17.2	Nebraska	11.6
Illinois	27.3	N. Hampshire	20.7	Alaska	15.9	West Virginia	11.0
Wisconsin	26.1	Indiana	20.2	Alabama	14.1	Kansas	10.6
Vermont	25.7	Maine	20.2	Iowa	13.7	Louisiana	9.1
Utah	25.5	S. Carolina	19.9	New Mexico	13.6	Mississippi	6.7

Source: College Board

TABLE A.4. Percentage growth in qualifying scores earned and changes in qualifying score rates, by state (and District of Columbia), public and private schools, 1997 to 2017

	State	Growth in number of qualifying scores 1997–2017	Percentage point change in exam pass rate, 1997–2017
1	Arkansas	1,280%	−17.9
2	Nevada	1,001%	−9.6
3	Texas	837%	−13.8
4	Washington	746%	+5.2
5	Georgia	730%	−7.0
6	Louisiana	669%	−24.0
7	Colorado	627%	−8.2
8	Arizona	601%	−4.6
9	North Dakota	589%	−11.9
10	Florida	559%	−4.0
11	Wyoming	558%	−5.3
12	Kentucky	556%	+0.5
13	Indiana	543%	+5.9
14	Missouri	543%	−9.6
15	Oregon	519%	−7.0
16	Nebraska	507%	−6.3
17	Oklahoma	504%	−14.7

TABLE A.4. (*continued*)

	State	Growth in number of qualifying scores 1997–2017	Percentage point change in exam pass rate, 1997–2017
18	North Carolina	491%	−6.3
19	Idaho	491%	+8.0
20	Minnesota	482%	+5.1
21	Alabama	471%	−14.3
22	Illinois	466%	−8.3
23	Maryland	446%	−8.2
24	**US**	**434%**	**−7.0**
25	New Mexico	413%	−20.2
26	Wisconsin	409%	−0.5
27	Tennessee	408%	−6.3
28	California	397%	−8.6
29	Kansas	391%	+9.1
30	Rhode Island	376%	−8.9
31	Connecticut	366%	−2.9
32	Ohio	359%	−1.0
33	DC	352%	−19.6
34	Michigan	342%	−1.0
35	Delaware	340%	−10.6
36	New Jersey	339%	−1.3
37	Iowa	338%	−6.4
38	Massachusetts	338%	−4.6
39	Mississippi	328%	−11.2
40	Virginia	328%	+1.9
41	Pennsylvania	323%	+0.2
42	South Dakota	302%	+16.2
43	West Virginia	293%	−5.2
44	Vermont	289%	+1.6
45	Maine	285%	−7.9
46	Montana	256%	−8.7
47	Hawaii	256%	−15.2
48	South Carolina	249%	+3.3
49	New Hampshire	236%	−0.9
50	Alaska	223%	−5.4
51	New York	206%	−2.1
52	Utah	135%	−3.0

Source: College Board

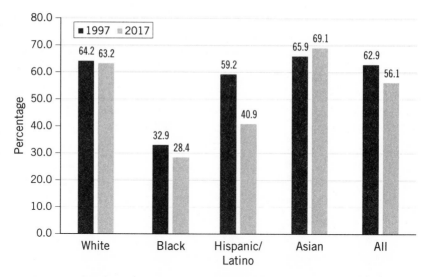

FIGURE A.2. AP qualifying score rates in US, public schools only, by race/ethnicity, 1997 and 2017.

"All" rate refers to all AP exams taken by US public school students, including races/ethnicities not shown separately here but recorded by the College Board: "American Indian/Alaskan Native"; "Native Hawaiian/Other Pacific Islander"; "Two or More Races"; "Other"; and "No Response." *Source:* College Board

Chapter 4

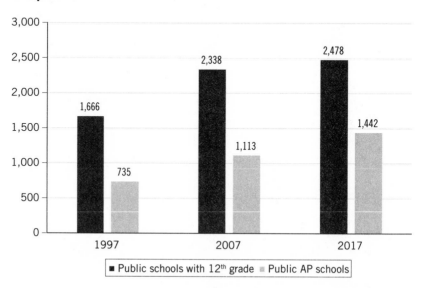

FIGURE A.3. Texas public high schools (offering 12th grade) and public AP schools, 1997, 2007, and 2017.

Sources: College Board and the Texas Education Agency

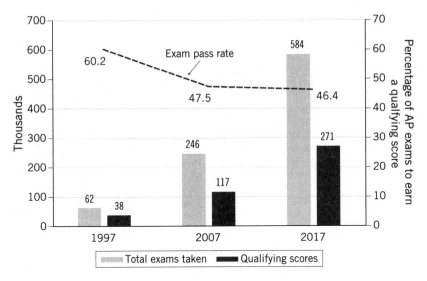

FIGURE A.4. AP exams taken, qualifying scores earned, and qualifying score rate, for public and private schools in Texas, 1997, 2007, and 2017.
Source: College Board

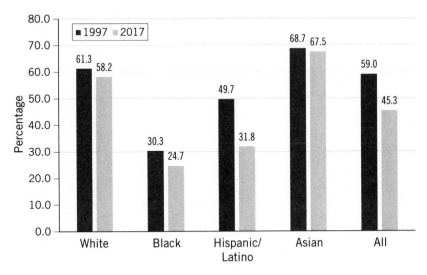

FIGURE A.5. AP qualifying score rates in Texas, public schools only, by race/ethnicity, 1997 and 2017.
"All" rate refers to all AP exams taken by Texas students, including races/ethnicities not shown separately here but recorded by the College Board: "American Indian/Alaskan Native"; "Native Hawaiian/Other Pacific Islander"; "Two or More Races"; "Other"; and "No Response."
Source: College Board

Chapter 8

TABLE A.5. Enrollment in AP classes, dual enrollment, and International Baccalaureate classes, public schools only, by state (and District of Columbia) 2015–16

	Enrollment in AP classes	Dual Enrollment	Enrollment in International Baccalaureate
Alabama	31,166	11,002	1,149
Alaska	4,308	2,120	580
Arizona	51,166	31,460	4,169
Arkansas	30,370	13,636	504
California	425,288	34,746	21,817
Colorado	53,962	19,233	7,282
Connecticut	33,033	15,329	656
Delaware	6,595	1,820	525
DC	4,183	58	44
Florida	195,563	55,254	13,822
Georgia	115,363	20,348	4,411
Hawaii	6,682	2,749	128
Idaho	10,815	16,486	1,729
Illinois	125,295	50,567	3,588
Indiana	54,131	70,807	2,625
Iowa	15,580	31,517	285
Kansas	17,490	24,423	1,538
Kentucky	44,659	18,167	752
Louisiana	23,099	17,843	665
Maine	8,428	2,229	485
Maryland	71,123	6,554	5,988
Massachusetts	55,368	3,125	2,295
Michigan	75,995	21,284	8,511
Minnesota	46,681	25,123	6,235
Mississippi	13,742	38,623	437
Missouri	33,289	9,341	2,328
Montana	4,671	2,950	969
Nebraska	12,967	13,019	271
Nevada	24,168	2,392	955
N. Hampshire	7,762	3,208	93
New Jersey	76,843	35,409	1,806
New Mexico	18,189	11,927	63

TABLE A.5. (*continued*)

	Enrollment in AP classes	Dual Enrollment	Enrollment in International Baccalaureate
New York	151,912	80,182	6,919
North Carolina	74,215	30,014	3,937
North Dakota	2,774	4,317	-
Ohio	59,443	50,420	2,884
Oklahoma	27,028	8,064	825
Oregon	26,958	27,049	6,310
Pennsylvania	84,786	25,327	2,248
Rhode Island	5,885	1,466	-
South Carolina	29,742	13,538	2,378
South Dakota	3,549	3,248	-
Tennessee	33,972	21,261	1,498
Texas	349,188	133,439	9,348
Utah	35,975	23,198	1,365
Vermont	3,816	1,845	-
Virginia	88,948	32,212	10,348
Washington	63,940	56,171	4,879
West Virginia	10,655	4,704	349
Wisconsin	55,283	45,968	2,839
Wyoming	2,743	4,863	475
US	**2,808,786**	**1,180,035**	**153,307**

Source: US Office for Civil Rights

Notes: These data were obtained from the OCR's district datasets for 2015–16, the first year in which districts were required to report dual-enrollment counts. Due to this new requirement, as well as state-to-state variability in dual-enrollment definitions and programming, numbers may be inconsistent. AP numbers here refer to class enrollment, not exams taken (different from what we report elsewhere using College Board data). IB numbers count students in grades 9–12 (or comparable ungraded levels) enrolled in the IB program.

INDEX

Italic pages refer to figures and tables

academic standards: AP as gold, 209–16; Asian students and, 167; black students and, 167–68; calculus and, 167; challenges to, 155–68; College Board and, 158–68, 169n13; Common Core and, 1, 156, 159, 192, 196, 202, 220, 229; degrees and, 2–3, 11; diplomas and, 158, 161, 167, 169n7; dual credit and, 159; equity and, 168; Every Student Succeeds Act (ESSA) and, 38, 156; exams and, 165–68; Florida and, 162; framework development and, 160–61; Goals 2000: Educate America Act and, 156; GPAs and, 158 (*see also* GPAs (grade point averages)); graduation and, 3, 157–58; Hispanic students and, 155, 167–68; Improving America's Schools Act and, 156; International Baccalaureate (IB) and, 159; matriculation and, 3; National Council on Education Standards and Testing and, 156; National Math and Science Initiative (NMSI) and, 164; New York City and, 164; No Child Left Behind and, 1, 103, 156, 159; Packer and, 162–63, 165–66, 168, 172–73, 176–78, 180; parents and, 95, 146–61, 164, 166–67; pass rates and, 167; physics and, 167; PISA and, 157, 159, 210; poor kids and, 159, 161; principals and, 162, 164, 166; qualifying scores and, 166–68, 183–85; quality and, 167 (*see also* quality); racial issues and, 167; reform and, 164; relaxation of, 157–58; revenue and, 166; rigor and, 157–60 (*see also* rigor); scoring and, 183–85; teachers and, 156–68, 169n7, 169n13; Texas and, 164; TIMSS and, 157, 159, 244; Title I program and, 156; white students and, 167
Achievement First, 116
ACT: academic gold standard and, 210; College Board and, 100, 185; dual credit and,

227; suburbs and, 100, 102; Texas and, 60, 62, 70n22, 250n33
Adler, Mortimer, 188
admission rates, 21
Advanced International Certificate of Education (AICE), 134, 234, 246n2
Advanced Placement (AP): academic standards and, 155–68; as agent of reform, 220–21; benefits of, 1–6, 144–45, 233–52; biology and, 12, 14, 73, 81, 88, 182, 189, 191, 238, *253*; calculus and, 57 (*see also* calculus); Capstone courses and, 35, 46–47, 97, 124, 172, 177, 203n5, 230; chemistry and, 12, 14, 92, 183, 191, 220, 238, *253*; College Board and, 2 (*see also* College Board); comparing options and, 148–50; competition and, 131–50, 232–33; course audit and, 41, 161–63, 174; criticism of, 209, 212–16; culture wars and, 188–203; early days of, 1–2, 4, 9–19; elite dropouts and, 170–85; English Language and, 35, 75, 81, 88, 91n22, 109, 117, 119, 196, 244, *253*; English Literature and, 34–35, 73, 81, 116, 183, 191, 195, 202, 226, *253*; Environmental Science and, 73, 75, 81, 217, *253*; European History and, 14, *253*; evidence/outcomes of, 234–39, 244–45, 247n4, 248n13, 251n45; exams and, 1–2 (*see also* exams); expanding at scale and, 78–83; expansion schools and, 81–83, 91n22, 92n23; framework development and, 160–61; *General Education in School and College* report and, 11–12, 189; gifted students and, 4, 21, 23, 37, 45, 94, 103, 112, 214, 220; as gold standard, 209–16; growth of, 15–19, 32–47; honors courses and, 18, 22, 24, 98, 100, 112, 141–42, 158; increased number of courses in, 29, 33–36; influence of, 1–4; Keller

A NOTE ON THE TYPE

This book has been composed in Adobe Text and Gotham.
Adobe Text, designed by Robert Slimbach for Adobe,
bridges the gap between fifteenth- and sixteenth-century
calligraphic and eighteenth-century Modern styles.
Gotham, inspired by New York street signs, was designed
by Tobias Frere-Jones for Hoefler & Co.